T0294338

REPORTING INDIA

INDIA

MY SEVENTY-YEAR JOURNEY AS A JOURNALIST

REPORTING INDIA

INDIA

MY SEVENTY-YEAR JOURNEY AS A JOURNALIST

PREM PRAKASH

EBURY
PRESS

An imprint of Penguin Random House

EBURY PRESS

USA | Canada | UK | Ireland | Australia
New Zealand | India | South Africa | China

Ebury Press is part of the Penguin Random House group of companies
whose addresses can be found at global.penguinrandomhouse.com

Published by Penguin Random House India Pvt. Ltd
7th Floor, Infinity Tower C, DLF Cyber City,
Gurgaon 122 002, Haryana, India

Penguin
Random House
India

First published in Ebury Press by Penguin Random House India 2020

ISBN 9780670093984

Typeset in Adobe Caslon Pro by Manipal Technologies Limited, Manipal
Printed at Thomson Press India Ltd, New Delhi

www.penguin.co.in

To my lovely parents, Smt Sushila Sabharwal and Lala Wishva Nath,
with whose blessings I completed this journey

Contents

Foreword

The 1950s were a heady time in India as it faced the birth pangs of Independence. A nation struggling to get moving after a heart-wrenching partition and 150 years of colonial rule. Those were times of abject poverty and hunger, anguish and pain. Yet, India then was the womb of a million dreams. There was fresh optimism in the air. A new India fuelled by restless youth was rising again. The world's largest democracy was on a long voyage of rediscovery.

Amid this turbulence, a young man fired by idealism followed his father and uncles, eminent photojournalists of their time, in their profession. He would be a chronicler of India's tryst with destiny. A camera is the 'save button' of history. Prem Prakash was to go on to become the first independent news cameraman-reporter of modern India. For seventy years, this indefatigable man has been an eyewitness to history as it was being made.

By the 1960s, Prem Prakash had become the India correspondent of the global TV news agency Visnews (later acquired by Reuters), and his small enterprise had come to be regarded as the first port of call for any foreign news channel or publication. Often, he would be the solitary cameraman recording people, places and events for posterity. Asian Films, as he christened his company—with its offices at 72 Janpath in New Delhi—soon became a favourite haunt for all purveyors of news. He was documenting India by the minute.

In my college days in the late '60s, I was an avid reader of the *American Cinematographer* magazine, because of my interest in cinema. One thing that always struck me was the tiny ad (the only one from India) it carried in every issue: 'Asian Films, 72, Janpath, for your filming needs in India.' At that time, I had begun writing in some publications and was roped in to start a magazine, *Tempus*. It was during those days that I first met him. Premji was sitting with a couple of senior journalists in earnest conversation. I introduced myself, and soon he was recounting his first-hand account of the 1965 war. I was enchanted by this amazing raconteur.

In due course, I went away to Mumbai to work in films. Once I got into TV in the '80s, my relationship with Premji and his news organization expanded beyond casual meetings. From then on, I would make it a point to drop in at his office for a cup of coffee, but more importantly to hear interesting anecdotes from this pioneering media person. I am happy that our friendship has blossomed over the past four decades. And we meet regularly now.

In our conversations, he would recall various milestone events that he witnessed in India and abroad. Many of these are told in this long-overdue memoir. He is perhaps the only journalist in India who hasn't just interviewed but has had personal conversations with every prime minister of India. He is as familiar with the leaders of today as he was with Pandit Nehru, Lal Bahadur Shastri, Indira Gandhi, I.K. Gujral, Rajiv Gandhi and Atal Bihari Vajpayee. He covered the wars in 1962, 1965, 1971 and 1999, and was a part of several entourages of presidents, prime ministers and other delegations of that time. He was there when Nehru suffered a heartbreak post the Chinese betrayal in 1962. He was in Tashkent when Shastri signed the ceasefire agreement and died mysteriously. He was in Bangladesh when the Pakistan Army surrendered. He covered Rajiv Gandhi's wedding. From riots and agitations to election campaigns, triumphs and celebrations, Prem Prakash has witnessed and recorded every heartbeat of India.

Among his most important contributions is the news agency ANI, which he set up in 1971. In the early '90s, Reuters bought a stake in ANI, and the latter soon became the dominant audiovisual news agency in South Asia. Today, ANI is among the largest syndicator of filmed news in the world and has over 300 correspondents and camerapersons working for it. Almost all international news organizations across 100 countries source their India feed from ANI.

We are living in a networked world, with over five billion people accessing news through different screens and mediums. News and information is the foundation of this always-on world. As our country sits on the cusp of a unique opportunity to become a geopolitical and economic superpower, the organization Prem Prakash set up decades ago will continue reporting the India story.

New Delhi   Amit Khanna
September 2020

Preface

My long professional journey began in 1952, when I set sail from Bombay on board the Italian ship *M.V. Neptunia* to Italy, from there onwards by train to Switzerland and finally, to Great Britain. One of our ports of call was Aden. Here, as a young Indian abroad, I was proud to find that my country's reputation was high. The Indian rupee was the currency most welcomed in shops and markets. None of the traders were interested in the pound sterling or the US dollar. The rupee was the currency of choice.

In Europe, too, I was happy to discover that India—my newly independent country, prospering under the able leadership of Jawaharlal Nehru—was highly regarded by everyone I met.

I had gone to Switzerland to attend a conference hosted by the Moral Re-Armament movement, for whom I worked as a photographer. I soon found myself very busy, working day and night at this very interesting gathering of delegates from all over the world. However, I did find time to travel across the country. It was during a trip to the city of Zurich that I met A.T. Pfister, who had set up an international news photo agency named ATP. He invited me to join his agency as ATP's representative in India—a position I was delighted to accept.

ATP was based in Zurich, the financial centre of Switzerland. There were an amazing number of banks in the city, many of which had wealthy Indians among their customers. The rupee was a hard currency, and at that time there were no restrictions on the movement of money from India.

Having heard about the fame of Swiss watches, I visited a few watch factories and was impressed by the hard-working technicians I met. I bought some low-end watches, as much as my wages permitted, for myself, my father, my mother and younger brother.

In Switzerland, I made another discovery—wine and apple cider. Despite working long hours, some of us youngsters did go out a bit. At one such picnic near the village of Caux, I first came across wine and cider. In India, of course, we had heard of wine, but most Indians who drank preferred hard liquor. Wine was regarded as simply fermented juice. Nonetheless, I quite liked the taste of wine and over the years enjoyed an occasional glass of wine in the company of friends. Today, India produces some very good wine and even exports it.

Another important lesson I learnt during that Swiss interlude: I enjoyed hard work. I never, not even for a day, felt too lethargic to get to work. It meant I was learning my trade, watching experienced operatives and listening to them.

From Switzerland I travelled through Europe until I arrived in London. It was here that I received a bit of a shock. Here, in the capital of the British Empire, it struck me that India was seen as nothing more than a land of snake charmers, elephants and princes. So ingrained was this belief that no argument could change this distorted view of India. After this experience, I was even more determined than before that I would spend a lot of my time towards ensuring that India's standing as a vibrant, energetic, modern nation was properly recognized.

Returning home towards the end of that year, I made an appointment with B.L. Sharma, then principal information officer of the Indian government, and sought accreditation as the representative of the photo agency ATP in India.

Thus began my professional career. At the beginning of 1953, I was accredited to the Government of India. This gave me easy access to no less a person than the prime minister of the country, Jawaharlal Nehru. The officials around the prime minister were friendly and cooperative. I requested permission to shoot a news photo feature on a day in the life of the prime minister. Mr Bhatt, the chief information officer, promised to mention the idea to Panditji, as Nehru was known to his friends.

To my pleasant surprise, I soon got a call from Mr Bhatt, who invited me to go to the prime minister's house to meet the people who could help me.

Upon arriving at the PM's residence, the first person I met was one Bimla Sindhi, a refugee from West Pakistan who was now on the prime minister's personal staff. I knew her quite well since she was a regular visitor to my father's photo shop, Ajanta Photo Studio, situated at 72 Queensway, now Janpath, New Delhi. (This was where I later began my own business—Asian Films—and where, in 1957, I established the Indian bureau of Visnews, the international television news agency.)

At PM Nehru's home, I received the most friendly welcome from Yashpal Kapoor, who was part of Nehru's personal staff. Yashpalji made me feel comfortable by addressing me as '*bachche*'—a term equivalent to 'son'—which he would use for the rest of his life when referring to me. It surprised me as to how trusting and informal the PM's staff was.

Later that evening, when Panditji arrived home, Yashpalji and Bimla Sindhi virtually held me by the hand when introducing me to the prime minister. I can never forget the amused reaction of Panditji looking at me—I must have looked too young and inexperienced to document a day in the life of a prime minister. But graciously, he did not say 'no', either because his staff had recommended me or because he was just being kind to a young lad. I was so excited about the prime minster giving me attention that I was willing to wait a while for his approval. After a few weeks, when I started pestering Yashpalji for a date, his reply would be, 'What's the hurry? Have a cup of tea.' But I started getting anxious about meeting my deadline.

I knew that Holi was a festival that India's first prime minister loved. This two-day festival of colours, when Indians celebrate the arrival of spring by sprinkling coloured powder and water on each other, is a photographer's delight. Every year, crowds would gather on the front lawn of Teen Murti House, the prime minister's official residence, during the festival. Panditji used to mingle quite freely with the crowds and join them in the celebration. It was so endearing to see him drenched in colours and enjoying the fun. He would then visit the homes of some of his cabinet colleagues to join in the festivities there.

I took a number of photographs of the prime minister playing Holi and then got the opportunity to photograph him whenever important visitors came to see him. It was a great start to my career. But soon, I moved on from still photographs—into the world of moving pictures and newsreels.

In 1957 I had the good fortune of being a founder member of the world's first global television news agency, the British Commonwealth International Newsfilm Agency (BCINA), which was set up by the Commonwealth broadcasters—BBC and Rank Organisation of the United Kingdom; ABC of Australia; and CBC of Canada.

The goal was that BCINA would provide worldwide news coverage to the three owner broadcasters and also sell it to TV networks throughout the world. Unfortunately, the name BCINA couldn't catch on internationally, and the term 'British' would occasionally be used by some nations to deny access. BCINA's telegraphic address was 'Visnews', and this was adopted as the name of the company. From the start, the agency began establishing bureaux in all the important world centres. Delhi was one of them.

Visnews became the world's first television news agency, delivering news footage to and from every corner of the globe. When it opened for business, there were no satellites, no Internet, no video or electronic devices. That meant moving international television news film via air cargo—a slow, cumbersome process, but one which worked well enough at the time.

While in London to discuss the establishment of Visnews, I worked out an arrangement wherein I would cover Asia from the Visnews bureau in India but could continue to pursue other journalistic endeavours. Thus, I was able to manage Asian Films, which ultimately became what it is today, Asian News International (ANI).

As the head of Visnews Asia, I was given the job of opening Visnews offices in various centres, starting with Singapore. In due course, that office became the regional centre for the distribution of content produced by Visnews, although Singapore in those days was almost like a small Indian town—far from the Asian financial and commercial giant it went on to become.

From Singapore I moved to Jakarta, the capital of Indonesia, ruled by another giant leader and freedom fighter of Asia, President Sukarno. And from Jakarta I flew to Hong Kong, a rather sleepy city at that time but soon to gain importance during the Cold War.

But while expansion of the Visnews bureaux was happening, the regional cold wars, Indo–Pak tensions, the unsettling of Tibet, China's incursions into the hitherto high Himalayan borders with India—all began to give a new dimension to news coverage that I had to focus on. The number of 'hotspots' in Asia was increasing.

India was now moving into the arena of realpolitik. Pakistan joined the United States in its Cold War against the Soviet Union. In return, the Pakistani armed forces began to receive massive American arms shipments. Peshawar emerged as the secret US Air Force base from where U-2 spy planes would fly over the Soviet Union.

Jawaharlal Nehru used diplomacy and friendship with China to try to contain the Chinese ambitions on India's borders. Panditji held the hand of Chinese premier Zhou Enlai and brought him into the Non-Aligned Movement. This at a time when communist China was not recognized by the United States and most Western nations.

Was there any other way India could have handled its relations with China? The answer to that question would in the long run lie with history. But at that time the mood in the country was to believe that if Nehru thought it to be in India's best interest, it must be so.

Such was the blind trust that Indians had in Nehru regarding foreign policy, that to think to the contrary would have been a betrayal of their national hero. By the time India became aware of China's real intentions, the latter had already built a road through Aksai Chin as a shortcut to Tibet. India had neglected the region and Panditji, speaking in Parliament, described it as an area where 'not a blade of grass grows'. Surely, barrenness should not have been sufficient reason to neglect such a strategic area but strangely, the media hesitated in asking too many questions, till it was too late.

India faced its first major crisis in its relations with China in 1962, when tensions between the two countries reached a new high. It began with the killing of an Indian border police patrol by Chinese troops. India had not moved its army to its borders with China despite China having done so; patrolling by Indian police was considered sufficient. However, the Chinese had already consolidated their position in the areas under their control. From that point on, India was fighting a rearguard action.

Nehru passed away on 27 May 1964, in many ways a broken man who realized that he was leaving India, a country he loved the most, with many unresolved issues. He had worked himself to death to restore some strength and pride to the Indian Army after the debacle of the war with China in 1962.

Lal Bahadur Shastri succeeded Panditji. As expected, the military ruler next door—Pakistan's General Ayub Khan—did not think much of India's humble second prime minister. He made his first provocative move in the Rann of Kutch, a marshy area on the western coast of India, in the state of Gujarat. That adventure by Ayub unleashed the first full-scale India-Pakistan war, during which the Indian forces crossed the border, threatening to overrun Lahore.

Shastriji's tenure as prime minister was a short one. His sudden death in Tashkent in 1966, during the peace negotiations with Pakistan, catapulted Indira Gandhi, Nehru's daughter, into the prime minister's office.

The senior leaders of the Indian National Congress opposed her, expecting her to follow their diktat—which she refused.

This led to the break-up of the party into two parts in 1969. The splitting of the INC, which had led the fight for freedom in India, shocked the nation. But Indira Gandhi was made of strong mettle. India's first woman prime minister, she fought her opponents like a tigress and served three terms.

I was in the thick of all these events, which played a momentous role in the shaping of Indian history.

Developments in television technology in the sixties resulted in rapid changes in the way news and visual material was distributed. Television was fast becoming the main avenue for delivering news. Daily TV news bulletins became the preferred source of information rather than the morning newspaper. It was a challenge which, I must say, Visnews and Asian Films met supremely well, establishing their leadership in the new television era.

The year 1971 saw a huge increase in India's TV penetration rate. Using satellites to transmit pictures, Doordarshan, the state-owned public service broadcaster, became a technologically advanced national television network. There was a hunger for news, yet it would be decades before private TV channels would be allowed to operate in India.

In Pakistan, the general election results of 1971 proved unacceptable to the Pakistani army and to Zulfikar Ali Bhutto, the leader of West Pakistan. A Bengali, Sheikh Mujibur Rahman, had emerged as majority leader—and rightly claimed to be the prime minister of Pakistan. But his claim was rejected by the powerful Pakistan Army and by Bhutto, leading to a massive crackdown on East Pakistan. Leaders of the Awami League, which supported Mujibur Rahman, were arrested.

The Pakistan Army began pushing the Hindu population of East Pakistan and the Awami League sympathizers into India. Soon, India had nearly a million people housed in refugee camps. India recognized Bangladesh's government in exile. The Indo-Pak war broke out in December, resulting in victory for India and the massive surrender of over 93,000 Pakistani troops on 16 December 1971. This was the largest surrender by any army since World War II, and it brought an end to East Pakistan as Bangladesh was born. It was the denial to Mujibur Rahman of his rightful claim to power that ultimately led to the fight for freedom in East Pakistan and to the creation of the new nation of Bangladesh.

I was in East Pakistan for weeks on end at the time, covering the events and seeing history being made.

By 1973 I had set up an independent television programme production facility in Delhi. India still had only one TV network, the state-owned Doordarshan, but I was still committed to my dream of starting an independent TV news service to tell the India story to the world.

When the satellite revolution hit India in 1991, there was an explosion of independent TV news channels. These channels were uplinked via satellites from places such as Moscow, Hong Kong and the Philippines and transmitted throughout India. Thus, much as the Government of India did not like independent TV channels, they were now here to stay, since their uplink hubs were outside India's borders.

India's first independent television news bulletin was uplinked from Moscow, by Siddharth Srivastava's ATN channel. They received a regular news service from Visnews and ANI. Visnews was later taken over by Reuters and became Reuters Television. In a further step forward, Reuters collaborated with ANI to distribute news from the subcontinent to the world. This is described later in the book.

A leading British correspondent once remarked that there are no full stops in India. This certainly applies to Indian news and politics. Sure enough, I found myself busier than ever before. The war in Afghanistan had become of major interest (I spent a lot of time in Afghanistan 1978 onwards, covering major events and travelling all over that country). News was now being moved in real time. Each day saw the emergence of new technology, with TV news channels scrambling to serve live reports to their audiences.

I have endeavoured in the following chapters to weave into a coherent narrative my experiences of covering India from the sixties to the new millennium. As an active journalist, with a career spanning five decades, and then in my work guiding ANI, I have witnessed, at first hand, the India story emerge, strengthen and thrive.

This is an eyewitness account of the huge advances I have seen the country make in its—and my—journey since 1947. It is also an account of the exciting changes we are witnessing now, adding momentum to India's march towards its destiny as a major economic and political power in the modern world—a destiny reflected in the emergence of ANI as India's premier television news agency.

I must also thank all those who coaxed me into writing this book and helped me with it. To mention a few names—my son Sanjiv, Smita, Ishaan, Peter Whittle, Amrit Maan, Colonel Jaibans Singh, Rashid Kidwai, Harinder Maan, Surinder Kapoor and Chandrakant Naidu among others.

1

Early Days

Rawalpindi, a lively city in the north of pre-Partition India, was where I was born. I have only hazy memories of that city because my father moved to Delhi long before I could form lasting impressions. But the pull of Pindi has, of course, remained as strong as ever. My father told me how our ancestors had moved from Central Asia to the Indian subcontinent, stopping first in Peshawar and then moving to Miani village near Rawalpindi—all now part of Pakistan.

India's education system in those days was very good. Though my father left school early, the school had imparted to him a well-rounded personality and given him a good hold on languages. He dropped out of school in response to Mahatma Gandhi's call to join the freedom movement. Part of my father's great influence on me lay in what he taught me about the India of those times.

My father was responsible for building and opening the first talkie (sound) cinema in Rawalpindi, called New Rose. He opened it for his maternal uncle, Lala Hans Raj Sawhney. This thread that linked our family to the world of film was to help shape my own career in later years.

India was a vast country but its population was small. People moved regularly from place to place, looking for new opportunities. However, in my father's case, it was the terrible recession of the 1930s that prompted the move to Delhi, the city that became the capital of India in 1911, when the British decided to move on from Calcutta.

My father's family settled in old Delhi, finding a new home in Kucha Natwan in Chandni Chowk. Old Delhi was very small compared to the sprawling bustle that it is today. Chandni Chowk was still the heart and hub of the city. I can never forget the daily routine when a 'mashak-wallah' would appear at around four o'clock in the afternoon in the middle of the street. The mashak was a bag of goat or sheep skin with an opening on one side from which water would be sprinkled to settle the dust and keep the street cool.

Later in the day, the kotwal, the head of the kotwali (police station), would emerge on horseback from the kotwali, followed by two constables also on horseback. They would slowly trot towards the mosque at the end of the street, then turn around and ride to the Red Fort before returning to the police station. This exercise would attract crowds of onlookers. This was a kind of demonstration by the authorities to show that law and order was being maintained and that the city was well under the control of the government and police. The police force was not large but sufficient for the population at that time.

As my father used to say, governments don't run by force. Ninety per cent of the respect for the government comes from what they call *iqbal*, or majesty.

The kitchen of our house was on the top floor, which meant my mother had to face daily raids from bands of hungry monkeys. One of our domestic helps would always be on hand for her to help keep the monkeys away, but the monkeys knew there was food in the kitchen and would not be deterred. (The monkey menace in Delhi has still not been resolved! It has spread so wide that even the Central Secretariat offices of the Government of India are overrun by hundreds of monkeys. The government makes special effort to keep the simians away.)

Another childhood memory of the city takes me back to an inkmaker's shop right below our flat. I would watch the men stir a thick black concoction, which they would spread on leafy sheets shaped like small tablets. They would then let these dry in the open until they hardened and became ink tablets. Adding a little water to them produced black ink.

There were a few private schools in Delhi for British children, but Indian children mostly went to government schools, where the standard of education was very high. My younger brother and I first started studying under a tutor, who came to our house to prepare us for school. We were admitted to a municipal primary school in old Delhi's Bhagirath Palace area. From there, we were moved to another municipal school at Kashmere Gate. I have happy memories of my schooling. The teachers were hard-working but severe punishment was the order of the day, even in primary schools. So you had to do well.

After finishing school at Kashmere Gate, I moved to the higher secondary school which was opposite our house in Chandni Chowk. When the term at my Kashmere Gate school ended, I was transferred to a different branch of the same school located in Gole Market in New Delhi. In Doctor's Lane to be precise.

My father had set up a photo studio in Kashmere Gate, a locality popular among the city's elite in those days. New Delhi was still being developed and many who lived there would come to this area for shopping. Close to Kashmere Gate was an area known as Civil Lines. In most Indian cities the British had built exclusive residential areas for their own comfort—and these were known as Civil Lines. It was here that the privileged lived.

The charms of Chandni Chowk

I grew up in Chandni Chowk, and I have some fond memories of my childhood there. Chandni Chowk was not as crowded as it is today. In the Mughal era, I am told, there used to be a canal flowing through what is today's main street. The canal was filled in sometime during the 1920s.

Kuchas in old Delhi are gated communities. Entering through their gates back in the day, it was as though one had arrived in a miniature city. The kucha had its own streets, shops, homes—everything. Our home was very close to the entrance of Kucha Natwan. Located here were several food shops, especially sweetmeat shops which were the pride of the residents of Chandni Chowk.

Even today, Chandni Chowk is famous for the delectable food it offers. Delhi's *bedvi* (called puri in Punjabi), made with wheat flour and other ingredients, is one such Chandni Chowk specialty that my family loved. It is served with potato curry cooked in Delhi style and Suji Halwa, with chutney on the side. This was our breakfast on many occasions. Another Delhi specialty is *nagodi*, a smaller puri which is filled with halwa and is eaten whole.

The reason I mention this is that on the rare occasion that I find myself eating these delicacies, it just isn't the halwa I savour, it is the flood of memories that comes gushing into the mind. Every family member had a favourite dish and whenever we had guests visiting, my father would send for some local specialty and my mother would make steaming cups of strong tea.

Cheek by jowl with the street food shops were the shops selling ittar or perfume. Their fragrance pervaded the whole street. The shops were mainly run by Muslims. One shop in particular had very kind owners who would call in young men like me and sprinkle some ittar on us.

Another thing unique about such neighbourhoods in those days was that we could hop across each other's terraces, balconies and verandas, and nobody raised any objections. There was no concept of privacy! The footpaths were wider and there were hardly any motor vehicles on the roads, so we youngsters were not bound by space or safety concerns.

Chandni Chowk had tram cars. Children from the kucha, including me, would run after a tram and jump on for a free ride. It was great fun. Life as a child was most enjoyable. We played in a playground behind the Town Hall. (The playground is now known as Gandhi Ground.)

There were murmurs of impending violence and trouble in the 1940s, but these did not seem to bother the family. In 1942, when the freedom struggle gained momentum and Mahatma Gandhi called on Indians to protest against the British as part of the Quit India Movement, there were demonstrations in Chandni Chowk. However, the police dispersed the protestors quite easily; the protests had lasted barely three days before Chandni Chowk was back to its old routine.

The street behind our house was lined with colourful shops—not just those selling perfumes, as mentioned earlier, but also a number of clothing shops. As you moved down the road, towards the Fatehpuri Mosque, on the left was Ballimaran, an area largely inhabited by Muslims. Ballimaran, too, was full of colour, with food outlets everywhere.

Right opposite Ballimaran, across Chandni Chowk, is Katra Neel. After the mutiny of 1857, when the British began taking over the properties of various officials working for the Mughal court and, in general, hounding Muslims and Mughal supporters, a lot of people were brought from the Punjab region, particularly Lahore, and moved into Katra Neel. The confiscated properties were auctioned by the British government and were mostly bought by the newcomers from Lahore. They became big landowners of Chandni Chowk and the kuchas. Among them, Chhunna Mal was reputed to be the biggest landlord of Delhi.

At the heart of Chandni Chowk stood a very tall clock tower. The British loved clock towers. They built them in most cities. They also placed huge clocks on the facades of railway stations. I don't remember if the clock installed in the Chandni Chowk clock tower was similar to the one at Big Ben in London, but I can clearly recall that the tower here was quite imposing. The bells chimed loud enough for people all over the neighbourhood to hear. Many a time, much to my mother's annoyance, I would use a stepladder to climb to the roof of our house to look at the clock tower. And I took great pleasure in her chiding me afterwards, 'You could have fallen and broken your bones.'

Nearby, to the right of the clock tower on the street leading to the Fatehpuri Mosque, was the majestic Town Hall. This heritage building still stands gracefully today, but no one seems to know what to do with it. It used to be the office of the city's municipality. The Delhi of today has many municipalities, and the Town Hall is hardly used. There have been many ideas on how to repurpose it. It would, for example, make a very nice hotel since it has gardens all around it. But it takes a long time to take decisions in our country . . .

Close to the Town Hall was the Garam Hamam or hot bath. Again, this was a tradition which came from Turkey or Central Asia, where there are public baths with hot water. Delhi gets pretty cold in winter, so these hot baths were a welcome facility.

I love the street in Chandni Chowk where I lived. Only once in the last few years, sometime in 2015, I took the metro to Chandni Chowk. Of course, the place I saw was not the Chandni Chowk I knew in my childhood. For one thing, it was difficult to walk on the crowded pavements. And the traffic was like it is in the rest of Delhi. I don't think I will go back to the street where I lived. Those memories should stay how they were, unsullied by the present.

My memories of my first school are very limited. The classes had only about thirty students and the teachers, mostly male, were addressed as 'Masterji'. Then, from the primary school in Chandni Chowk, I was moved, along with my younger brother, to another primary school in Kashmere Gate because that was closer to my father's photography studio.

The major shops those days used to be at Kashmere Gate, which was the first big shopping centre in Delhi. This market grew in importance when the British moved into Delhi after the mutiny, and again after 1911, when Delhi was declared the capital.

I remember the governor general's house, built near the Civil Lines, where the University of Delhi's North Campus is located today. The university vice-chancellor's office was once the governor general's house. It is in this house that Lord Louis Mountbatten is said to have proposed to Lady Mountbatten. I remember, too, the Secretariat building and the Assembly House, which now serves as the Legislative Assembly of the state of Delhi.

I really enjoyed my schooling in Kashmere Gate. Being there gave me the chance to frequently walk to the photography store that my father and his elder brother had opened. It was fun to be there and there were cinemas just down the street. There was also a sweet shop near the school and we used to visit it often to enjoy Delhi's speciality, the bedvi. The shopkeeper's name was Mitthan. Later, when I joined Hindu College, I found that Mitthan's shop was right next to it.

My parents moved to New Delhi sometime during the mid-1940s because Kashmere Gate was losing its charm. New Delhi had been built. It was the time of World War II. Lots of American troops had arrived in India and some were stationed in Delhi. By this time my father had opened his photography store at 72 Queensway and had two other businesses, one at Parliament Street and another, a restaurant, in Connaught Place.

I must give you give you my impression of Connaught Place, which was once the most beautiful shopping centre in the world. I would often go around CP. Even in summer you could go around the market because the walkway is like a circular veranda—shaded, absolutely comfortable. It remained so till the late sixties, when it began to decay. In the evenings, some friends and I would take a leisurely walk around and then go to one of the restaurants, like La Boheme, which was in the outer circle and run by Nirula's. They had a lovely Chinese restaurant on the mezzanine floor. Eating there meant you felt like you were in a dining car of an Indian Railways train, the decor was such.

I would regularly go to my father's studio at Queensway and gape at the American soldiers who came to get their photographs taken. Their barracks were nearby and the Americans had all kinds of offices in the Queensway area.

Life in New Delhi was quite different from what it was like in Chandni Chowk. Close to our flat in CP's outer circle was the Railways Playground where I went with friends to play cricket.

That was how I was introduced to the sport that I, and the rest of India, love.

Meanwhile, my father built his own house in Karol Bagh. I am not sure why he chose that place because the area was more expensive than Sundar Nagar in Lutyens's New Delhi and other places. A lot of the areas in New Delhi were regarded as unliveable because of large open spaces but Karol Bagh was a lively place, a little posher than old Delhi. So, we moved to Karol Bagh. By that time, the war had ended and the Americans were leaving.

During the war, the government had requisitioned the school building in Anand Parbat which belonged to Ramjas School. So after the war the school moved back here from Doctor's Lane. Living in Karol Bagh was very convenient for me as it gave me easy access to Anand Parbat and to my school, which occupied a beautiful old heritage building set in lovely grounds. Here again, the teachers would make every effort to ensure that students did well in exams, and I did well there.

Every year at my school, there was an inspection by a British education inspector. That was quite an event in the school with the principal and teachers under a lot of stress, hoping that the school make the grade. There were other activities too. I joined the boy scouts and I was awarded a few medals—one for cooking! I love my amateurish cooking even today.

I thoroughly enjoyed going to camps with the scouts. One such camp was in Tara Devi, just below Shimla. It was my first visit to the region. We went to by train to Kalka, then took the Toy Train and stayed at the Tara Devi Hostel. It was all great fun. I ranked second in my school-leaving exams.

College days

At the Hindu College, my first day was quite interesting. I was warned about seniors ragging junior students to intimidate them, and I arrived at the college a bit apprehensive but seemingly bold. The college had a huge bicycle stand where I saw some seniors waiting. They grabbed me and took me to the cafeteria. There, they ordered samosas, tea and cold drinks and handed me the bill. Thank God I had enough money to pay for it all!

But I made some lifelong friends. Among them were my dear friends Inder Sharma, Dr Pabley, Bhagirath Bhalla, Kanwar Rajender Singh, Madan Nayyar, S.D. Pandey, Satya Dev Sharma; and the girls were Aruna Sharma, Indira, Nirmal Randhwa, Urmila, Swaran Kapoor. Inder later married Aruna. Kanwar Rajender Singh married Indira. Swaran was a close friend, but when I went away to Europe we lost touch. We stayed friends all our lives, marriages, children, grandchildren, bereavements—we have been through it all on the road of life.

I took an interest in the Boat Club and became the secretary. The Yamuna River used to be so beautiful back then. When I see the river now, overflowing with effluents, it makes me weep.

In those days, I used to love taking a boat on the Yamuna, rowing down to the railway bridge and then rowing back upstream to the club. We had a large membership at the Boat Club and competed in an annual race with St Stephen's College. We always did well in this contest because we took our rowing and boating seriously.

I also liked debating. We had an excellent teacher named Professor Premchand who used to preside over what was known as the Hindu College Parliament. My friend Inder was elected our 'Prime Minister' that year, and I became his 'Home Minister'. Professor Premchand used to coach us in public speaking and he taught us how to debate effectively. It was a splendid training ground for later life.

When I was in the second year, we all went to the launch of the National Union of Students in Bombay. There, I was elected to the national executive, with Ravi Verma as the president. He was later to become a minister in the cabinet of Morarji Desai. He was a Congressman at heart and a great gentleman.

After arriving back in Delhi from Bombay, I wrote a complete report on the launch of the National Union of Students. I detailed properly how a nationwide body of students had become a reality.

That was, in a way, my first attempt at what was to become my career later on: journalism. I am happy to say that my report was greatly appreciated by the college principal and the staff in the common room, as well as by other professors and teachers.

I graduated from college in 1951 with excellent grades and distinction in three subjects. I was keen to begin my career in photography and news. But my father wanted me to study further. A compromise was reached, and I was asked to work in the family owned photo studio.

My first cousin, a news cameraman, offered me apprenticeship as his assistant and soon afterwards my father introduced me to an outstanding documentary maker, Dr Pathi, who took me to Kullu, where he was shooting. He took me on as his apprentice, and that proved to be a great learning experience for me.

The visit also opened my eyes to what was happening in post-Independence India. There were no hotels in Kullu back then and we were staying at a 'circuit house', which is a kind of guest house for senior civil servants and those recommended by government officials.

One day, the caretaker of the circuit house came crying to Dr Pathi. The man was upset because the wife of the district commissioner had taken away expensive carpets from the circuit house and replaced them with ordinary ones. The man was scared that he might be accused of stealing the carpets. As a young lad, I was shocked to hear this. The circuit houses, I am told, were so well-furnished that carpets used to be imported from Persia and they were, of course, very expensive. I have never forgotten that unhappy event—my first brush, as an adult, with government corruption in free India.

Independence on the horizon

Memories of the dawn of independence are still etched on my mind. The year 1946 was when we all started looking forward to independence with great expectation. I was a boy but I heard all the stories told by the adults at home and in the neighbourhood. It was a strange time. The Americans had left New Delhi. The city was being deserted and some British troops were also leaving. I remember the summer of 1946 and the later years when Delhi was practically emptying out.

There was a lot of speculation in the air. I had the good fortune, even at that age, to see Mahatma Gandhi. He was staying in what was then known as the Bhangi Colony of New Delhi, during the period of the independence negotiations. I was there, helping my cousin Ved Prakash film the event. (I still feel that the area's name, Bhangi Colony, was derogatory and discriminatory towards the people who kept New Delhi clean; the word 'bhangi' was used as a pejorative for lower castes.)

I will always remember the sight of Mahatma Gandhi and the other great Indian leaders I saw at that time. Until then, I had only heard about them or seen their photos in newspapers. But I will never forget the day I actually saw them.

As a young boy of around fifteen, it was quite an experience for me to stand by the side of Ved Parkash as he covered the arrival of the Congress leaders to meet Gandhiji, about the ongoing freedom talks with the British. Pandit Jawaharlal Nehru, Maulana Azad, Sardar Patel and others arrived one after the other. We then went into the room where they were sat on the floor, with Gandhiji at the other end of the room. Gandhiji was dressed in his dhoti and was sitting with papers in his hand. My first impression was that he looked very thin and small. Even as I held the light for the camera, my eyes were on Mahatma Gandhi, who looked like a sadhu to me. Filming and photography took place for just a few minutes during which the leaders were either quiet or talking jovially. Gandhiji remained quiet all through.

I also had another occasion to watch Mahatma Gandhi when he came to the meeting of Asian Relations Conference held just before Independence. Gandhiji came to address it, as usual, in his dhoti. This Conference was attended by many figures from across Asia who were leading independence movements in their countries.

As India moved towards independence, tension was building in the air. There was talk of partitioning the country into two. A new viceroy, Lord Mountbatten, had arrived in New Delhi. He was said to be very friendly with Jawaharlal Nehru, who was heading the interim Indian government at that momentous time.

The whole country, and particularly Delhi, was brimming with anger at the thought of partition. The proposal was straining the relations between the Hindu and Muslim communities. There were no riots at that time, only tensions. Then came that great night of independence. We were all glued to the radio as India became free. There were great celebrations. My mother made home-cooked sweets to distribute in the neighbourhood, but there was a sense of foreboding about troubling times ahead, even though we had become a free nation.

Riots ruin freedom delight

The next day, 16 August 1947, brought with it tragic stories. Riots had broken out in Punjab. We heard stories of people crossing the new border and walking towards India. Photographs of the first migrants arriving in Delhi from West Punjab appeared in newspapers. There was an attempt by the government at that point to stop them from entering Delhi, but that did not work.

Once they came to Delhi, riots broke out. People in the city were angry at seeing the refugees arriving en masse. But the new arrivals had left their homes, businesses and everything behind in Pakistan and were not mentally or physically capable of handling a hostile response.

When people from West Punjab arrived in Delhi, having lost their homes and belongings in Pakistan to Muslims there, they were angered that many Muslims were living in Delhi and had not vacated their homes to leave for Pakistan. In their conversations with residents in Delhi, they said that they had left West Punjab because they were told that all Muslims were leaving Delhi to come to the new country of Pakistan, and that getting accommodation in north India would thus be no problem for them. Hence they were livid that many Muslims had chosen to stay back.

Riots broke out in the city when the refugees and the original inhabitants couldn't control their anger over the shock of what they had lost and what they were potentially going to lose. The crowd that later turned into a mob clearly wanted the Muslims to leave their homes. The government evacuated several thousand Muslims to camps for their safety. Their homes thus vacated were occupied by the refugees from Punjab. Their logic was simple: Muslims must go and take their homes in Pakistan. The swap, they felt, was legitimate. The riots also resulted in several Muslim families leaving the city on their own for Pakistan after making arrangement with refugees from Pakistan about exchange of homes. Lala Yodh Raj, chairman of the Punjab National Bank, exchanged his palatial house in Lahore with an equally palatial house on Hailey Road in Lutyens's Delhi which belonged to a Muslim family.

I watched in horror from the top of the Tropical Building, people rushing here and there in anger, going towards Paharganj, where a sizeable population of Muslims had settled. Many of the Muslims thought that they had no option but to leave for Pakistan.

Tropical Building was situated in Block-H of Connaught Circus, as Connaught Place was once known. (It is still there.) The building was owned by Tropical Insurance Co. Ltd of Calcutta. This insurance company had been started by Lala Shankar Lal, an associate of Netaji Subhas Chandra Bose. Lala Shankar Lal was also the chairman of the company. He was sent by Netaji to Japan as early as 1939 to make contact with the Japanese leaders.

According to building rules in Lutyens's Delhi, the ground floor was reserved for shops, the first floor had offices and residential flats were on the second floor. My father had moved to a flat in Tropical Building and had left Chandni Chowk when the business moved from Kashmere Gate to 72 Queensway. Though it was a two-room flat, it was spacious enough, with a large terrace where we slept at night during the summer. There were no air conditioners or coolers in those days. Thus, when our relatives exiting west Punjab arrived here, they were all able to sleep in relative comfort on charpoys or stringed cots under open skies at night. Of the two bedrooms, we used one as a sitting room.

Among the flood of arrivals were all our relatives from Rawalpindi. Our small flat in Connaught Place was suddenly cramped with relatives. Since it was summer, everyone could sleep on the terrace in the open. We had a huge terrace and lots of cots. One of the families staying with us was that of my father's uncle, Lala Hansraj Sawhney, who was a leading advocate in Rawalpindi. We all managed extremely well. Mother and the other women would cook food and everybody was in good humour, even though many had left their old lives behind.

Lala Hansraj Sawhney had left behind his prized possession, his entire library. He was hoping to go back one day, which, as was now clear, was never going to happen. But the Royal Air Force was helping evacuate people from West Pakistan, and it so happened that my father and my cousin were covering this airlift for foreign broadcasters. My father was able to hitch a ride on an RAF plane to Rawalpindi for him and his uncle to bring back whatever they could.

I was told that when they got to the house in Rawalpindi, they found it occupied by a friend of Sawhney Sahab who was shocked to see them. He was not happy but could not refuse them entry. So they were able to bring back a few trunk loads of books. They were so heavy that one of the RAF officers asked my father, 'Hey, hey! What have you got here? Stones or what?' And that's how Sawhney Sahab's library came back to New Delhi.

Soon, riots engulfed all of Punjab. Trains filled with slaughtered people arrived at and departed from stations. It was all very tragic and no one knew how to stop it. I remember reading at the time—and my father talking about it—that Prime Minister Jawaharlal Nehru himself came out on the streets to try and control the crowd and help the police. Of course, he was taken away by his security detail because the crowds had become very angry.

After a few seemingly endless weeks, things settled and Sawhney Sahab found accommodation in the Pearey Lal Building in Connaught Place. He moved in there and life steadily got back to normal. But his family had lost everything. My own family lost everything in the village of Miani in west Punjab, including the land and the house that stood there. There was also a house we owned in the Naya Mohalla in Rawalpindi which was also gone.

Another memory of Partition is of people with loud speakers in cars and jeeps, driving around the area and making announcements regarding the mass exodus from west Punjab to India. They said we needed to airdrop food for the refugees. Everybody was expected to cook food and pack it very securely so that the parcel would not burst open when dropped from the air.

So all families, all households, everyone in the neighbourhood and, in our own house, my mother and all the women who had come over from the 'other side' (we still couldn't call it Pakistan) and were staying with us, made parathas with aloo, added some achar (pickle) and wrapped it in a very strong cloth packing.

From our home, dozens of food packets were given to the people collecting them. The packets were loaded in jeeps, taken to the airport and airdropped to feed the advancing crowds. This mass migration created more tension and bitterness among communities, as photographs started appearing in the newspapers each day of the sea of humanity moving towards India.

Groups of people on both sides were attacked as they moved. There were horror stories of women being kidnapped and taken away. I remember reading how Lady Mountbatten and an Indian minister named Rajkumari Amrit Kaur travelled to what had become Pakistan to see if they could find abducted women and try and bring them back safely.

It was tragic. The mayhem continued for a while until, at last, people began settling down. Having left their homes across the border, many had come to Delhi, to Amritsar. A large number had even gone to Kashmir. Sadly, they were rejected again because Kashmiris didn't want them there, thinking their presence might trigger more riots.

There were losses in our family too. My father told us of one Lala Amolak Ram who entrusted his friends with the task of escorting him to the railway station. Instead, they attacked him and escaped with all his money. He never reached the railway station. Such things happened frequently and left deep psychological wounds on Punjabis—wounds which, I am afraid, remain to the present day.

But my family was, of course, settled in Delhi. Our suffering was indirect and could be borne.

Take-off in the profession

I began my career as a news photographer. I chose to work on photo features, which gave me the opportunity to write while I took photographs.

The Illustrated Weekly of India was the country's leading pictorial magazine. It was published in Bombay and was extremely popular. I started submitting my features to them and was thrilled when they carried my first feature with three pages of photographs. More such features followed. In a very short while, even at my young age, I was gaining a reputation as a photojournalist.

At the same time, I was taking whatever news photos I could in and around Delhi and submitting them to the local newspapers. I was thrilled when *Evening News*, the evening newspaper of *Hindustan Times* with a large circulation in Delhi, carried a picture taken by me.

Seeking international exposure, I contacted the London news photo agency Planet News and began submitting photographs and news features to them. The *Illustrated London News*, a prestigious London magazine, also carried my photos. Meanwhile, I became one of the prime contributors to the *Illustrated Weekly of India*.

I once covered a trade union meeting at the Talkatora Gardens in Delhi, addressed by a British delegation. My photograph of that meeting was published by *Evening News*. Soon afterwards I got a telephone call from an Englishman named Roger Hicks, who had been at the meeting. He had seen the photograph in the newspaper and invited me over for a cup of tea. I was quite excited because it was my first encounter with a foreigner, apart from the ones I used to meet at my father's studio.

I found that Hicks was a representative of the Moral Re-Armament (MRA) movement, about which I knew nothing. He explained how they were trying to generate interest in the movement and asked if I would care to attend their forthcoming assembly in Switzerland and perhaps work with their photographic team. All my travel and accommodation expenses, he told me, would be borne by them.

I gave the idea some thought. It looked like a great opportunity for me to learn how English people went about the business of photography and journalism. I was also impressed by Roger Hicks and his colleague David Young, who would accompany me to Switzerland. I said I would certainly talk to my father about this and get back to him. My father gave me the go-ahead and told me not to worry about New Delhi but to work hard on my future. Thus began a new chapter in my life.

A milestone

The invitation to attend the Moral Re-Armament Assembly in Switzerland was an early milestone in my long professional journey. It was the summer of 1952. Hicks told me that I had to take a ship from Bombay in three weeks' time. I didn't have a passport but he introduced me to a senior ICS officer, Krishna Prasad, who signed my passport application form, which was rushed to the police station at Kashmere Gate for background check and verification. I received my passport one week later. There was no requirement for a visa to the UK in those days. But one required a visa for Switzerland, which could be obtained from the Swiss embassy in Delhi.

My whole family came to see me off with garlands, as was the tradition, at the railway station in Delhi. My cousin Ved Prakash escorted me to Bombay where Hicks had made arrangements for our comfortable stay. Finally came the day when I had to board an Italian ship bound for Genoa in Italy. I was to go from there to Switzerland, where the conference was taking place. And later to London.

So there I was, a twenty-year-old lad starting a new journey to unknown lands.

Sailing from Bombay, I looked at the Indian coast as we steadily moved towards the Arabian Peninsula. At our first stop, Aden, I went ashore and bought a few things from shopkeepers who asked to be paid in rupees, not dollars or pounds. The Indian rupee, as I have said before, was a strong currency, even stronger than the US dollar. At the time of India's independence, one Indian rupee was equal to 1.12 US dollars.

I made a few friends on that voyage but I still remember one fine lady named Sangeeta who took me under her wing like an elder sister. She was going to Milan to her brother, having divorced her husband in Delhi. I had heard about divorce but was astonished to hear that such things happened in India too. The ship took us to Alexandria and from there to Italy. I went on to Milan, where I bid goodbye to Sangeeta.

In Milan, I was welcomed by some of the Re-Armament people. The next day, I took a train to Switzerland and arrived at Montreux. From Montreux, a mountain train took me to a small village called Caux. The place had a huge assembly hall and hotels mainly catering to guests attending conventions.

I was welcomed by David Channer, head of the photography division of the organization, who escorted me to my room. I was to share the room with David who, later, became a lifelong friend. This was the beginning of another stage in my career.

I was well settled at the Grand Hotel with my room-mate. David would wake up early every morning to meditate. He followed this with a diary-writing session, which he called 'guidance from God, listening to the inner voice'. David told me that this was how he focused and prepared his plan for each new day. It was my first experience of this kind of discipline. Thereafter, I would sit with David and work out my own plan for the day—whether it was writing letters to the family, work, or going sightseeing, you decided what you wanted to do during the day and that became your plan.

I was fascinated with all the new photographic equipment in the office. I would put it to the enthusiasm of youth that besides taking photographs every day I would spend a lot of time in the darkroom to ensure everything was done correctly. I knew this was a crucial step to producing top-quality photographs. You had to master everything, from developing negatives and making prints to composing pictures. It meant a great deal and I learnt a lot.

I sent some pictures back to India and some were published, much to the delight of my friend Roger Hicks. I made great friends during my time in Switzerland, and it was as though I'd been given an acknowledgement for my hard work when I was invited to dine with the organization's founder, Frank Buchman.

He talked of my joining his organization, but I was unsure if I wanted to make that commitment as yet.

Switzerland was beautiful, but let me tell you about the first shock I got in that country. I was on a train to Montreux. When I left the train I realized I did not have my camera. I rushed to the station master's office to report my loss. He alerted the next station but nothing was found. The station master said there were some Italian thieves on the train and perhaps they had taken it. I was heartbroken. I wrote to my father and told him what had happened. He promptly responded, saying the camera was fully insured. He sent me a form, which I completed, signed and sent back. I received the full value of the camera before I left Switzerland.

Off to Paris and London

From there I moved to Paris. Since I had very little money, I decided to explore Paris by foot. To this day I remember almost all those streets and areas. I wanted to see the historical places I had read about in books. It was such an exhilarating stay for me, and I have often revisited Paris whenever time and opportunity allowed.

After three days in Paris, I took the train to London. In those days there was no tunnel under the English Channel, and the whole train, with all its passengers, had to be loaded on to a ferry, transported across the Channel and then taken off the ferry at the other end.

I shared my compartment with an elderly American gentleman. I had the lower berth and offered it to him, at which he was delighted. The next morning we chatted, and it turned out that he was the founder and chairman of America's leading weekly newsreel, *News of the Day*. He gave me his business card, told me which hotel he was staying at in London and asked me to meet him to discuss the prospect of working for him in the United States.

When the train chugged into London, I was met by someone from the MRA. He took me first to Berkeley Square and to a house which had once belonged to Lord Robert Clive, also known as 'Clive of India'.

I was finally taken to 39 Charles Street, Mayfair. The house belonged to General George Channer, who had worked in India and was the father of my friend, David Channer. It was only later that I learnt that Mayfair is part of west London, one of the most expensive areas of the city. Unfortunately, I was still suffering from the cold I had developed in Paris and wasn't allowed to leave the house for five days.

When I felt well enough, I made a beeline for the hotel where that kind gentleman from *News of the Day* was staying, but much to my disappointment he had already left for America. There ended the first part of my dream. But I have always believed in a Punjabi saying my mother taught me, '*Rabb jo karda ae, changey wasdey karda ae* (Whatever the Lord does, is for your good).'

I returned to learn that my colleagues had organized a job for me at a London studio. I joined the next day and learnt a lot about studio photography. Later, I went with them to the field, covering news events. I also went to the Rank Organisation film studios and spent a fortnight there, working on some of their newsreels.

By December 1952, I had already celebrated my twenty-first birthday in Switzerland. I was happy, but London in winter was a very dark place. Each house had a basement full of coal, used for heating purposes. Every chimney belched out smoke, making London perhaps the world's most polluted city. Englishmen kept two detachable shirt collars with them at all times: one for the day and another for when they went out in the evening. Even breathing in that city was painful. That very year many people in London died from what they called smog—a deadly mixture of smoke and fog which hovered over the city.

I stayed in London for two more months, but my main memory of the city is of waking up in the dark and going to sleep in the dark. I did go out a bit, but London was very foggy and you did not see much sun.

As my time in the UK neared its end, I made plans to return home. Roger Hicks was disappointed that I had decided not to continue with the MRA. I was grateful for all he had done for me, but it was time to get back to India, to get back home.

And so I took my first flight. I flew on an Air India Super Constellation to Bombay via Paris and Rome. I spent the night in Bombay and took another Air India flight, albeit on a smaller plane, to Delhi. In Delhi I was welcomed by all my friends, family and some of my father's staff with garlands.

The next day I asked my father to introduce me to B.L. Sharma, who was his friend and the principal information officer of the Government of India. I was ready to go to work. I had a business card from the ATP photo agency and a letter stating that I represented the company in India. B.L. Sharma took me to the press facility officer and asked him to process my credentials.

Two weeks later I was accredited to the Government of India and my career had begun.

2

A Bright Start under
Nehru's Benign Watch

I was just about twenty-two when I reached an important milestone in my professional journey. In 1953, I was accredited to the Indian government, of which Pandit Jawaharlal Nehru was the prime minister. To be able to cover news concerning the Government of India and its ministers at that time, one needed accreditation from the Press Information Bureau (PIB).

Fresh from its newly won freedom, India was a rather innocent nation—perhaps still overawed by the memories of British rule. There were no security threats of the kind we see today. Getting accredited to the central government was a much simpler affair in those days, perhaps because there were not too many journalists in Delhi. The accreditation usually came through after security clearance by the police. The PIB worked as the main department of the government for journalists looking to get information about or access to various government departments.

Being a freelancer and reporting for the Swiss news agency ATP, I soon learnt that Jawaharlal Nehru was in great demand internationally. The PIB accreditation brought me close to the prime minister's household, where I got along very well with the staff, particularly Yashpal Kapoor and Bimla Sindhi.

Nehru effect

I had open access and made frequent visits to the prime minister's house, and soon Panditji would treat me like a family member. I was a young, lean guy at that time, and quite uninhibited. I spent a lot of time in that magnificent house, Teen Murti Bhavan. Panditji's wise guidance played a major role in my career.

As a photographer, I used my own Rolleicord, a very small German camera that outperformed the ones used by more senior cameramen around me. All other cameramen in those days used Speed Graphics, huge American plate cameras. Panditji was always amused to see me working with my small camera and was quite pleased when he saw the results. He was very photogenic, which made my task easier in a way!

The other photographers were dismissive of me at the start but soon found that I was making my mark with the Rolleicord. The old veterans were sceptical. Their motto was, 'Yeh ladka kahan se aa gaya (where has this lad come from)?' My photos were getting published everywhere, so within a year they, perforce, admitted me into the News Cameramen's Association (NCA), a position earlier denied to me as I was too junior. Not only did they admit me, they later elected me general secretary. I then led the association, and to make it really effective I ensured that NCA got affiliated to the Indian Federation of Working Journalists (IFWJ).

Some of the photographers had thought that by admitting me into the IFWJ, they would inveigle me into getting them access to Panditji's house. But I didn't misuse my access to the PM; it was for purely professional work. The photographers wanted the government to stop the sale of the PM's pictures at cheap rates, because it was hurting their own prices. But the government wanted the PM's pictures to be made available to all, including Indian publications that could not afford the exorbitant prices of private photographs.

Panditji took a keen interest in my work, knowing my pictures would be seen abroad. Throughout his tenure as prime minister and external affairs minister, he personally took note of India's image abroad, even though this was the job of the publicity division of the foreign office.

I vividly recall an American network asking me to get the prime minister's view on what the twentieth century would hold for Indian children. Panditji was very fond of kids and agreed to do the interview. I borrowed a movie camera (which could record sound) from a foreign network in Delhi and, following official suggestion, set it up in his house.

As he sat down for our exchange, he asked me the subject of the interview and how I intended to handle it. Raw as I was, I simply handed him the cable from the American network. He read it and suggested that I first start the camera, then ask the question, go back behind the camera and record his reply. The interview turned out to be a big hit in America.

Another unforgettable moment from that time was when I acquired my own sound camera, an Auricon Cine Voice. I asked the prime minister for an interview, to be shot with my new camera, and I was instantly given the permission to set it up in Nehru's Parliament office. I was allowed just fifteen minutes to do the interview. Before starting, I told Panditji that my camera would only run for two-and-a-half minutes, whereafter I would need to change the film. He was very accommodating and ensured that his replies were not too long.

The interview lasted for well over half an hour. Panditji's dreaded secretary, M.O. Mathai, was making angry gestures at me from outside the office. He wanted me to come out. It was Mathai's job to ensure that no one spent more than the stipulated time with the PM. He had earned the reputation of being a tough person. But as he tried to interrupt the interview, I refused to look at him. When the interview ended, he told me that I had encroached on the prime minister's teatime. Nonetheless, when Mathai came in, Panditji asked him to arrange tea for me too. Over tea, he asked me all about my new camera and inquired when I would get a bigger one.

Movies versus television

My main aim now was to move into television news. Television had made its appearance in the West during the 1950s. But people who owned television sets in Europe at that time would lock up their precious new devices, which is exactly what happened during the early television days in India. Television as a medium did not have the reach or popular appeal of cinema newsreels. My father launched India's first independent newsreel soon after Independence. There is a story behind that event and how it happened.

In 1942, after the Congress party had voted not to cooperate with the British in pursuing the war, many Congress leaders found themselves in jail for supporting the Quit India Movement. However, the British war effort was promoted by the popular cinema newsreel *Indian News Parade*, controlled by the British government, and proved very popular in gathering Indian support.

The interim government of India, which was in place by 1946, did not approve of this newsreel. It was felt that *Indian News Parade* had defeated the purpose of Congress party's non-cooperation call. So the government shut it down. This left a vacuum in the cinema newsreel sector. My father filled it by launching his own version, called *Eastern Movies,* which ran for two years.

Within a couple of years after Independence, the honeymoon period of India's new government was over. People became critical when cases of corruption began to surface. So the Indian government once again decided now to launch its own cinema newsreel, *Indian News Review.* They felt the need to educate people and inform them about government activities. But this time, unlike under British rule, they brought in a law requiring cinemas to devote twenty minutes of screen time to government newsreels—ten minutes of news and ten minutes of documentary. It meant cinemas were forced to run twenty minutes of government propaganda as well as ten minutes of material from my father's *Eastern Movies.* In those days, Indian movies invariably ran for three hours.

Soon, the cinema owners realized this was unviable. They were losing time for commercials. They told my father that, although *Eastern Movies* was very popular unlike the government-sponsored *Indian News Review*, they could not afford to run it any more. So that brought about the death of *Eastern Movies*.

The idea of going back into that business continued to nag at me. The big American and British newsreel companies already had their own staff in India, so I looked elsewhere. I eventually went into business with two foreign companies—Warner–Pathé News in America and Deutsche Wochenschau in what was then West Germany.

I loved working in the newsreel world again but the days of cinema newsreels were coming to an end in 1957. I began to think seriously about television. I heard that the newsreel companies Paramount News, Warner–Pathé News and Rank Organisation were thinking of forming a television news agency. I decided to get involved.

Thus it was that in 1957 I landed in London to join the founding team of the British Commonwealth International Newsfilm Agency Limited (BCINA). By strange coincidence, the first editor of the BCINA was Tony Whyte, son of Sir Allen Whyte, who was the first speaker of India's Central Legislative Assembly that came into being following the Government of India Act of 1935. The act created bicameral legislature at the centre—Federal Assembly, or Lower House; and Council of State, Upper House, like the Rajya Sabha of today.

It was not long before it became clear that the name BCINA did not convey the company's purpose, and that the word British in the name made it seem like a government agency. So the name was changed to Visnews (Visual News), which was BCINA's telegraphic address. Ultimately, this is what became the world's greatest television news agency. I am so proud to have been a part of the team that founded Visnews, and I will cherish this association all my life. The agency was later taken over by Reuters and became Reuters TV. It is still the world's largest TV news agency.

Beyond snake charmers

I had seen India's image projected abroad as a country of snake charmers and elephants. This image, as I was to find later, was deliberately chosen by the British to humiliate India. Once, when I was invited to the home of a nice gentleman who was a BBC cameraman in London, I was amused to find that my friend's children had expected me to be dressed like a 'Red Indian' and were afraid of meeting me. This may be an odd incident, but it has stayed with me.

Thus, when preparing to launch my own agency—later to become ANI—my aim was to correct this distorted image of India, and I believe I have succeeded to a considerable extent in doing that, for ANI today has a global reach.

Global breakthrough

I made contact with a French newsreel company, Gaumont Actualités, who were keen to get film material directly from India. Political pictures, being treated as commodities, could hardly move from India in those days. One had to get a permit from the Reserve Bank of India (RBI) to be allowed to send photos or newsreels abroad, apart from a special customs clearance. I managed to get these, even though it meant huge paperwork and sending quarterly reports to the RBI.

I had already been to West Germany and found Deutsche Wochenschau equally eager to receive items from India, particularly feature items to keep their audiences aware of the real India.

One of the first stories I was asked to cover for Gaumont Actualités was about the situation in the French colony of Pondicherry in southern India. The French had made all-out efforts to colonize India and had fought wars with the British. Finally, they could only stay in a few enclaves like Pondicherry, Mahé and Karaikal. I discussed the idea with Kewal Singh, India's political agent in the territory, and he thought I should include coverage of the anti-French agitation starting to erupt there. I said I would.

My first predicament, as a young fellow who hardly knew the bureaucratic rules of India, hit me on this important assignment when I landed in Madras on the way to Pondicherry to find I needed a Pondicherry–India passport, which the authorities in Madras were refusing to issue. However, I knew some officers in New Delhi who would willingly help young journalists. One such officer was Mr Bhat. He put his foot down and said the passport should be issued without delay. It was, and I continued my journey to Pondicherry.

It was a quiet place with a lovely seafront. I met Kewal Singh and toured around to assess the situation. I met the French governor, who explained how happy the people of Pondicherry were with the French. 'They are French citizens,' he said. The French authorities were quick to realize that the story I was filming could get them into trouble with their government back home in France. They also got to know that I was meeting the dissidents against French rule. Kewal Singh read the signs and warned me to be careful.

I was to film a ceremony at which the French governor was to raise the French flag—a symbol of French authority in the region. Kewal Singh drove me to the event but told me to keep my bags in the car, ready for a quick getaway after the filming—before the French could lay their hands on the material I had shot.

Back in Delhi, I edited and dispatched the film to Gaumont Actualités, just the way they wanted it—all about Pondicherry, its location, etc. Then I cut a documentary about the anti-French demonstrations to be shown in India. It was all about French rule in Pondicherry and was titled *Towards Freedom*. Kewal Singh mentioned the idea to the prime minister, who welcomed it. This was my first foray into documentaries aimed at promoting the real India and serving the national cause.

It soon became evident to the French that India was firm on getting back the French enclaves in India. The Indian government released my documentary critical of the French on the day talks opened with the French regarding this issue. The documentary became a major influence on the French delegation.

When the talks ended, it was agreed that Pondicherry and other French-occupied areas would be transferred peacefully to India. I covered that event in the prime minister's office. As I left, Kewal Singh came running after me.

'Wait, Prem,' he said. 'The prime minister wants you.'

I went back. Panditji was smiling and said: 'Shabash. Well done.'

National objective

I realized then that honest, straightforward journalism, used properly, can play a major role in serving national objectives. There was no turning back now.

The visit to the French-ruled colony in Pondicherry and subsequently to Portuguese Goa helped me understand the cultural differences between the British, French and Portuguese occupants of Indian territories. The French appeared quite suave to Pondicherry residents, while the Portuguese had left the Goans emotionally attached to them. Though people may have resented foreign rule, both the French and the Portuguese made many friends in India. Goa was not a colony, but a province of Portugal. And Pondicherry was like a province of France.

Both the Portuguese and the French mixed freely with the locals, even marrying them. They did not treat these places as their colonies. The British in India were generally aloof and practised discrimination in certain areas of life. There were coaches in trains meant only for the British. Thus, there never was any bonhomie with the British as one could see in Goa with the Portuguese or in Pondicherry with the French.

It is a matter of record that when the French and Portuguese departed India, practically all the Goa and Pondicherry locals who could travel left, respectively, for Portugal and for France or other French colonies. When I covered the liberation of Goa, I found the Goans were really upset that India had moved in.

Nehru's style and ideas

I have long believed that as a leader, Jawaharlal Nehru represented the hope of a great majority of Indians. He had his failings. But he had the vision needed to develop a newly independent nation and for India to join the international community on equal terms. He truly loved India and the people of India trusted him implicitly.

Upon taking over the government, Nehru did not nationalize many private industries except for the aviation sector. And, even when turning Air India into a national carrier, Nehru ensured that J.R.D. Tata continued as chairman of the airline he had originally founded. Nehru had a very high regard for J.R.D. Tata—not only for his work as an industrialist but also as a civil aviation expert. Thus, Air India's quality of service and reliability was not disturbed even after nationalization. Although it was a very small airline compared to giants like Pan American Airways and British Overseas Airways Corporation, Air India was considered to be one of the world's finest airlines during its time under J.R.D. Tata.

Panditji did not believe in wasting money on nationalization but in using government funds to create new assets. He believed in Fabian socialism, promising equitable distribution of the nation's assets and gains.

The Fabian Society of Britain believed in socialist economy minus the Marxist revolutionary approach to it. They believed that socialism could be introduced in society through democratic means. Prominent Fabian thinkers included Harold Laski, who had an influence on Nehru. Thus, giving up the free market economy that the British had left behind, India's first prime minister slowly began implementing a socialist economy in the country.

However, Fabian socialism brought communist-style controls on industrial growth for the first time. The government now decided which areas were to be taken into the public sector and which were to remain private. British companies continued to function and operate as before because they were, after all, covered under Indian laws.

Among the institutions nationalized were insurance companies and a giant Life Insurance Corporation was created. There had been far too many insurance companies and quite a few had collapsed. This meant heavy losses to the people insured. As citizens began losing faith in the institution, Nehru nationalized the sector to restore their confidence in the safety of the investment. The Life Insurance Corporation was created to serve the whole country. LIC's guiding principle or motto, *yogakshemam vahamyaham*, is a Sanskrit phrase which loosely translates into English as 'your welfare is our responsibility'. It is drawn from chapter nine, verse twenty-two of the Bhagavad Gita.

An occasion I have never been able to forget—and which haunts me still—is when I filmed an interview with Panditji about the population explosion. I asked him pointedly why the government was not doing anything about the population of India growing at a rapid rate. Panditji replied that it was really not a major issue and that with full industrialization India could well support twice the size of its then current population. I have often wondered whether he knew or realized that our population was growing at an exponential rate. The government's inability to meet the needs of the growing population was perpetuating poverty. Over the years and, more so, after the removal of the Fabian socialist-style economy, a large middle class has emerged in India, although poverty remains the harsh reality for about one-fourth of our population.

The royal couple visits India and Pakistan

The first major international visit during Panditji's term was in 1961, when Queen Elizabeth II and her consort, Prince Philip, the Duke of Edinburgh, visited India and Pakistan. Queen Elizabeth II became the head of the Commonwealth upon the death of her father, King George VI, on 6 February 1952. The queen's visit was to be the first by a British monarch since the Delhi Durbar of 1911, organized for King George V. King George had then been invited to be crowned as 'Emperor of India'. It was here that King George declared that Delhi was to be the capital of India. Until then the British had been ruling from Calcutta.

I was part of a pool of photographers covering the royal tour. The queen was welcomed by Panditji and President Rajendra Prasad and was greeted everywhere with great enthusiasm. I was astonished to see the number of people who had travelled to Delhi to see the royal couple en route from the airport to the President's House, where the queen stayed. I also had the privilege of travelling with Prince Philip when he went ahead of the queen to preview places on her itinerary.

The tour was extremely successful, and Panditji ensured that the royal couple enjoyed it. It was so successful that the queen chose to make a private visit to Jaipur to meet the maharaja of Jaipur, Sawai Man Singh, and his gorgeous consort, Gayatri Devi. The state of Jaipur had long since become part of Rajasthan, and the maharaja was known as 'Rajpramukh'. The Jaipur royals organized a huge durbar and reception for the queen and Prince Philip. They both arrived riding an elephant. It turned out to be a very colourful event, with everyone in the durbar and reception dressed in royal finery. Princely India was alive again.

Queen Elizabeth and Prince Philip also toured other parts of the country. The maharaja and maharani of Jaipur organized a *shikaar* (hunting expedition) for them in Sariska. I think they killed eight tigers. This was feudal India at its peak.

The entire event was a visual treat for international publications, but the sheer audacity of privilege that was on display left me feeling quite uncomfortable.

Splendour of Swat

The queen then travelled to Pakistan, starting in Karachi, where General Ayub Khan put on a big show for her. For me, the highlight of this trip to Pakistan was a visit to the North-West Frontier Province (NWFP), including the state of Swat. At that time, it was a small principality and its head was known as the amir. The general had chosen this region because his son was married to the daughter of the amir of Swat.

Nestling in the Karakoram mountain range, Swat is a beautiful part of the subcontinent with a tremendous Buddhist history. However, what I saw at that time was that the amir of Swat and the rest of his family, like General Ayub Khan, were more British than Muslim in their demeanour, and even in that remote area I didn't see any purdah among the ladies of the amir's household.

But as we know from recent history, it is the same place where people tried to kill Malala Yousafzai. It is quite confounding to think how a place that had been so advanced for so long could become the site of the attempted murder of a young girl. But that's a different story to be discussed in some other context.

We were conducted on the royal tour of Pakistan by an Anglo–Indian officer, F.D. Douglas, who was the principal information officer of Pakistan. He said he knew my father very well and was very pleased to see me. He confessed that it was because he remembered my father that he authorized our Swat visit. Otherwise, Swat was said to be closed to Indians.

Of course, the Pakistan of that time was not what it has now become. Yes, the Kashmir issue was there, but we were not out to break each other's heads over that.

In the tribal areas towards Landi Kotal and Khyber Pass in NWFP, I was amazed to see the names of all the Indian military contingents which had served there. I was surprised and charmed. Landi Kotal, though part of Pakistan, was a free-trade territory. No Pakistani laws or customs duty were applicable there. It was known as 'Ilaqa Ghair' or foreign territory. Even today, the tribes on both sides of the Pakistan–Afghanistan border are autonomous. They didn't recognize British rule, and they don't recognize the Pakistani government as such.

The British worked out a very sophisticated system via political agents, who would ensure tribal leaders were happy and distribute allowances—bribes, really—to keep them from violent retaliation against the British. The tribals amassed weapons and ran Landi Kotal as a free-trade area, but the British did not interfere.

At Landi Kotal, the other thing that surprised me was that all the goodies in the world were available at rock-bottom prices. Smuggling was rife across the Afghanistan border. Goods, smuggled across on camel trains, found their way into Pakistan and were transported in the cars of government officials, into cities like Peshawar, Rawalpindi and Lahore, to be sold at much higher prices.

In the Khyber tribal area, I could sense the hostility that the locals felt towards Pakistan. There were three of us Indian journalists on that tour, and we became very wary of people in that region. Yet the royal tour to Swat was an experience to cherish.

From Swat we came to Lahore, via Peshawar, and stayed in a hotel that once happened to be the house and residence of the former chairman of Punjab National Bank, Lala Yodh Raj. A gentleman received us at the hotel. He said he was waiting for us because he had been told three Indians from Delhi would be staying here along with other members of the press party. In no time, he was telling us how he hated Pakistan, hated Pakistani officials and regretted the day he arrived in that country. It was very embarrassing for us to hear his tirade against Pakistani officials, the government and the kind of country it was turning into. He said so in the presence of the officials.

He rued the day he left Delhi. One sentence I can never forget was: '*Janab aap gundo ke mulk mein aa gay hain. Aap kyon aaye yahan par? Main toh inko zeher khilana chahta hoon . . . Aapka khana mere ghar se aayega.* (Sirs, why have you come to this country of ruffians? I want to serve them poison . . . Your food will come from my home.)'

The gentleman especially wanted us to tell Lala Yodh Raj in Delhi that he was looking after the temple in the house and that a Hindu family came there regularly to perform puja. Such was the level of understanding and love between some people in the two countries. No doubt the gentleman looked after the three of us very well. He would tell us how he would spend his evenings at the

Chelmsford Club in New Delhi, among very civilized persons. And here he was among ruffians!

I was born in Rawalpindi, and this was the first time I was returning to the land of my birth, now a different country. Did I feel a twinge of regret or empathy? I don't really know. I was just too busy working and maybe was too young to be sentimental about such things. Even the fact that I now had a Pakistan visa on my passport did not seem a big deal.

The queen then went to Nepal. Travelling with her to Nepal was another great experience. That tour remains a great memory for me, as one of those happy occasions covering India and the subcontinent. This was a time with no tension and no talk about war.

Nehru's sagacity

The people of India went out of their way to welcome the royal couple. Indian hospitality blossomed into its best. There was no evidence of any bitterness towards colonial rule or hostility towards our former rulers, only a certain sanctity of protocol prompted by traditional warmth for the guests.

Besides, it had been more than thirteen years since Independence. The transfer of power had been facilitated by friendship between two men—Nehru and Mountbatten. If there was any rancour, it was defused by Nehru. After all, the Indian leadership had allowed Lord Mountbatten to continue as governor general while the nation formulated its Constitution.

Remember, after the overthrow of the white regime in South Africa, Nelson Mandela distinguished himself by ensuring that there was no reverse apartheid. The native South Africans didn't retaliate, and everything legitimate in the old system that was nonetheless in favour of the 'whites' was allowed to continue because Mandela displayed that magnanimity. Was there this kind of sagacity in India's attitude? I would say Nehru set the precedent that Mandela followed. Mandela was, in a way, inspired by Nehru as much as he was by Mahatma Gandhi.

Brits opt out of service

Nehru, as I said, did not nationalize British industries. Strangely, however, at Independence, the British nationals who formed the bulk of the Indian Civil Service opted to leave India.

It should also not be forgotten that the Mountbattens—and particularly Lady Mountbatten—were popular for their work among refugees at the time of Independence. Edwina went to refugee camps. She helped to bring back abandoned and separated Hindu and Sikh women from West Pakistan to India and helped to send Muslim women left behind in India back to their families in West Pakistan.

Perhaps not many Indians remember it, but the Mountbattens did make a remarkable effort to counter the anger felt among various groups. Their actions helped reduce anti-British feeling considerably.

People ask me if I had captured anything on camera of that anger and its manifestation in riots and disturbances.

No. I was too young. In 1947, I was a young boy.

3

The Nehru Magic Wanes

At the end of the 1950s, history was taking a different turn.

The McMahon Line in the north-east was drawn during the British rule as India's eastern border with Tibet. It was demarcated in Shimla, in 1914, after the British government of India signed a treaty with Tibet. Long before that, on 12 November 1893, the Durand Line had been drawn to demarcate the border between India and Afghanistan. This was done after an agreement between Sir Mortimer Durand and Abdur Rahman Khan, who was the ruler of Afghanistan.

Ladakh had been neglected by the erstwhile ruler of Jammu and Kashmir. The British also paid scant attention to that area, which was strategically significant because it bordered Tibet. Since there was complete peace between India and Tibet, there had hardly been any activity on the border. Once the accession of Jammu and Kashmir took place in 1947, Indian police started patrolling areas in Ladakh, including the border with Tibet. They found that the Chinese had not only moved significantly into Indian territory but had even built a road in Aksai Chin, which was news to the newly formed Indian government as well as to the Indian forces in the border area.

Chinese invade vast areas

In 1959, a large Indian police patrol was challenged by the Chinese. Fighting erupted. Nine Indian policemen were killed and some taken prisoner. As usual, Indian authorities protested, but the Chinese laid claim to the area.

Tragically for Pandit Nehru, the Chinese returned the dead bodies of the Indian policemen on the eve of his birthday. So Panditji did not celebrate his birthday on 14 November 1959.

A point of no return, I felt, had now been reached between India and China. The prime minister tried to play down the importance of the area when, in one of his interventions in Parliament, he declared that 'not a blade of grass grows there'. In retort, a senior Congress leader, Mahavir Tyagi, pointed at his own head, saying, 'Nothing grows here. Does it mean it is to be given away?' Was Panditji trying to prepare the nation to surrender that territory to China? Perhaps. But the Chinese had already determined that the area belonged to them.

After this major incident, the Indian Army was directed to protect the border. The situation remained grimly quiet. Clearly, Panditji was making every effort to deal with it diplomatically. Looking back, most historians have termed the Indian prime minister as being romantically naive, but those of us who had faith in him were ready to believe in the power of diplomacy. The Chinese, of course, were quick to move into Tibet.

In 1961, the Portuguese enclave of Goa, in western India, became a centre of interest. The Indian leadership felt this could be dangerous for the nation. The Americans had been fighting in Vietnam, and Hong Kong had become a holiday centre for US soldiers. The ongoing American military presence in South Korea and its increasing involvement in Vietnam prompted some reports to suggest that Goa might be turned into an 'R&R (rest and recreation) base' for American troops, bringing the Cold War to India's doorstep.

Goa liberated without fuss

It was probably then that Prime Minister Nehru decided to liberate Goa, and the issue was handled by the then defence minister, V.K. Krishna Menon. Goa was a sleepy little territory with a tiny airport from where planes flew to Karachi via Colombo and on to Lisbon, Portugal.

On 19 December 1961, India sent a large contingent of troops to the Goan border and moved in. Portugal hardly had any military presence there, so it was an easy operation, especially since the governor of Goa had decided not to put up a fight.

I went to cover the story but found that the Indian Army would not allow journalists to accompany them. Once again, I had to call on an old school friend for help—a young foreign office diplomat named S.K. Singh. He solved my problem by giving me the 'password' I needed to cross into the war zone.

The next day, 20 December, a few of my journalist friends and I reached the point by road from Belgaum where we were met by the military police. At first, they tried to stop us, but I insisted that we had to go in.

'*Bakwas karte ho!* Password *bolo* (You are talking nonsense! Say the password),' the officer said. We gave the password and crossed into Goa.

Our big problem was that we had no transport. We managed to hitch a lift, but the guy drove us straight to the police station. Some Portuguese police officers were there, but they didn't bother us. And so, we drove on. We were taking a huge risk, because we had heard that the Portuguese had planted landmines on the roads to stop or slow down the march of the Indian Army. Luckily, the local villagers had spotted this activity and put up little flags along the highway, marking the places where the landmines had been laid.

We were able to reach the banks of Mandovi River in Panjim and cross the river by ferry. We caught up with the army just as they were accepting the Goan surrender. The same officers and the same intelligence guys who were against having us there now welcomed us cheerfully, asking how we managed to get in.

So that was my first experience of covering a war. A war that was really not fought.

Kerala takes a left turn

When the second general elections in independent India were held in 1957, the Indian National Congress suffered its first setback, with the loss of the state of Kerala to the Communist Party of India (CPI). The party had been banned soon after Independence. At that time, Joseph Stalin suspected Nehru of continuing to harbour soft feeling towards Anglo-American ideas of democracy and governance and was suspicious of Nehru's tilt towards the West. He also called upon the CPI to bring about a revolution. The CPI seemed to respond to Stalin's appeal and was soon banned. Later, this ban was withdrawn and the CPI could fight elections in Kerala.

The emergence of communist power in Kerala under E.M.S. Namboodiripad was seen all over the world as the beginning of the end for Indian democracy, before the communists take over India. This was a cause for concern, since the Cold War between the West and the Soviet Union was now beginning to intensify.

Indira Gandhi had been elected the president of the Indian National Congress while her father was the prime minister. My own feeling in later years was that this was done by elements in Congress who didn't have the courage to face Nehru directly. They thought they could use her. But they would discover that she had her own ambitions.

In one of his remarks to the press, Panditji had said he did not very much appreciate the idea of having to sit down for breakfast with the Congress president—his daughter—every day!

Against the wishes of many, Indira Gandhi started work on her plans to overthrow the duly elected government of Kerala. A so-called agitation was launched there. The Congress party joined forces with all those who were on the war path with the communist government of Namboodiripad. They included the Catholic Church, which was at loggerheads with the government over the education bill that curbed their power; and the Muslim League, who were promised portfolios in the new government if they supported the Congress.

I travelled to Kerala to cover the story. It was an odd place. For one thing, it was under prohibition. Now, I loved a drink or two in the evening, so I asked the hotel staff where I could get the stuff. They told me I could get it in the city.

'How?' I asked. 'The city is under prohibition.'

They said there was a very big bar next to the police station. I couldn't believe it.

They said, 'No, no, no! You go there. There is a curtain . . . Just lift the curtain and go inside.'

Yes, it was very true! I couldn't believe my eyes. There were lots of men sitting around tables. That's when I found out that Keralites love their brandy with soda.

One of the local journalists, who had helped me in getting to know the area and the goings-on there, told me about Kerala: 'Sir, don't worry. This is not politics in this state.'

'What do you mean?' I asked.

He said, 'It is just a big industry here.'

That was the first time I heard politics referred to as an industry.

Then I met Namboodiripad, leader of the Kerala government, and was very impressed by the clarity of his thought and the sense of purpose he had in what he thought was the path India should follow.

The Congress aligned with communal elements to campaign against an elected government. The agitation was organized in such a way that the central government in Delhi was eventually able to dismiss the elected government in Kerala. This was done through a presidential proclamation on 31 July 1959.

Was there any violence during the agitation? None that could warrant pulling down an elected government for any good reason. Demonstrations and protests, yes, but there was no destruction of public property. Nor did the state government resort to any repression in cracking down on protests.

Another example. When the communists were trying to advance their cause in Calcutta, there was some kind of demonstration every evening around four o'clock, near the governor's house. There were clashes with the police. The demonstrators would burn a tramcar or bus, and it would make headlines all over India. Such demonstrations involved a few hundred people and had little public support. People would be happily playing cricket or football just about half a mile away.

Kerala was no different. But with people's aspirations being trampled on undemocratically, one saw Kerala finally turn into a left-dominated state. This happened because the Congress party under Indira Gandhi's leadership turned very hostile towards the government of Kerala. The agitation was not really called for. Finally, Nehru's hand was forced to dismiss an elected government.

Ties with China turn sour

After the easy job of liberating Goa, the central government probably believed that India's army was strong enough to deal with any external threat. That belief was to be put to the test soon enough.

Relations with China were deteriorating. A visit by the Chinese prime minister, Zhou Enlai, along with his deputy in 1960 was designed to defuse the tension between the two countries. The Chinese leaders were not only to meet the Indian prime minister but other leaders of the Indian National Congress and members of Nehru's cabinet.

It was said to be so important that India's leading newspaper editors—Frank Moraes, S. Mulgaokar and D.R. Mankekar—came out of their offices to cover the story alongside their reporters. I was also running helter-skelter, getting as many visual stories as I could.

The talks opened at the prime minister's house. Panditji and Zhou Enlai were supposed to have good personal relations, but when I was covering the talks I saw considerable tension between the two leaders. The term body language is a modern construct, but we had developed a cameraman's way of spotting unease between world leaders. The talks broke down. The die was now cast. India demanded that the Chinese withdraw from the areas they had occupied.

In mid-1962, when he was travelling to Sri Lanka, Nehru was answering questions from newspaper reporters, and in one remark he said that he had asked the Indian Army to evict the Chinese aggressors from Indian territory. It was a huge statement. The Chinese construed it as almost a declaration of war on China. Things moved very fast after that.

The Chinese amassed their troops along the north-east and in Ladakh. Skirmishes began to erupt between the Chinese and the totally ill-equipped Indian outposts, which were occupied by the Chinese, one after the other.

Many reporters and photographers from the international press moved towards Tezpur, in the foothills of what was then the North-East Frontier Agency (today's Arunachal state). The Indian Army in those days was governed by a World War II mentality in relation to censorship, and we were refused entry.

I sent a telegram to the prime minister's office saying that the media was not being allowed to go to the front line. Panditji immediately cleared the press to be taken to the scene of action. But that did not end the matter. When I again tried to cross the front line I was told I could not proceed. On asking the reason, I was told that photography was not allowed. Yet another missive to Delhi, and I was allowed to go in.

I was offered a seat in the jeep which was leading the advance but ended up in another jeep with the chief public relations officer of the Indian Army, Brigadier C.L. Bharadwaj. My friend George Verghese, deputy editor of *The Times of India*, was in another jeep. We steadily moved forward.

The condition of the Indian Army was pitiful. Straight from the plains of the Punjab, units arrived to find they had insufficient transport. They were marching up a mountain in lightweight summer uniforms, in the wrong boots and with inadequate weapons. Even as I was filming this, I was filled with a sense of foreboding: this was not going to end well.

We eventually reached Bomdila and spent the night at the divisional headquarters where General Kaul, the corps commander, came to brief us. He was an odd character in many ways.

We press people naturally wanted to be at the right place at the right time, so we asked to be taken up the hill, at the heart of the action. General Kaul started showing us what kind of photographs the army would prefer. He was still thinking in terms of World War II when many such pictures were staged, miles from the action. But the world of journalism had moved on. You did not do that any more. Both George Verghese and I laughed at the idea.

Looking to explore the area, George and I ventured up the mountain at night. As we moved up, we noticed lights ahead of us, up in the distance. What did it mean? George's guess was that it was an Indian patrol. My own feeling was that perhaps the Chinese could be outflanking the Indian positions. The next day we were moving towards Sela. That's where the Indian Army was expected to block the Chinese advance.

Again, the sight was painful to behold. Mountain guns were being dragged up and installed in a great hurry. I met Brigadier Balraj Badhwar, the husband of a cousin of mine. He was overseeing the placements of the artillery that was to back the troops atop Sela and keep the enemy back. On my way back from Sela I again met Brigadier Badhwar. Both George Verghese and I had carried a lot of tinned food with us. We presented it to the brigadier and his men. That was the last I saw of Brigadier Badhwar. Later, when the Indian Army was outflanked and overrun, we were told that Brigadier Badhwar and some other officers with him were ambushed and killed by the Chinese after the ceasefire.

It is tragic, but I must mention that the elder brother of Brigadier Badhwar was also in the army. Major Shrishti Badhwar was killed in unprovoked firing by the Pakistanis at Nekowal on 7 May 1955, when he was escorting farmers who tilled the soil on this side of the Jammu border. This was among the early instances of trouble between India and Pakistan, and it was a major news story of that time. Panditji visited the home of the widow, Mohiniji, to express his condolences to our family. Our family has been closely associated with the Indian Army and takes pride in it.

Troops that had been flown in and marched up to Sela were digging trenches. Here was the enemy almost on top of us and we were still digging trenches. The Chinese simply came at us in waves. A huge Chinese propaganda campaign had already demoralized the Indian military. That is what the Chinese did in Korea. Indian troops fought bravely enough, but this was a different terrain.

When we got to Misamari, George and I heard that Sela had been lost and that the Indian Army was on the retreat. In panic, somebody spread the word that the Chinese could be advancing towards the plains of Assam and that they might land paratroopers. General Kaul ordered the withdrawal of the Corps Headquarters from Tezpur, which in fact meant the retreat of the army from Tezpur. Kaul also tried to play the hero by flying into the war zone to rescue the divisional commander who was fighting up there.

Prime Minister Nehru went on the radio that night with a speech about the setback to the army, saying his heart went out to the people of Assam. All of us sitting in Tezpur that night wondered if India had given up the northern bank of Assam. Later events proved that it had, as orders were issued to evacuate Tezpur and other cities in the north.

People shut their houses and shops. There were tragic scenes of people crying as they left. The banks of the Brahmaputra reminded me of pictures of Dunkirk. The Indian Army and other paramilitary forces were spread out on the riverbanks, hoping to find some way to cross to the southern bank. Thousands of them. It was a heartbreaking sight.

Tea planters started abandoning their gardens. Basically, all these tea planters were from north India or other parts of the country, not from Assam. It was this background which later led to the differences between the Assamese and the non-Assamese. British planters didn't leave.

Assam was already facing an influx of illegal immigrants from what was then East Pakistan (now Bangladesh). Later, the All Assam Students' Union carried out an agitation against illegal immigrants. They wanted local jobs reserved for the Assamese. Thus we now see that most tea estates in the region are well-managed by the people of Assam. In the current situation, it has led to an agitation against the Citizenship (Amendment) Act and the National Register of Citizens. The reason being that the Assamese see all Bangladeshi Hindus being given citizenship of India under the new law. They won't mind that, but they want the Bangladeshi Hindus out of Assam and into West Bengal.

It was very fortunate that, during World War II, the Americans had built airstrips all over the north-east. This included an airstrip at Tezpur and a huge hangar, which became an active airport where planes from Delhi or Calcutta could land to evacuate whoever could be airlifted out. Within a matter of thirty-six hours, large numbers had been evacuated.

George Verghese and I refused to leave Tezpur, despite the warning of the Indian Army which did not want anyone to remain. None of the other journalists were keen to stay, but we refused to leave. We were the only two Indian journalists to stay there. We spent the night very comfortably in the Planters Club, where we had, of course, planted ourselves.

In the morning, as we came out, we found the vast grounds of the Planters Club filled with a mass of people. They thought we were Indian officials who were still in charge. But who were these people? It turned out they were prisoners who had been released from the local jail. The fleeing administration had opened the jail and the nearby mental asylum.

A very dear friend of mine, Narender Sikand, was manning the main ferry across the river, and he told me he would not move his ferry until I was on board. He would not leave me behind.

I was working for Reuters in those days. There was no way to send the pictures back, so I asked one of the foreign reporters to take my written copy across the river to the nearest post office for transmission. The reporter was shocked to see my copy going to Reuters. He felt his copy would be exclusive in British newspapers and elsewhere. But this was not to be. However, being a good professional, he took my copy, laughed and said, 'You owe me a beer.' He could have easily not transmitted my story, but such was the solidarity among journalists those days that we even helped our competitors.

So for the next five days, if I remember right, the world saw and heard whatever was going on in Tezpur and at the north bank of the Brahmaputra from me and, as far as India was concerned, from George Verghese.

The Chinese withdraw

Curiously, the Chinese decided not to advance further and declared unilateral ceasefire. They began to withdraw from the North-East Frontier Agency (NEFA) and move back to the McMahon Line. Clearly, the Chinese had accepted the fact that the territory was, at best, disputed and not theirs.

After a few days, Panditji arrived in Tezpur and asked to see me. He knew that George Verghese and I had stayed till the end. I told him all that I had seen in NEFA, Sela and other points, where everyone only talked about the Chinese coming in waves.

I further told Panditji that our Indian troops were full of energy despite all odds and willing to fight, but I felt the Chinese had outflanked them. Thus the move to vacate the north bank of the Brahmaputra in Assam and Tezpur was perhaps made by the Indian Army in panic. George Verghese also spoke to Panditji.

The Chinese withdrew unilaterally and India recovered NEFA, now known as Arunachal Pradesh. As Indian forces and administration began to move back into Tezpur, some of us went with them and saw the armed forces clearing the dead bodies still lying on the roadsides. It was a sad sight all the way to Bomdila.

Later, the government appointed a commission under General Henderson Brooks to inquire into what went wrong in the fight against the Chinese. The report was commissioned directly by the prime minister. Yet, when it was submitted, no one heard anything from it. That report has still not been made public.

It was one of the most emotionally exhausting stories that I have covered. War is always a difficult story to tell, and this was to be a learning experience for me.

The fall of NEFA and the unilateral ceasefire by the Chinese had broken Prime Minister Nehru. Though his own party was baying for his blood—his detractors in the party held his policies towards China responsible for India's defeat—the people of India did not join in, even though they were shocked at what had happened. There was no mass agitation against Nehru as a consequence of the defeat of the Indian Army.

That itself, perhaps, had an impact on the prime minister's health. I watched him work overtime to rebuild the Indian Army he had once naively neglected. Emergency commissions were announced to recruit officers and train them in six months for the job as the army was being expanded. New officers were recruited. Whether he had to beg or borrow, the prime minister was determined to acquire the armaments he needed from around the world. Nehru worked day in, day out, and I, on my many visits to the PM's residence, would find him working late at night, clearing all kinds of bureaucratic files.

He even compromised on the Non-Aligned policy vis-à-vis the United States when he asked for an American aerial umbrella, as he perhaps felt that our own air force, with its limited power, was not capable of defending our skies against the Chinese. United States Air Force planes arrived in India. This was strange. Here we were, a country still refusing to join on the side of the Americans in the Cold War yet forced to compromise because of the Chinese threat.

John F. Kennedy was assassinated on 22 November 1963. The same day several senior Indian Army generals were killed in a helicopter crash in Kashmir. Five top officers, including Maj. Gen. Nanavati, Lt Gen. Bikram Singh and Lt Gen. Daulat Singh, were among the six killed in the helicopter crash. Why were so many senior officers travelling together in a helicopter? The prime minister was taken aback with this loss. An order was issued soon after, prohibiting senior officers from travelling together in this way.

Both these events had a profound impact on Panditji, who was very fond of the Kennedy family. JFK had assured Panditji of the United States' full support. For Panditji, the assassination of yet another personal friend (Gandhiji being the other) was hard to bear.

I asked Harry d'Penha at the prime minister's office for Nehru's reaction to Kennedy's assassination. When I said that I needed the reaction before seven o'clock—not long after news of the assassination had come in—d'Penha doubted if that could be done. I didn't explain to him that the media request I was making was for broadcast abroad, where statements of all world leaders would be played. I was irritated that this had to be explained to a PMO official. I just asked him to forward the request to the prime minister. And sure enough, I was given time to install the camera in the PM's reception area.

Panditji was, at that moment, seeing off the speaker of Parliament, Sardar Hukam Singh. Noticing me waiting with my camera in the lobby, Sardar Sahab offered to leave, but Panditji, stickler as he was for certain protocols, saw the speaker off personally before coming to me for the interview. He looked very tired. As he started to answer my question, he almost fell asleep. I had to touch him gently to wake him up and tell him I could not present the Indian prime minister to the world in that state.

Panditji's only remark to me was, 'You have disturbed my thought.' I apologized, put some pillows around him, reworked the frame so that the pillows would not be visible and started all over again. We finished the statement in two and a half minutes.

As he was leaving, Panditji turned back and asked me, 'Prem Prakash, *yeh saat baje ka hukum kya tha* (What was this order for me to give the interview by 7 p.m.?)' Obviously, he had himself seen my request.

I explained to the PM that I had to get back to the office, write the dopesheet to explain my pictures, rush to the airport and place the news film package on a BOAC flight to London at ten o'clock that night. As I have explained earlier, there was a lot of bureaucracy involved in being able to send news film package abroad. I explained to Panditji that if the package were to miss the flight, all our effort would go to waste. That's why 7 p.m. Panditji nodded and asked me to rush with the film. And I did get my film on that London flight.

Thanks to the prime minister's efforts, the Indian Army was steadily being modernized, expanded and strengthened, and its manpower was being doubled. Panditji took complete charge of it and travelled extensively to see his other nation-building projects make progress.

But his health was giving way. On 7 January 1964, he suffered a mild stroke while attending a Congress party meeting in Bhubaneswar, Orissa. When he returned to Delhi, some of us had gone to Palam Airport to film the PM's arrival to the capital, as we always did. But for the first time photographers were not allowed on the tarmac. We were asked to wait outside the airport. No explanation was given. Indira Gandhi received her father with a large shawl, which was draped over him, and when he emerged from the airport in his car, he gave a watery smile to us as we clicked away, totally unaware about his feeble health.

It is my belief that in the twenty months that he lived after October 1962, Nehru did a great deal to restore the defence capability of India and strengthen the Indian Army. He felt personally responsible for its earlier decline and needed to reclaim the confidence of the Indian people. Nehru became very conscious of the problems he would be leaving behind, including Kashmir, Tibet and relations with China.

He released the former chief minister of Jammu and Kashmir, Sheikh Abdullah, who had been imprisoned. The two had continued to be friends. Nehru wanted Sheikh Abdullah to go to Pakistan and Pakistan Occupied Kashmir to see if the issue of Kashmir could be resolved. After being released from jail, Abdullah came to Delhi and stayed with Panditji before going to Pakistan. Having seen off Sheikh Abdullah, Panditji walked towards the back garden of his house, where a young Dalai Lama was waiting for him.

The Dalai Lama had come to see him—a memorable meeting, which I covered for international television. My report showed Panditji taking the young Dalai Lama for a walk in the back garden of Teen Murti Bhavan. The Dalai Lama held Panditji by his left arm, which had been paralysed after he suffered a stroke. I still remember that walk, and my filming it, as a great moment for the two men. Panditji was very fond of the Dalai Lama and was saddened by what China had done in Tibet.

It appeared that the prime minister was trying to talk to him to see in what way he could help with Tibet. Nehru had promised the Dalai Lama, on his very first visit to Delhi, that Tibet would remain autonomous. But this was something Nehru had been unable to achieve. Besides, the Chinese were annoyed by the way India had managed to get the Dalai Lama out of Tibet.

Nehru had been scheduled to visit Tibet when Panchen Lama, the second-highest Lama in Tibet after the Dalai Lama, was also there. Crowds gathered from all over Tibet to welcome 'Chogyal', elder brother—that's how the Indian prime minister was known in Tibet.

The Chinese did not want Nehru in Tibet. However, before the Chinese could depose the Dalai Lama or do anything else in Tibet, the Indian intelligence services had alerted the government in Delhi of China's intentions. Because of that information, Indian operatives were able to initiate the rescue of the Dalai Lama, who was brought after a ten-day journey through Tibet to India.

By now, the Indian Army had been raised by Panditji to half a million men. Weapons such as automatic rifles had been acquired. While the Americans were refusing to supply certain equipment, Nehru was getting them from Russia.

The army was regaining its confidence as, following the 1962 debacle, the whole business of politically motivated promotions and other inefficiencies ended. We were lucky that we still had men like General Sam Manekshaw surviving in the army before they could be purged by the political elements running the Congress at that time.

At the outset of his term in office, Nehru had ignored the modernization of India's armed forces. He believed firmly in his political theory that, following the horrors of World War II, no nation would resort to war to solve international disputes. That ideology lay in tatters when China attacked India's borders and an ill-equipped Indian army proved no match for them.

The light goes out

I was at the prime minister's house on 24 May 1964, when he fell critically ill and, soon afterwards, passed away. It is my belief that it was the Chinese attack and the Indian defeat which cut short his life.

Frank Moraes, among the great editors of his time, made some very acute observations in his exhaustive book *Witness to an Era*. It would be apt to quote an excerpt here:

> After the Dalai Lama's entry into India the era of Hindi-Chini Bhai-Bhai was definitely over. A fusillade of notes between Delhi and Peking preceded the fusillade of fire. On 20 October 1962 the Chinese mounted a massive offensive at dawn around the Thagla ridge on the McMahon Line and simultaneously in Ladakh.
>
> Nehru, with his proclamations of undying friendship for China, found it difficult overnight to adjust his sights and he reacted characteristically with the petulance of which he was sometimes capable: 'Throw them out,' he ordered. The rest is history.

On 27 May 1964, the day Nehru died, a friend in the Ministry of External Affairs said to me, 'He really died two years ago. He died when the Chinese crossed our frontier.'

Panditji had now passed away.

It was not easy for me, as well as for most of the country, to come to terms with that fact. I had spent so much time at his home, watched him do so many great things for India. So many conversations! I had worked extensively on an acclaimed BBC film, *Nehru: Man of Two Worlds*, for which I travelled with him and stayed at Anand Bhavan, his ancestral home in Allahabad.

As I covered the events surrounding his death, my mind travelled back and forth. It was difficult for me that day to handle the camera. But I had to do it. It was my professional duty.

India was virtually at war on two fronts, with Pakistan and China. There were the unresolved problems on the Tibet–China border. And there was Kashmir. India's development was, no doubt, well underway, but the economy had gone from bad to worse since the British left. Still, Nehru loved the country, and the country loved him.

A dispatch in the *Guardian* newspaper said this of him:

460,000,000 people in this country that has been forged on the anvil of this one man's dreams and conflicts were plunged into the nightmare world which they have, in the last decade, come to dread as the 'after Nehru' era.

But the real tribute to Nehru—a tribute that touched my heart—came from Atal Bihari Vajpayee, the Bharatiya Jana Sangh leader at that time. It is worth reading today:

Bharat Mata is stricken with grief today—she has lost her favourite prince. Humanity is sad today—it has lost its devotee. Peace is restless today—its protector is no more. The downtrodden have lost their refuge. The common man has lost the light in his eyes. The curtain has come down. The leading actor on the stage of the world displayed his final role and taken the bow.

In the *Ramayana*, Maharishi Valmiki has said of Lord Rama that he brought the impossible together. Though Panditji was an agnostic in his life, we see a glimpse of what the great poet said.

He was a devotee of peace and yet the harbinger of revolution, he was a devotee of non-violence but advocated every weapon to defend freedom and honour.

He was an advocate of individual freedom and yet was committed to bringing about economic equality. He was never afraid of compromise with anybody, but never compromised with anyone out of fear. His policy towards Pakistan and China was a symbol of this unique blend. It had generosity with firmness. It is unfortunate that this generosity was mistaken for weakness, while some people looked upon his firmness as obstinacy.

I remember I once saw him very angry during the Chinese aggression when our Western friends were trying to prevail upon us to arrive at some compromise with Pakistan on Kashmir. When he was told we would have to fight on two fronts if there was no compromise on the Kashmir problem, he flared up and said we would fight on both fronts if necessary. He was against negotiating under any pressure.

Atalji's tribute was in Hindi, and he concluded when he reminded the parliamentarians:

Sir, the freedom of which he was the general and protector is today in danger. We have to protect it with all our might. The national unity and integrity of which he was the apostle is also in danger today. We have to preserve it any cost. The Indian democracy he established, and of which he made a success is also faced with a doubtful future. With our unity, discipline and self-confidence we have to make this democracy a success.

The leader is gone, the followers remain. The sun has set, now we have to find our way by the light of the stars. This is a highly testing time. If we all could dedicate ourselves to the great ideal of a mighty and prosperous India that would make an honourable contribution to world peace forever, it would indeed be a true tribute to him.

The loss to Parliament is irreparable. Such a resident may never grace Teen Murti again. That vibrant personality, that attitude of taking even the opposition along, that refined gentlemanliness, that greatness we may not see again in the near future. In spite of a difference of opinion we have nothing but respect for his great ideals, his integrity, his love for the country and his indomitable courage.

With these words, I pay my humble homage to the great soul.

4

Lal Bahadur Shastri Fills the Void

With the passing of Jawaharlal Nehru, Gulzarilal Nanda took over as interim prime minister. The Congress party meanwhile proceeded with the formal election of the next leader of the country. Party president Kamaraj Nadar led prolonged discussions with senior Congress leaders, held mostly in a small room at Teen Murti Bhavan.

During his lifetime, Panditji had clearly indicated that Lal Bahadur Shastri should be his successor. He inducted him into the cabinet to administer the prime minister's office as a minister without portfolio. Many of us could see the signs that the next PM would be a camera-shy man and not much of an orator as compared to Panditji, and we used to wonder what it would be like in the future to cover the PM's events.

Shastri was first elected to the Lok Sabha in 1952 and was subsequently made minister for railways and transport. His probity and integrity in public life was recognized by a particular event in November 1956, when he resigned as railways minister, taking moral responsibility for a train crash in Tamil Nadu in which some 142 people were killed.

This selfless act saw Shastri's popularity surge. Nehru reappointed him to the ministry for home affairs in 1961, where he gained a reputation as a skilful mediator. Nehru described Shastri as a man of the highest integrity. The Congress party finally chose Shastri as Nehru's successor, and he was duly elected by the parliamentary party before being sworn in on 9 June 1964 as India's second prime minister. The Congress party had carried out Nehru's wish.

My association with Shastriji went back a long way. We interacted a lot when, as a member of the Delhi Union of Journalists (DUJ), I was called on to form a cooperative society with the job of finding housing accommodation for journalists. With the imposition of Fabian socialism, which Nehru adopted from the United Kingdom, it was no longer possible for private developers to offer land or houses for sale. The government had created the Delhi Development Authority in 1957 to deal with housing needs. Fabian socialism, though its proponents claimed it was different, functioned almost like a communist state economy. The only concession given was, perhaps like in communist countries, to allow a group of people form a cooperative and acquire a piece of land from the government to develop for their own purposes.

Houses for journalists

When Shastri was the home minister, my colleague, the late B.C. Saxena, and I would call on him regularly to plead for land to be allotted to the cooperative society. But in India it is not easy to get people to work together. While the DUJ society was the largest of the four journalist societies, there were three other associations of journalists—Press Association, Press Trust of India Employees Association and Times of India Officers Association. It was quite a headache, but finally recommendations were made and the four societies were told to join hands, to form a coordination committee and select a piece of land from the plots being offered.

I remember Shastriji would discuss matters in a very friendly way. He would ask if we would be able to run the cooperative society. *'Aap log chala paoge isko? Bahut badnami ho jati hai aise kaam karne mai* (Will you be able to run this? Such ventures can bring much embarrassment to the persons running them).'

We assured him that we could manage, and we did manage. For me and B.C. Saxena and the others, led by the late K. Subrahmanyam, getting this enterprise launched was no mean feat. We were able to deliver 325 plots to 325 journalists in what is today one of the prime locations in New Delhi. It was almost a jungle in those days!

Naming the colony called for much deliberation. There was a huge debate between two camps: journalists who worked for the Hindi media and those in the English-language press. I suggested the name Gulmohar but many thought it to be Urdu and inappropriate! But the late J.M. D'Souza, manager of the *Times of India*, Delhi, argued very convincingly for the colony to be named Gulmohar Park.

Nonetheless, others still opposed the name on the grounds that it was Urdu. Some thought the name should be Journalists Colony. But finally, the name Gulmohar Park was approved, although we compromised again and ended up with Gulmohar Park Journalists Colony. It was Shastriji's great gift to the journalists of Delhi.

Instant popularity

Shastriji was often compared with his predecessor and criticized for his perceived shortcomings, though he was very tolerant of such criticism. This was evident even when Panditji was alive. Shastriji was comfortable in allowing Panditji to take the lead.

One instance I remember as an eyewitness. I happened to be in Panditji's house when, on 27 December 1963, serious trouble broke out in Kashmir over a relic of Prophet Muhammad which had gone missing. It was known as the Moi-e-Muqaddas (the Hair of the Prophet). There were riots, anger and inquiries about where the relic had gone.

It was midwinter in north India. Panditji asked Shastriji to go to Kashmir and sort out the issue. As Shastriji was leaving after his last briefing, Panditji stopped him and asked, 'Lal Bahadur, *tumhare paas kuchh* overcoat *ya garam kapde hain ke nahin* (Do you have any warm clothes to wear in Kashmir)?' Then he added, '*Achha thehro, main abhi aata hoon neeche* (Wait, I will just come down).'

Panditji rushed back inside, returned with his own overcoat and gave it to Shastriji. It was a funny sight because when Shastriji wore it, the overcoat covered him all the way down to his feet. But it was with that overcoat that he went to Kashmir.

The issue in Kashmir was quickly resolved. It emerged that the mother of Bakshi Ghulam Mohammad, then chief minister of Jammu and Kashmir, had fallen seriously ill and wanted to have a *deedar* or a holy witness of the Moi-e-Muqaddas. Obviously, she could not go to the mosque in her condition. So the Moi-e-Muqaddas was taken to her house.

That created a crisis because visitors to the mosque were outraged by its disappearance. There was a public outcry. But Shastriji intervened and ensured that the relic was returned to the mosque.

Economic crisis

The nation was already in serious economic crisis when Shastriji took over. Following the war with China in 1962, expenditure on rebuilding the armed forces was increased. It began to hurt the economy and prices began to rise.

Shastriji was keen to reform the economy. Sales tax used to be a big issue in those days. Lots of people all over the country were evading taxes. I remember Shastriji pointing out that his own family sometimes said that if they bought things without a receipt they could avoid sales tax.

But before the sales tax problem could be dealt with, the man across the border—Pakistan's General Ayub Khan—started creating trouble on the western frontier. The general used to make fun of the new Indian prime minister and thought he could now easily deal with India because 'this diminutive fellow' would lack the will to handle a border incursion.

General Ayub Khan launched his first adventure into the Rann of Kutch, a huge, barren expanse in Gujarat inhabited by wild donkeys. This area had been the subject of earlier disputes, but in April 1965 Ayub moved in quickly, taking India by surprise.

However, the Indian Army reacted promptly and defeated Pakistan in an armed confrontation that lasted till the end of April.

When I went there to cover the skirmish, the starkness of the desert was something new for me. I hadn't shot in a desert earlier. I saw a mirage for the first time in the Rann of Kutch. But of course, the Indian victory over Pakistani invaders was the real news story here. Having failed in its attempt to beat the Indians in this barren tract of land, Pakistan announced, in May 1965, its willingness to settle the dispute. Britain interceded, and the two sides, meeting in London, reached an agreement on 30 June 1965 to withdraw their forces to their original positions.

Pakistan's first military adventure after Nehru had failed.

Pakistan's misadventure

But General Ayub and his coterie had other ideas. Disappointed with the failure of his campaign in the Rann of Kutch, the general turned his attention to Kashmir. The Pakistanis had seen the Indian Army lose the 1962 war against China but thereafter had been kept in check by Nehru's diplomacy and denied another chance of military aggression during his lifetime.

True to their familiar strategy, the Pakistanis again started with infiltration, just as in 1947, when they had sent armed hordes of infiltrators to invade Kashmir. Now, under what was to be known as 'Operation Gibraltar', Ayub Khan sent regulars of the Pakistan Army (dressed as Pathan tribesmen) into Kashmir, hoping to foment revolution from within.

As news about this incursion started coming in, I flew to Srinagar to cover the story. Not far from the Srinagar airport, the car I was in came under sniper fire. Two bullets hit the car, but the driver kept going. It was clear that some of the infiltrators had managed to reach the outskirts of Srinagar city.

The people of Kashmir were certainly not pro-Pakistan, despite some politically motivated activists demanding a referendum.

Even if a referendum had been held, India would have won. But that's a different story altogether.

The infiltrators had reached the outskirts of Srinagar, but they had failed to enlist support of the local population. Srinagar city was put under night curfew, although movement of inhabitants was allowed. In the next few days, the rest of the press corps and I—we were staying at Nedou's hotel—saw that the local population was keeping the authorities apprised of reports of such infiltrations.

Each day, dozens of bodies of infiltrators were brought to the military area. Fighting infiltrators in civilian areas was not as simple as it may sound. India had to make sure that the civilian population was not affected, and it succeeded in that purpose. Indeed, the infiltrators themselves were shocked to find the civilian population not offering support or refuge to them, as was expected by their bosses in Rawalpindi.

It was evident that this Pakistani gamble had failed.

As the Indian Army began clearing the infiltrators, it moved towards Haji Pir Pass, from where the infiltrators had moved into Kashmir. It began to push the Pakistanis behind to clear the area and succeeded in capturing the Pass. It was a great victory. I climbed to the top of the Haji Pir Pass when the Indian Army took it.

With Haji Pir Pass securely in the hands of the Indian Army, Pakistan's passage into the valley had been closed and their desperate, last-ditch efforts had failed.

Atop Haji Pir Pass I watched one such battle where the Pakistan Army attempted to fight back, but Indian soldiers, well-supported by artillery, inflicted heavy casualties on the enemy. And yet, amid all those Indian victories on various battlefields, nothing had prepared me for the sight of dead Indian jawans and their injured comrades. These remain among my saddest memories.

With the Haji Pir Pass gone, the Pakistan Army was now making an all-out effort to capture the 'chicken's neck'—a tiny area under Indian control which connects the Indian mainland to Jammu and Kashmir. Had Pakistan succeeded in doing that, the Indian

Army's communications between Kashmir and India would have been broken.

Befitting reply

It was at that point that Shastriji took the decision to move Indian forces across the international border to attack Lahore and Sialkot. With this decisive move, Lal Bahadur Shastri took Ayub Khan and his people completely by surprise. They had not expected India to raise the stakes. I rushed from Haji Pir Pass to cover India's move into Pakistan at Sialkot.

For the first time in its history, the Indian Army had crossed an international border, and it showed that India was in an aggressive state of mind. The army moved swiftly towards Lahore and Sialkot. The Pakistanis were being beaten, and their incursion into Kashmir had been successfully repelled.

Arriving in Jammu, a small press party and I were conducted by the army towards the battlefield by no less a person than General Rajinder Singh 'Sparrow', one of India's most senior and decorated generals. A group of us accompanied the general to an active tank battle, during which he very proudly showed us the outskirts of Sialkot.

Suddenly, four Pakistani Sabre Jets appeared in the sky. With our little press party and the general in clear sight of those Sabres, we all thought this was the end for us.

As the fighter jets circled and dived to attack, we made a dash for nearby trenches. His troops protected the general by piling their bodies on top of him. For the next twenty minutes or more the four Sabres kept circling and diving, and firing.

My younger brother, the late Om Prakash, was with me. We were together in a trench. I told him, 'My God! Both of us are here. What happens to the family if we both die?' The Sabres would come down and pour all their ammunition on us—but, miraculously, nothing hit us.

Soon, Indian anti-aircraft guns went into action but could not bring any plane down. When the four enemy jets turned back and the all-clear was sounded, it was found that all they had achieved was a few bullets into the jeep of the general's aide-de-camp, Captain Chauhan of 16 Cavalry. Capt. Chauhan took some bullets in his leg. That was the extent of the damage inflicted by the much-vaunted Sabre jets. The Pakistani fighter pilots had failed even to hit the tanks that were like sitting ducks in that area.

As we all gathered after the four jets had left, General 'Sparrow' said it was clear what kind of air force the Pakistanis had. It seemed to me that, for all the noise they made about the super airplanes they got from America, the Pakistani Air Force didn't know how to use them.

During the Indo–Pak war of 1965, very small Indian planes— like the Gnat fighter jets—made a mark by bringing down a number of Pakistani Sabres. In the end, what mattered was the man behind the machine rather than the machine itself.

Meanwhile, as the war continued, Indian forces moved towards Sialkot and Lahore. But now, international pressure was applied and a ceasefire was declared on 22 September 1965. A colleague, Ravi Bedi, and I drove towards the ceasefire line to join the press party that was being escorted there. As it happened, we were slightly late. But that meant we were able to drive all the way to the ceasefire line by ourselves, without being confined to what the conducting army officer might have wanted us to see.

As I reached the ceasefire line it became all too clear that there had been a bloody battle during the night. The ceasefire line was on the Ichhogil Canal, and Pakistan had made attempts to cross to the Indian side. Dead bodies of Pakistanis were still lying all over the battlefield; most were handed back to the Pakistanis.

One of the Pakistani colonels had been captured and his people were shouting from the other side, asking if Colonel so-and-so was among the dead or injured since they had not seen him. He had been captured and was later returned to Pakistan, when the POWs were exchanged.

Shastriji's popularity soared to new heights. He was now the hero of India—the man who had dared to attack Pakistan and emerged victorious, thus restoring the reputation of the Indian Army, which had suffered so badly in 1962.

Gains boost morale

Having won this round, Shastriji settled down to other things, like building pressure for peace talks. He made it plain that India was not prepared to give up the areas it had reclaimed in Jammu and Kashmir. The logic was simple. It was India's territory, and we would only vacate it in exchange for whatever territory of ours they had taken in Rajasthan.

Even though Shastriji had managed to survive American arm-twisting, the Soviet Union began to apply diplomatic pressure, forcing Shastriji to agree to India-Pakistan talks being held in Tashkent in Central Asia.

January is very cold all over north India, but it is extremely cold in Central Asia and particularly in Tashkent. The prime minister, along with his senior ministers—the defence minister, Y.B. Chavan; foreign minister, Sardar Swaran Singh—and all senior officials, took an Air India commercial flight to Tashkent. Prime ministers never took special flights in those days; they used commercial flights. And journalists did likewise, meeting their own expenses.

An Air India flight to London was specially diverted and we all landed in Tashkent for the talks. As was the custom in the Soviet Union in those days, Shastriji was given a special dacha, as they call it—a dacha being basically a cottage in one of their holiday resorts.

As the Tashkent talks opened, the question of vacating the areas captured by India in Kashmir arose. India was firm. It was not going to vacate areas won in Jammu and Kashmir because they were Indian territory. But throughout the talks the Soviet Union put heavy diplomatic pressure on Prime Minister Shastri.

Soviet pressure mounts

By the time of the Tashkent talks, the PM's office had relaxed their media norms a bit and journalists had easier access. So I spent most of my time waiting around Shastriji's dacha for events to unfold. If the prime minister was not talking, I arranged to meet other ministers. One day, I remember, Alexei Kosygin, the Soviet Union's foreign minister, arrived and made a beeline for his Indian counterpart, Sardar Swaran Singh.

I could hear very clearly as I walked behind the two foreign ministers. Kosygin was holding Swaran Singh's hands and pleading: 'Please, Swaran, I want you to have this thing signed and agreed.'

Great negotiator that Sardar Swaran Singh was, he simply replied: 'I can only convey what you want, but I cannot advise him. He is the leader and he makes up his own mind. He decides and we carry out.'

Kosygin kept on insisting. I understood then what game the Russians were playing. They had a problem with the fact that Pakistan was now part of an alliance with the Americans, who had been allowed to set up a secret air base in Peshawar. From here, American U-2 spy planes flew over the Soviet Union. All Soviet nuclear facilities were in Central Asia. Their nuclear testing was done there, and their future space program was formulated there.

The Russians were very keen to try and prise Pakistan away from the United States, using the Tashkent talks as a lever to get Pakistan out of America's embrace. This might have been farfetched, but in hindsight the Soviet Union and its ministers were surely making strenuous efforts to see to it that India acceded to Pakistan's demand to return all the territories in Jammu and Kashmir. The Indian Army strongly opposed the idea.

For India, the question of vacating Haji Pir Pass did not arise; it was crucial to the defence of India's borders. So the talks finally broke down with Shastriji refusing to sign. The entire press party was told to take it easy that day and go shopping.

Advantage conceded

While we were shopping, some Soviet officials suddenly appeared and asked us to rush back. The agreement was about to be signed at around 4 or 4:30 p.m. We were all taken aback. What had happened?

I have never been able to figure out what pressure forced Shastriji and the Indian delegation to sign the Tashkent Declaration. One person whose mind I could not read was the Indian ambassador to the Soviet Union, T.N. Kaul. He was supposed to be very close to, and very friendly with, the Soviets. Was it he, perhaps, who had influenced the prime minister? Or was there any bigger threat from the Soviet Union which had forced India to sign?

Anyway, the agreement was signed. I along with my dear friend, the late N.S. Thapa of the Films Division, approached Shastriji, requesting a meeting with him later in the evening before returning to Delhi. He said yes, we could come to the dacha and talk. Basically, we wanted to film Shastriji at work. We shot some footage without asking him anything about the agreement he had signed. We then went back to our hotel and called it a night.

Shastriji passes away

Past midnight, we were all woken up by telephone. A voice told us: 'Your prime minister is dead. Please come down.'

I couldn't believe this. What had happened? Everyone was stunned. What could have caused the death of the prime minister when he had looked so healthy hours before? It was true that Shastriji was a heart patient, and for a heart patient to go into that kind of cold climate and enter such negotiations under extreme mental pressure was risky. But one has to understand this in a historical perspective. What must have been playing on the mind of the prime minister when he agreed, against the advice of the army, to sign the agreement?

We waited outside the prime minister's dacha all night in freezing cold. Early in the morning, the body was brought out and the coffin was carried towards the plane. Ayub Khan also gave a shoulder to the coffin as the procession moved towards the airport.

Thus ended the short tenure of a prime minister who had earned immense popularity. Here was this diminutive man who had achieved the impossible and registered his name in Indian history for all time.

Shastriji's sudden death shook India badly. Once again, Gulzarilal Nanda became the caretaker prime minister (as he had done after Nehru's death). The Congress party sat down to choose a successor. For once, K. Kamaraj was unable to make a case for Mrs Gandhi because Morarji Desai was laying claim to the position of prime minister.

Nevertheless, the new contender emerged—Nehru's daughter, Indira Gandhi. It was Shastriji who had, in his wisdom, inducted Mrs Gandhi into his cabinet as the minister for information and broadcasting.

The Indira era begins

The general view of the party at that time was to have her succeed Shastri. But it was challenged by Morarji Desai. This led to a vote by the parliamentary party in which Morarji Desai was defeated. Indira Gandhi thus became Lal Bahadur Shastri's successor as prime minister of India.

Shastriji's departure also meant in many ways the passing of a certain generation of political leaders. Those in control of the party belonged to a bygone era. They were brought up in a different political culture. Mrs Gandhi's election marked a fresh beginning.

The general opinion was that she was selected because party leaders thought they could control her. But little did these experienced politicians realize that Indira Gandhi was no pushover. Having emerged as leader of the party and as prime minister, she would be very much her own person. After all, she had been the Congress president during her father's time and knew the party inside out.

5

A Tough Start for Indira

Indira Gandhi assumed prime ministership at a very difficult time. She had to handle the fallout resulting from Lal Bahadur Shastri's agreement in Tashkent. The nation was angry at the withdrawal of its forces from areas, such as Haji Pir Pass and the mountaintops of Kargil, that the army had captured with great sacrifice. The mystery surrounding Shastriji's death added to the general anguish.

Bihar was facing near-famine conditions with a very severe drought. There was acute food shortage and India depended on imports of food grains, which were not sufficient since our foreign exchange resources were poor.

This was a big news story that would have international implications. I had started making pitches to editors, so that they would send me to Bihar soon.

Mrs Gandhi sought help from the US and the country agreed to supply food grains under a US law known as PL-480. Under this law, which had been adopted by the US during Eisenhower's presidency, India was to pay for the food grains in rupees. The money was to be used by the US for its embassy or other agencies in the country. President Lyndon B. Johnson shipped 16 million tonnes of wheat and 1 million tonnes of rice to India. The aid was welcome, but it came with a rider: liberalize the economy. That was not acceptable to Mrs Gandhi.

Indira Gandhi had to avert a famine and avoid bankruptcy. The Indian rupee was very weak at that time. The official exchange rate of the US dollar to the rupee was 4.70, whereas in the market a dollar was being traded at Rs 10. The rupee was devalued when I was in Ladakh, covering the Indian and Chinese troops facing each other across the Pangong Lake, the world's highest and largest salt water lake with lovely blue water. It is situated at an altitude of 4,350 metres. The devaluation of the rupee came as good news for me up there. I must have been among the few Indians who welcomed this devaluation, even though it was not done to the level of the market rate. I used to receive only Rs 13.30 for a pound, as my salary from Visnews came in pounds sterling. The market rate used to hover between Rs 30–40. I was now to receive Rs 21 for a pound after the devaluation. Well, I thought to myself, some relief.

Mrs Gandhi now started dealing head-on with the drought in Bihar, to save the people there from famine. In order to contain the media coverage of this issue, a meeting was called by Ashok Mitra, the then information secretary and among the last of the British-trained ICS officers in service. (In the colonial era, the Indian Civil Service was an institution controlled by the British; after Independence it was renamed the Indian Administrative Service or IAS.)

At this meeting, all the heads of the official media, such as the Films Division, Press Information Bureau, Photo Division, All India Radio, etc., were present. I was the only non-official attendee, because I represented Visnews, an international television agency. Among the ministry's biggest concerns was how the world would view the Bihar situation and that the international reaction might not be very complimentary.

Nearly everyone sitting around Mr Mitra at that meeting was a media giant and each recommended that Bihar be closed to the private media with only official media handling the coverage. I listened in complete silence and did not offer any comment. At this point, Mr Mitra turned to me and asked: 'Mr Prakash, you have been very quiet. What is your view?'

I said, 'Sir, the people sitting around are very senior to me, with a lot of experience. But in all humility, I do not agree with them.' I said my view was very simple: the tragedy in Bihar had not been created by any actions of the government. This was nature's calamity. If the government was seen not doing enough to meet the crisis, then however much you try to shield Bihar from public view, the outside world would soon find out. That could damage the government's image.

On the other hand, if the government was seen working to bring help to those affected, it was important to let the world read about it in their newspapers and watch it on their television screens. After all, there were famines during the British era, when millions died. If nobody died in Bihar from want, India would be seen to have achieved something quite remarkable.

There was complete silence around the table, until Mitra responded to me: 'I accept what you are saying. Bihar won't be sealed. We will ensure that the world gets to know how we are handling the situation.' Thereafter, the meeting got adjourned.

As I got up to leave, Mr Mitra asked me to stay on. He then asked me, 'Can I call you by first name, Prem?' I replied, 'Sir, you are so senior. It will be an honour for me.' He asked when I would be able to travel to Bihar to bring back the first reports. Very soon, I responded, as the story had already begun playing.

I came back wondering whether I should go there by myself as a Visnews correspondent or take another foreign correspondent with me. My dear friend Tony Cane's name came immediately to mind. He was the head of the Australian Broadcasting Commission (ABC) in Delhi. I had helped ABC set up their office in Delhi. ABC was very close to Visnews and a major subscriber. I thought working together would ensure a much wider coverage. Besides, if I worked alone, it might be felt that, as an Indian, I was presenting a biased report.

I called on Mr Mitra to apprise him about my plans and told him that I proposed to travel to Bihar by road along with Tony Cane. I have never seen a government official as excited as Ashok Mitra got when he heard my plans. He said he would ensure that all the district commissioners on our route were made aware of our itinerary and that they would cooperate in every way possible.

Travelling from Delhi, I saw for the first time what is known as the Indo–Gangetic Plain. For miles till infinity there was flat land, with no undulations. As history tells us, once foreign invaders managed to reach Delhi, there was no stopping them through these plains.

We found conditions in Bihar extremely difficult, with farmers in some places carrying buckets of water to the parched soil. But the hopeful sight was that the aid programme of the central government was working efficiently. Prime Minister Indira Gandhi had not left the situation solely with the Government of Bihar but was taking direct interest herself to ensure that relief work was reaching the stricken areas even in remote villages.

Food was distributed in each and every home in these villages. Drinking water, too, was delivered regularly. Filming the plight of the people left me very sad but hopeful that the government was making sure no one died of starvation.

If Mrs Gandhi herself had not taken full responsibility for dealing with the Bihar drought, matters could have gone awry. Independent India thus managed to save itself the ignominy of what could have been a severe famine.

This is how Mrs Gandhi started her journey of her premiership.

Then, other events came over the horizon. After the economic downturn, the rupee's devaluation and the Bihar drought, the general election was around the corner.

In many ways the 1967 general election marked a watershed in Indian political history. A lot had changed since the 1962 general election: India had been mauled by China and forced to withdraw from the territories of Kashmir it had recaptured from Pakistan, thanks to the Tashkent Declaration. The period had seen two prime ministers pass away. This was also Mrs Gandhi's first election as prime minister. There were doubts among the mass of India's voters about her abilities, as other senior Congress leaders were still around.

Mrs Gandhi led the election campaign as fiercely as she could and managed to win the polls for the Congress, albeit with a small majority. The party could only win 283 seats in a house of 520, whereas in the 1962 election it had won 361 seats. Thus, it was by a very narrow margin of thirteen seats that the Congress emerged as winner.

The setback in the general election led the old guard in the Congress to project this as a defeat of Mrs Gandhi, for her inability to lead the campaign properly. They felt she could either be eased out of the party or made to follow their diktat. But this was not to be. She was not a person who would take orders from anyone.

After Mrs Gandhi had taken charge as prime minister, the senior leaders of the party—S.K. Patil, K. Kamaraj and Atulya Ghosh—led by the then Congress president, S. Nijalingappa, began asserting themselves. They resented her, for they thought she was not in tune with the party. But a conflict between the party and the prime minister was nothing new. Even Nehru had differences with Acharya Kripalani and others in his time. I met many of Mrs Gandhi's colleagues, and they were senior to her. Each had very strong views on her ability to lead them. Some were very sharp in their criticism. The nature of discourse had changed in the party from Nehru's time to Indira's.

Indira shows her mettle

Mrs Gandhi pushed ahead with her plans to eradicate poverty in India. To deal with the issue, she initiated a dramatic ten-point programme, seeking social control of the banking sector, nationalization of general insurance, nationalization of the import-export trade, public distribution of food grain, curbs on monopolies, limits on urban incomes and property, better implementation of land reform and an end to privy purses and princely privileges.

In the meantime, Morarji Desai, who ran a parallel power centre, enforced the Gold Control Act vigorously. This made the prime minister and the government extremely unpopular. A great many jewellers committed suicide when they found they could not obtain gold. The public mood had become volatile. Nonetheless, Mrs Gandhi continued with her agenda, convinced that tough measures were necessary.

In May 1969, the president of India, Zakir Husain, passed away. He was the first president to die in office. V.V. Giri, the vice president, became acting president. In 1969, as his term moved towards its end, a fresh election was required. A Congress working committee met in Bangalore to consider the candidates. Mrs Gandhi was inclined towards V.V. Giri continuing as the president, but the party preferred Neelam Sanjiva Reddy.

To outsmart the party, Mrs Gandhi proposed Babu Jagjivan Ram, a member of the lower caste. This meant that she was ready to withdraw her support for V.V. Giri. I felt Jagjivan Ram himself was not very interested, since he was already a minister. He had his ambitions. Had he agreed to be president it would have meant the end of active politics for him.

Mrs Gandhi tried to pitch the idea that it would be a really apt tribute to Mahatma Gandhi, during his centenary year, to elect a member of the Scheduled Castes to the highest office of the country. Again, the working committee overruled the prime minister and stuck with Sanjiva Reddy. I was given to understand that there were allegations of misdemeanour against Sanjiva Reddy and that he had made remarks critical of Mrs Gandhi.

Sensing what she was up against, Mrs Gandhi returned to Delhi. There, she encouraged V.V. Giri to file his papers as an independent candidate. This is the only instance since the promulgation of the Indian Constitution that an independent candidate not only contested the presidential election but went on to win it.

Giri's candidature was openly supported by Indira Gandhi. She had facilitated it by asking the MPs to vote 'according to their conscience'.

This election could have been the undoing of Mrs Gandhi. She had taken a huge gamble. I was there in Parliament House when the votes were counted. V.V. Giri lost the first round. Soon, those who were considered Indira loyalists started leaving the counting centre thinking her candidate Giri was losing the election.

Then the counting began for the second preference vote. Here, Mrs Gandhi scored heavily. Those voting 'according to their conscience' gave the second preference votes to Giri. The Congress party had officially decided to give the second preference votes to C.D. Deshmukh, endorsed by the Jana Sangh and the Swatantra Party.

The results showed that 163 Congress MPs had cast their second preference votes for Giri. He also secured a majority in the electoral college with eleven out of the seventeen states, although the party was in a majority in twelve of them. This indicated that support for Giri was widespread across the nation and his victory was not dependent on the backing of communists and regional political parties.

Mrs Gandhi's supporters managed to polarize the electorate between the left and right and to reject the candidature of Deshmukh in the second preference vote. V.V. Giri won the election narrowly, scoring just about 15,000 votes over Sanjiva Reddy. The old guard of the Congress had been defeated and Mrs Gandhi emerged all-powerful. Giri's success confirmed, howsoever narrowly, Indira Gandhi's authority.

Her advisers, like P.N. Haksar, and her new allies among the Young Turks, including my friend and mentor Inder Kumar Gujral, formulated the ten-point programme floated at the Bangalore session. Now, the fight between the prime minister, who wanted to control both the government and the party, and the leaders who controlled the party, was out in the open.

The party seemed destined for a split. The Congress Working Committee met in Delhi to take stock of the situation arising out of the defeat of its presidential candidate. But was this just a review meeting or were the older leaders looking to go further? Either way, it was not to Mrs Gandhi's liking. She felt that they might try to censure her and ask for her resignation.

In the end, she absented herself from the party meeting. (I saw all the party leaders sitting there and waiting for her.) Instead, she called a separate meeting which included a large group of her supporters calling themselves Requisitionists. They met at the prime minister's house in a direct challenge to the main party.

These meetings continued for several days. On one occasion, Nijalingappa, the president of Congress, was physically attacked when he came to the party office. He was not hurt but was stopped from entering the office by those demonstrating in favour of Mrs Gandhi.

The die was cast. The grand old party, for the first time since its formation, broke into two: Congress (O), which was led by the traditionalists; and Congress (R), with the 'R' standing for Requisitionists.

My editors in London, including the editor-in-chief, Tony Whyte, congratulated me in a long message on the story of the Congress split for being able to explain to lay viewers around the world how a lady had emerged on top of the world's largest democracy. Incidentally, Tony Whyte was born in India, at the house of the speaker of the Indian Parliament on Akbar Road. His father, Sir Allen Whyte, was the president of the Legislative Assembly when it was created following the 1935 Government of India Act.

Sir Allen Whyte's portrait used to be hung in the lobbies of Parliament. I had the good fortune of meeting him in London while he was alive. He remembered many Indian parliamentarians, including Motilal Nehru, extremely well.

The group which took over Congress (R) included many young people, among them my dear friend I.K. Gujral. They became known as Mrs Gandhi's 'kitchen cabinet'—a group of advisers who, though they didn't hold any official posts, were considered to be extremely influential because of their proximity to the PM.

I remember that, in an interview, Mrs Gandhi had termed parliamentary democracy as moribund and not suitable for India. Years later she toyed with the idea of introducing a presidential system. The idea was dropped, but the fact that it was floated at all suggested she was always looking to consolidate her power.

And so, in 1969, Mrs Gandhi emerged as a leader in her own right. She was now running a minority government in Parliament.

Those in Congress (O) were acting like the opposition. They had to, but were unable to, bring about a vote of no confidence because she had the support of the Communist Party—which was a very large political outfit at that time—and many other left groups. Some kind of vote of no confidence was brought later on, but it was defeated.

Strengthened by her position both as the president of her party and prime minister of India, Mrs Gandhi called for elections in 1971—a year ahead of schedule. Apart from having to deal with the harsh fallout over the hugely publicized ten-point programme, she was also dependent on the support of the left parties, who were adamant on demanding the nationalization of big banks. She announced the nationalization of banks and embraced it as her own decision.

The government nationalized fourteen banks with the objective of providing easy loans to the poor, the farmers and small businesses. Taxi drivers became very prominent in the distribution of these loans.

Under pressure from the communists and left-wing parties, Mrs Gandhi also cancelled the privy purses of the maharajas, even though these were given to the former princes under a treaty. This naturally led to a lot of opposition from feudal elements all over India but it was a decision that the left approved. The vast population of India was hardly bothered.

Jawaharlal Nehru had once openly stated in parliament that he would not waste money on nationalizing private sector companies or foreign businesses, but Mrs Gandhi reduced the majority stake of foreign investors in India to 40 per cent, giving in to the pressure mounted by the left-wing parties that were supporting her. Thus, foreign investment fled from India and was no longer forthcoming.

How the world reacted to this move did not matter to Mrs Gandhi. Her goal was to gain support at home and to win votes. Mrs Gandhi called for elections in 1971 on the back of all these populist actions. She refused to go into any coalition or arrangement with those who had supported her minority government. In the end, Congress (R) romped home with a very comfortable majority. Congress (O), belonging to the old guard, was rendered insignificant.

At this stage, Mrs Gandhi shed all the support she was getting from the political left and set out to pursue her own agenda, which included reshaping the country's economy. But she could not revive the economy, nor attract foreign capital.

6

Bangladesh on the Horizon

Even as the government assumed charge in Delhi, with Indira Gandhi winning a very comfortable majority, events elsewhere were taking a strange turn.

In the election held in Pakistan, Sheikh Mujibur Rahman's Awami League, which was largely based in East Pakistan, secured a majority of seats. Thus, Mujibur Rahman became eligible to become prime minister of Pakistan. However, this was not to the liking of the authorities in West Pakistan or of the army, which controlled the country through martial law. Rebellion erupted in East Pakistan in support of Mujibur Rahman, calling for the Awami League to be given charge of the country.

Zulfikar Ali Bhutto, leader of the Pakistan People's Party, supported by the army and the people of the dominant Punjab province of Pakistan, suggested a strange 'two prime ministers' compromise, with two leaders controlling the two parts of Pakistan. But this was not acceptable to the Awami League.

In a historic speech in Dhaka on 7 March 1971, as the crisis in Pakistan over government formation grew, Mujibur Rahman threatened that the mass protest, launched in East Pakistan by his party, would become a movement for liberation. He declared: '*Ae baar sangram, mukti sangram* (This time the battle will be the battle for liberation).' He was very clear in his mind that any struggle this time against the high-handedness of the Punjabi-dominated West Pakistan and its army would need a fight to the finish.

The Pakistan administration reacted swiftly. The army general, Tikka Khan, was sent to East Pakistan as governor. Soon after his arrival he ordered a complete crackdown on the Awami League and arrested Mujibur Rahman and other leaders. (Mujibur Rahman was transferred to a jail in West Pakistan.)

Widespread riots broke out. The military authorities prepared for a further clampdown. Hundreds were killed. And now the whole world became aware of events in East Pakistan as they became prime-time global news.

Birth pangs for Bangladesh

While political campaigning for the 1971 general election was taking place all over India, Pakistan—a country under martial law and ruled by President Yahya Khan—was going to polls for its own National Assembly elections.

East Pakistan had always been a volatile part of Pakistan—ethnically, culturally—and in fact was totally different from West Pakistan. The two had never moved together, especially after Jinnah, the founder of Pakistan, during his visit to East Pakistan shortly before his death in 1948, proclaimed in Dhaka that Urdu would be the national language of the new state of Pakistan. The people of East Pakistan objected strongly. They were proud of their own Bengali language and culture. Language riots broke out and were curbed, but Bengali remained the language of East Pakistan. To placate the people of East Pakistan, an offer was made that Bengali be made the official language of Pakistan along with Urdu.

During a visit to East Pakistan to cover cyclone damage there, I had noticed and felt the hatred that divided East and West Pakistan. East Bengal, which came to be known as East Pakistan, was originally part of the huge province of Bengal in the British days. At the time of Independence, the province of Bengal was also partitioned. The Muslim-majority East Bengal was separated from West Bengal, which, with its capital Calcutta, went to India.

East Pakistan was thousands of kilometres away from West Pakistan, with the vast land mass of India in between. Yet East Pakistan remained a part of Pakistan, albeit under heavy police and military control. In early 1969 there had been riots in East Pakistan. The Pakistan government described them as a conspiracy to secede from Pakistan. Mujibur Rahman had been released from jail in February 1969.

The elections for Pakistan's National Assembly, held in December 1970, saw the Awami League emerge as the majority party, capturing 167 out of 313 seats of the house. This came as a shock to West Pakistan and its military rulers. The Awami League also won 288 out of 300 seats of the East Bengal Legislative Assembly. Now, the Awami League, in the true democratic sense, was the real representative of the people of Pakistan.

Quite rightly, Sheikh Mujibur Rahman staked his claim to govern Pakistan as its prime minister. This certainly was not acceptable to the president and martial law administrator, Yahya Khan, who was now joined by Zulfikar Ali Bhutto.

They refused to allow Mujibur Rahman to become prime minister. Bhutto even refused to accept any solution suggested by Mujibur Rahman to solve the impasse. Negotiation and talks between the two sides chugged along all the way to March 1971, with Mujibur Rahman still being denied his right to be prime minister. That was when Zulfikar Ali Bhutto, backed by President Yahya Khan, proposed an unheard-of solution: having two prime ministers of Pakistan, namely himself and Mujibur Rehman. Bhutto was not in favour of autonomy for East Pakistan, wishing instead that it continue as a colony of West Pakistan.

The two leaders, along with Yahya Khan, met in Dhaka in March 1971. But the talks failed. Mujibur Rehman issued a call for a nationwide strike across both East and West Pakistan to enforce the result of the December elections. Yahya Khan ordered General Tikka Khan to fly to Dhaka and take charge of East Pakistan as governor. More troops were flown into East Pakistan. Pakistan's all-powerful army had clearly negated the elections of 1970.

On 7 March 1971, Mujibur Rahman, in the face of an emerging critical situation, addressed a huge rally in Dhaka. He asked for the lifting of martial law, for the army to be confined to the barracks and the transfer of power to the elected leader of the Assembly before 25 March. At the same time, the Bengali judges refused to swear in Tikka Khan as governor, although this certainly did not deter the military rulers, either in Rawalpindi or in Dhaka.

Allowing Mujibur Rahman's deadline of 25 March to pass, Tikka Khan launched his genocidal crackdown on East Pakistan. Mujibur Rahman was arrested during the night of 25 March and immediately flown to West Pakistan, where he was put on trial and sentenced to death for sedition.

Unilateral independence of Bangladesh

The Awami League had announced on 25 March that 'Bangladesh was now a sovereign and independent country' and confirmed it in Chittagong on 26 March—now celebrated as Independence Day of Bangladesh.

General Tikka Khan's next act was to expel all foreign journalists from Dhaka. He then cracked down on East Pakistan with full military might. His first targets were the political leaders—many of whom managed to escape just in time. He then attacked the University of Dhaka in the most brutal manner. Student agitators in general and Hindu students in particular were his targets. They were lined up and shot dead.

I was to later see a video of these killings, taken by a professor who had a house opposite the ground where the students were murdered by the Pakistan Army. Such an act against unarmed citizens was nothing short of a war crime.

As Tikka Khan launched the crackdown, I was asked by my editors in London to move to the Indian border with East Pakistan and cover whatever I could. I knew it was not as simple as it sounded.

I decided to travel to Calcutta by train to give myself some time to think. Durgadas Chatterji, my cameraman colleague in Calcutta, met me at the Howrah Station. The next day, we drove together to Benapole, the border outpost on the road to Jessore.

It seemed all quiet. Pakistani border guards stood vigil. All the world's press and television had converged on Calcutta as the news spread about the genocide in East Pakistan. Over the next two days, Durga and I watched foreign TV teams cross the border, only to see them return after an hour or so.

We felt we were being beaten by these foreigners who seemed able to get into East Pakistan while we could not. Meanwhile, we covered other border points from where a trickle of refugees were making their way into India.

Suddenly, on the third day, we found there were no border guards on the Pakistani side. Durga and I thought for a moment and then decided to walk across. The Indian guards asked us to be careful in case Pak soldiers were hiding. But we found nobody on the other side. The border outpost was vacant, with a Bangladesh flag installed there.

We managed to get a lift and headed towards Jessore. But the driver refused to take us all the way and dropped us at a tea shop. Inside, we found people listening to All India Radio and felt reassured. I, as a Punjabi who could not speak Bengali, had to be very careful because the Bengalis were purportedly against the Punjabis, as most of the Pakistani soldiers were from west Punjab. So my colleague Durgadas Chatterji did all the talking, and I kept quiet. I could, of course, follow Bengali and later that year began to speak the language.

Durga managed to get us another vehicle, and we made our way to Jessore. On the outskirts of the town, a shock awaited us. Dead bodies of civilians lay on the road and by the roadside. We were told they had been killed by the Pakistan Army the previous night.

We moved into Jessore and found it deserted. All the shops were closed. We went to the railway station to look for a map of the town and managed to make contact with a bunch of Mukti

Bahini—the Bangladeshi 'liberation army'—volunteers, who showed us around.

They took us to a spot where they had lined up several 'Biharis'—the Urdu-speaking residents of East Pakistan. They were to be shot. This was jungle law now. We decided not to stay and asked to be driven back to the border. My God, what a drive it was! Almost at jet speed. But we reached the border and crossed back into India.

The film we had shot was to be the first look the world would have of the scene in East Pakistan. The pictures told the story of the genocide that was being inflicted all over East Pakistan. Our film left for London that night, together with my eyewitness account, carried all around the world the next day by Reuters. All this visual material was released by Visnews to its subscribers globally.

Early next morning Durga and I again headed for Benapole. From there we explored the countryside and found people who were abandoning their homes, fearing the military would attack them. Women were the special targets of the essentially Punjabi-dominated Pakistan Army.

The sight horrified us. More dead bodies and another deserted village. As we rushed back we were told that the 'Razakars' were nearby. The Razakar force was a religious paramilitary raised by the Pakistan Army (comparable to today's Islamist terrorists in Pakistan). Tikka Khan had created it to spread terror among the population in general and among Hindu villagers in particular.

Our next foray was towards Chuadanga, which was declared the provisional capital of the new state of Bangladesh. The town was ruled by an Awami League leader, popularly known as 'Two Gun Haq'. Mr Haq used to carry two revolvers in his hands! The town was awash with Awami League flags and was under the firm control of the Awami League, the local police having given up.

Getting into East Pakistan, covering the genocide and coming back with the pictures was far from easy. One had to rely on whoever on the other side was willing to help—hoping not to be betrayed to the enemy. Two journalists from Calcutta making a similar foray had been captured and killed by the Pakistan Army.

Durga and I decided to go to Khulna next. As we crossed the border, we ran into a camp where volunteers of Mukti Bahini were being trained for war. It was all very basic, but we found the young men to be very enthusiastic.

Durga and I were joined by a young man called Mantu, who was to be our guide. We found Khulna deserted. We were taken to see the police station. In retrospect, I think we were lucky because the chief of the police was a Bihari whose officers had rebelled. He was expecting the worst for himself. Or else it could well have been the worst for us!

And lo and behold—we soon landed in serious trouble at the house of a local MNA (member of the National Assembly). He was the only Muslim League candidate from East Pakistan to be elected to the National Assembly. He thought we were perhaps the advance party of the Indian Army. Rumours were all over Khulna that the Indian Army was marching towards the city via the bridge where local police force had more or less given up.

Convincing him, letting him believe that we were indeed the advance party, we managed to move quickly from there to the bridge. Several policemen were preparing trenches in case the Pakistan Army attacked them. Crowds of people with their belongings walked past them on their way towards the border. As I pointed the camera at them to record their flight, they raised their hands as though the camera was a gun!

I now asked the jeep driver to take us back to the Indian border. He refused and tried to take us once again to the MNA's house. At this stage our guide, Mantu, showed him his camera bag, which he said was loaded with bombs, and threatened to blow him up. To our relief, the fellow was frightened enough to drive us back to the border.

Once on Indian soil, we heaved a sigh of relief. That had been a close shave. Having sent my story off to Reuters, I locked myself in my room. I just wanted to thank the Lord for having brought us back safely. I have often wondered what would have happened to our families if this day had turned out against me and I had been killed. There was every possibility of that happening, because first we landed at the police station and then at the house of a pro-Pakistan MNA.

To this day I feel lucky to have survived that foray into East Pakistan. That story and my coverage of the situation resulted in loud protests from Pakistan. They claimed that Reuters and Visnews had made illegal entry into what was still Pakistan. I must say, however, that ordinary Bengalis in East Pakistan were all very protective towards me and Durga.

Late one night, as I was about to go to sleep, I got a call from the principal information officer of the Indian government, M.L. Bhardwaj. He had just checked into the Grand Hotel in Calcutta. He asked me over to his room to discuss something urgent. He wanted to know about all the Bangladeshi leaders I knew, including those who were interacting with the press on behalf of the leaders of the Awami League.

I told him about the young man Badshah, press secretary to Sheikh Mujibur Rahman. The Sheikh treated Badshah as his son. Bhardwaj met him the next day and it was decided that Badshah would invite the international press and escort them to a point on the East Pakistan border where the provisional government of Bangladesh was to be presented by the Awami League leaders.

Shrouded in secrecy, the plan went through smoothly the next morning. We were all escorted by Badshah to the border and then crossed over into what was still East Pakistan. We reached a village where a huge stage had been raised. The leaders of the Awami League appeared and a provisional government of Bangladesh was announced. They declared their determination to continue the struggle till Pakistan withdrew from their country.

The Bangladeshi flag was raised, and the meeting ended with the chanting of Tagore's 'Amar Sonar Bangla', which was later adopted as the national anthem of Bangladesh. It was historical footage that I had shot, but when one is shooting one doesn't realize the magnitude of such things. The mind and the eye are focused on the image, the sight and the sound.

By this time, the Pakistan Army's crackdown had proved effective and Dhaka was said to be quiet. The Pakistan government now became concerned that film and news reports of the genocide in East Pakistan were getting to the outside world. It lodged more protests with Reuters—that we were entering East Pakistan illegally and that Reuters and Visnews must stop this illegal activity.

Our mission was to tell the world the truth—and we succeeded. The stories and pictures from East Pakistan greatly influenced world opinion in favour of Bangladesh's fight for freedom. The world came to know of the atrocities and genocide being committed by the Pakistan Army in East Pakistan. But nonetheless, by the middle of April, Tikka Khan had managed to secure the border, making it impossible to enter East Pakistan from the west.

After covering the endless flow of refugees heading for India, I decided to go back to Delhi for a while. In Delhi, my friend S.K. Singh, head of the external publicity division in the Ministry of External Affairs, jokingly remarked: 'So you have ended this war for the moment.'

I realized then that the government had been monitoring all my telex messages and reports going to Visnews and Reuters. And that these had become a major source of information about what was going on in East Pakistan.

Around that time, eastern India was getting hit by pre-monsoon rains, also known as nor'westers. It rains very heavily in these storms, which added to the difficulty of dealing with the influx of refugees. The Indian government had already opened several refugee camps. The refugees were not only Hindus. Muslims were also being pushed out by the Urdu-speaking Biharis. My coverage of the refugee camps and the human tragedy continued. The world began to understand the huge problem India was facing. Among several global figures who came to India to see for themselves the refugee situation was Senator Edward Kennedy.

East Pakistan's military was now at full strength, but Mukti Bahini was making life difficult for them. Its guerrilla attacks were restricting the movement of the Pakistan Army to main roads and cities.

At he same time, it was clear that India could not afford to keep over a million refugees in its care. East Pakistan did not want them back. In fact, more and more were pushed into India. The refugees wanted to go back—but only after the Pakistan Army had left.

Events were moving quickly. It seemed that an all-out war and the defeat of Pakistan was the only way India could send the million-plus refugees back to their homes. However, war was not an immediate option because of the monsoon rains. There are a great many rivers in East Pakistan and they rise rapidly during the monsoon. Sending in the army was not an option at that time.

Meanwhile, Mukhti Bahini was increasing in numbers. Its attacks on the Pakistan Army were causing serious damage to the morale of the Pak troops. Furthermore, India was now supporting Mukti Bahini in its fight.

In November, Indira Gandhi undertook a tour of world capitals to raise this issue and apprise the world of what Pakistan was doing to its people. She returned from her tour fairly satisfied with the global response. However, the Americans under President Richard Nixon and the Secretary of State Henry Kissinger were hostile to India.

Precautionary orders were given to the Indian Army to prepare for action to ensure that the mass of refugees left India and went back to their homes. In West Pakistan, Mrs Gandhi's tour was clearly seen as a bid to prepare the rest of the world for military action by India. It was assumed an attack would be launched in December. On analysing India's intentions, President Yahya Khan initiated pre-emptive attacks on Indian Air Force bases.

On the night of 3 December, Pakistani aircraft attacked a number of such bases and started the war on India's western border. The targets of the Pakistan Air Force were airbases at Amritsar, Ambala, Agra, Awantipur, Bikaner, Halwara, Jodhpur, Jaisalmer, Pathankot, Bhuj, Srinagar and Uttarlai. It was immediately repulsed by the Indian Army, which simultaneously moved into East Pakistan, outflanking the Pakistan Army there.

When the attack began, I was in Agartala, covering developments on that side of the Indian border. I was with Brigadier Shahbeg Singh at his headquarters. One of the most highly decorated Indian soldiers, he was now head of counterinsurgency operations, responsible for training the Mukti Bahini. Also present at his headquarters was Brigadier Osmani, who was later to be the chief of Bangladesh Army.

The Mukti Bahini was fighting pitched battles against the Pakistan Army in this sector and inflicting heavy damage. I was most impressed to see how well their training prepared them for action. To be sure, they severely dented the morale of the Pakistani soldiers and paramilitary.

India recognized the government of the new state of Bangladesh on 6 December 1971, while contingents of the Indian Army moved into East Pakistan. Since Mukti Bahini had already dampened the spirits of the Pakistani troops, when the Indian offensive began our forces moved quickly. The Pakistan Army was soon in full retreat, being attacked by the local population as well as by the powerful Indian military.

The United States threatened to intervene on Pakistan's behalf. It moved its Seventh Fleet towards the Bay of Bengal, bringing with them the threat of nuclear attack. President Nixon and Henry Kissinger hated Mrs Gandhi and her power, as she was seen to be close to the Soviet Union and was the leader of the Non-Aligned Movement. At the same time, the Soviet Union was backing India's action in East Pakistan.

By 14 December it was clear that the Pakistan Army was in no position to continue fighting. General Sam Manekshaw, chief of the Indian Army, called upon the Pakistan Army to surrender or face annihilation. General J.F.R. Jacob of the Indian Army flew into Dhaka, to finalize the terms of surrender, which was to be unconditional, with India guaranteeing Pakistani troops protection against almost certain annihilation by Mukti Bahini.

As the army advanced, I flew into Calcutta, from where I travelled with General Jagjit Singh Aurora and General Jacob to cover the surrender ceremony, held at the race course in Dhaka. Pakistan surrendered to the Indian Army and Mukti Bahini. General Aurora signed for India and General Niazi, commander of the Pakistani forces, signed on behalf of Pakistan. It was a heady feeling for us journalists covering those last few days of the 'Fall of Dhaka'. I will never forget the faces and expressions of common people who saw an end to their misery.

India moved the Pakistan Army into cantonments, where some 93,000 soldiers laid down their weapons—the biggest surrender since World War II. Again, these were historic events that I covered, but at that time uppermost in my mind was the thought that I had to quickly shoot and send the pictures to London.

Indira Gandhi was now the greatest, much-celebrated heroine of India. The prime minister received a standing ovation in Parliament following the unconditional surrender by the Pakistan Army. In Dhaka, the Bangladesh government took charge.

Meanwhile, Sheikh Mujibur Rahman was still in a Pakistani prison, with a death sentence hanging over his head. It is said that the Pakistanis had dug a grave near his prison cell. Mrs Gandhi acted firmly and ensured his release in January 1972. Mujibur Rahman flew to London and from there to Delhi on his way back to Dhaka.

Mujibur returns

Mujibur Rahman's arrival in Dhaka was big world news at the time, and practically all major media networks, including the BBC and the other global news channels of the United States and Europe, were present in Dhaka to cover his arrival and the massive welcome he was going to receive. I was there too, with my full team. All the networks together had chartered a plane to take their filmed material to Bangkok for processing and satellite transmission, since there were no processing facilities in Dhaka.

I knew beating the competitors on such a story was not going to be easy. Thus I advised John Tulloh, the Asia-Pacific editor of Visnews, who was waiting for my material in Bangkok, that I was going to edit the story myself as I filmed and restrict the footage to 400 feet, i.e. ten minutes, which was the time we had booked for the satellite feed in Bangkok. No news channel ran a news item for more than three or four minutes.

I did my filming at the airport as Mujibur Rahman's plane landed, with leaders of the interim government waiting for him to alight. I had managed to get at the foot of the aircraft as the Sheikh appeared from the plane to wild cheers of the crowd at the airport. After his welcome by the interim government leaders, he got into an open truck to drive through the city for the parade ground where he was to address a mass meeting.

I travelled with the cavalcade for a couple of miles, covering the huge enthusiastic welcome, and then walked back to the airport. I got my package ready and handed it over to the pilot of the chartered plane as we waited for the other journalists to arrive. Several managed to turn up just before the flight took off, and despite my protests the flight was delayed by half an hour to give them time to get their packages ready. The plane then took off for Bangkok.

The next morning, as I was getting ready to go for breakfast, I received a cable from John Tulloh in Bangkok, congratulating me for covering the whole story so well in ten minutes. He told me that while other journalists' material was still being processed, ours was already on the satellite and reaching everyone. We had managed to stay ahead of the competition. The other channels had to use breaking-news material from Visnews.

The next day, Mujibur Rahman took charge of the government of Bangladesh. The war had left India with 93,000 POWs to care for. India also moved quickly to send the refugees back to their homes in independent Bangladesh. As the refugees prepared to leave, they were given enough food and money to restart their lives and were carried back happily in convoys of trucks. I had earlier shot films that showed them trudging into India with hopelessness on their faces. Now, they had hope.

After prolonged negotiations, India and Pakistan agreed to discuss the issue of repatriating POWs. Formal talks opened in Shimla in July 1972. Bhutto arrived there with his daughter, Benazir.

Among the POWs were several civilians, including a soundman of Visnews from Karachi who happened to be in Dhaka the day it fell.

The talks did not proceed well. India was looking for a solution to the Kashmir issue during the talks, so as to end hostilities with Pakistan for all time. It is my view that India lost all the advantages it had gained through its victory in December 1971, because our negotiators failed in the game of brinkmanship. The talks had run into stalemate, with either side refusing to sign any accord. Bhutto was not prepared to concede anything that could resolve the Kashmir issue. I thought at that moment, as did others, that the talks had broken down. Yet we were taken by surprise when the announcement came that the Simla Accord was to be signed. It happened late at night. India lost a major opportunity to resolve the Kashmir issue, because it fell for the promises made by Bhutto.

Pakistan recognized Bangladesh, which it would have done sooner or later. But, more importantly, it got back its POWs without addressing the Kashmir issue. Bhutto and his delegation were not willing to concede anything, but I believe to this day that he would not have gone back without ensuring the release of the Pakistani POWs. The families back home in Pakistan wanted them back.

All he conceded was to not harp on the term 'ceasefire line' in Kashmir and agree to the term Line of Control. This meant that India could retain areas like Kargil, which it had retaken in 1971. The Kargil high peak outside the town, captured by India in 1965, was returned to Pakistan after the war under the Tashkent Agreement. However, India recaptured it in 1971, and it has been part of India ever since.

Bhutto kept reassuring India that while he was very dependent upon the army, once he took full control of the government he would ensure friendship with India. But he certainly did not have the backing of the Pakistan Army in proposing such an understanding.

Once its POWs were back in Pakistan, the Pakistan Army again began its nefarious activities against Bangladesh and India. It did all it could to destabilize Bangladesh. In Kashmir, it fomented internal disturbance.

The Pakistan Army later hanged Bhutto on a little-known charge—that Bhutto had orchestrated the murder of a political rival. But in fact they hanged him because they felt he was responsible for the separation of East Pakistan.

And at home, Indira Gandhi faced widespread criticism for signing the Simla Agreement without sorting out the Kashmir issue.

7

Democracy's Darkest Hour

The twelfth of June 1975 was like any other summer day in Delhi—
hot and humid with frequent power failures adding to the discomfort.

Then there was a bolt from the blue. Suddenly, teleprinters in
the newsrooms of media offices began clattering out a news alert
from Allahabad. The verdict had been delivered on a lawsuit filed
by the opposition's defeated candidate, Raj Narain, against Mrs
Gandhi's election to Parliament in 1971. It was announced by Justice
Jagmohan Lal Sinha. Prime Minister Indira Gandhi's victory from
Raebareli had been set aside by the Allahabad High Court following
an election petition alleging malpractices and corruption.

Congress was stunned. Journalists rushed to the prime minister's
house. I was there too, along with Surinder, my colleague. Large
crowds had gathered to support Mrs Gandhi, while senior Congress
leaders went in and out of the house. Mrs Gandhi did not come out.

The court barred Mrs Gandhi from holding elected office for six
years, but it stayed the execution of the verdict to give her time to
appeal against the judgment, if she chose. The media was as stunned
as the government. Several were of the opinion that she should
resign. By now, however, it was clear that she would put up a fight
and go into appeal at the Supreme Court.

After Indira Gandhi's comprehensive victory in the 1971 Lok
Sabha election, her rival, Raj Narain, had challenged the election

result in the Allahabad High Court. The case had dragged on. Raj Narain insisted there were corrupt practices, but in fact there were none, except that one of Mrs Gandhi's confidants, Yashpal Kapoor, whom I had known from Panditji's time, was just as powerful as he used to be. This indicated that the bureaucracy believed that she hadn't given up as yet. Raj Narain—the 'joker in the pack', as he was known—was elated at the verdict and demanded her resignation.

Yashpal Kapoor's resignation came a few hours after the election was called, and he had already begun participating in the election campaign while employed by the foreign office of the government, something that the law does not permit. This was at best a technical or bureaucratic irregularity.

The case had already been argued and judgment was due towards the end of May. But the judge delayed it for some unknown reason. It was alleged that some Congressmen approached him to try and influence him in Indira Gandhi's favour, making things worse for her. The judge was clearly peeved at this approach by the people whom he considered Mrs Gandhi's agents.

Justice Jagmohan Lal Sinha had been avoiding public appearances for quite some time. He stayed home and called his stenographer to dictate his judgment. To guard against leakage, the judge insisted that his stenographer stay in his house. The day the dictation was completed, he asked the stenographer to disappear. That was 11 June 1975.

These are all known facts. The judgment was to be announced the next day, 12 June. Everybody across the nation was waiting. The judge arrived in court at 10 a.m., and within five minutes he allowed the petition.

The news spread like wildfire all over India and beyond. A news flash said that the court had allowed Raj Narain's petition and found Mrs Gandhi guilty of corrupt practices. The judge then read out the judgment pronouncing Mrs Gandhi guilty on the basis of a simple technical error. It was like pronouncing a death sentence on someone for jaywalking.

But who was Yashpal Kapoor? What kind of person was he? What was his importance? He had been very close to the Nehru household from Panditji's days. He moved seamlessly between government office and service to the Nehru-Gandhi family, mistaking both to be the same.

I must make a personal comment here. Remember, feudal families have a tendency to foster sycophants—people who would praise them. Yashpal Kapoor was a past master in the art. He was the literal gatekeeper to the household. Bureaucrats, ministers, media—everyone had to pass his scrutiny before getting access to the family.

Mrs Gandhi brushed aside all hints at possible corrupt practices by officials around her. At some point, when confronted with a question at a press conference as to why she was not taking steps against corruption, she had replied that corruption was a universal phenomenon. That sent a message down the line to the corrupt bureaucracy that it was okay to indulge in such practices so long as you did not get caught with your hands in the till.

After the Allahabad judgment, Mrs Gandhi was expected to resign. But she stood firm and said she would not do so, not till she went to appeal to the Supreme Court. The opposition took to the streets to protest at her challenging the judgment. This, to my mind, was totally unfair. You cannot prevent a person from exercising all their legal options. Demonstrations by the opposition, primarily led by the Jana Sangh, were not that big. These also did not resonate with the people, as by and large everyone felt that Mrs Gandhi had every right to go in for appeal.

Behind the scenes, the coterie surrounding Mrs Gandhi made sure she did not quit. They worked to foil the High Court order while waiting for the Supreme Court ruling. More and more corrupt self-seekers surrounded her. The party was being run by the likes of Dev Kant Barooah, who kept singing paeans to her greatness. Barooah came up with the sycophantic slogan 'Indira is India'.

The party organized rallies outside her house using rented crowds. They kept attacking 'the forces that were bent upon destabilizing India'. No one mentioned the court order.

The Supreme Court, in its judgment on 24 June 1975, upheld the Allahabad High Court judgment, adding that Mrs Gandhi could continue as prime minister for six months and attend Parliament but not vote there. Subsequently, on 7 November 1975 (during the Emergency), the Supreme Court overturned Mrs Gandhi's conviction in the Allahabad judgment.

Obviously, during those six months, following the Supreme Court's conditional stay order, the prime minister's office would be occupied by a person who was not really authorized to be there because of the Allahabad High Court order. At least this was the sensible way of looking at it—if the prime minister was disqualified she ought to resign, as the opposition insisted while holding their demonstrations.

The unrest was beginning to affect the country's stability. The government had come to a virtual standstill, and many bureaucrats felt they were carrying out the orders of an illegal government.

The night before

The die was now cast. On 25 June, I covered a huge rally at Ramlila Maidan addressed by the highly respected opposition leader and freedom fighter, Jayaprakash Narayan, who demanded Mrs Gandhi's resignation. He called upon the armed forces and the civil services not to obey orders from a government he thought to be illegal.

That same night, the president of India, Fakhruddin Ali Ahmed, who had just been flown back from Malaysia, proclaimed a state of civil emergency. Thus the court orders were overturned. Constitutional provisions were invoked to deny civil liberties. Indira Gandhi had decided to brazen it out. She had chosen power over propriety, and her rule would continue.

Rationale missing

Censorship was imposed on the press. The next morning most dailies carried front pages with large blank spaces. Power supplies to newspapers were cut that evening. Information adviser, H.Y. Sharada Prasad, who was supposed to be our link with the government, came to the Press Information Bureau in the evening to advise the media about the Emergency, the imposition of censorship and how their stories might be cleared.

I protested strongly. I asked how they would censor television and newsreels. I said the Emergency was a fact but it was not meant to put people out of their jobs. In any case, the government had absolutely no facilities for censoring visual material.

It needed processing laboratories, viewing rooms and other technical backup. None existed in Delhi. Even in Bombay, such things existed for the film industry but not for television, nor for the 16 mm film we used. The government's own television was set up as an experiment, working only in black and white with few facilities. In fact, the government's TV centre relied on me. They had no laboratory, and we—Asian Films—were the ones who provided them with the necessary facilities.

Since the censors could not see any film I shot, I suggested they refer to the dope sheet which went with every film. It listed the contents of the footage and the story it told. I told Sharada Prasad that he could use the dope sheets to assess the content and decide which items should be censored and which should be passed. It would have to be dealt with in mutual trust.

That agreement was arrived at, and television news items were censored on the basis of the dope sheets. If anything objectionable was found, i.e. the censor's instructions had not been carried out, the person or the organization concerned would not be allowed further consideration. It was strict but worked.

Sharada Prasad had realized the huge negative impact abroad if television newsfilm reports were banned outright. So, this was his solution. Harry D'Penha, the recently retired principal information officer, was called back from Bombay to be the chief censor. Life became very difficult for us, but I told my colleagues—Surinder, Jagdish and others—that we must understand and deal with this terrible period. One could either hit the streets in protests, get jailed or else circumvent the system and get our news reports out, as cleverly as possible. The country had not come to a standstill and although censorship had been imposed, the media mostly functioned within the framework of stringent rules.

The government certainly censored some of our items. For example, we went to Chandni Chowk where the first demonstrations against the Emergency had taken place. The police had beaten the demonstrators mercilessly. The censor said we could not release the newsreel report. They censored it. We couldn't send the story out. Period.

I will not forget certain instances. Once, as we were leaving Chandni Chowk, some inquisitive people stopped our car near Gurudwara Sis Ganj Sahib because they had heard of a lathi charge and the beating of demonstrators. They asked what was going on. One gentleman, a Sardarji, said something that stings even now. In chaste Urdu he said, 'Why are you asking them questions? Can't you tell they are journalists? They are not allowed to speak.'

They were disappointed in the media, the political class and the administration for not resisting, and yet there was empathy towards us.

Within a short while the authorities started working on strange things, like the beautification of Delhi. It began with Jama Masjid. Bulldozers were brought there to evict small shopkeepers from the area around Jama Masjid. Surinder and I went there to cover it.

Communist leader Subhadra Joshi stood there with the others, watching people being evicted. The government did nothing to ensure the poor vendors were given time to salvage their goods. It was shocking. Bulldozers destroyed shops without giving shop owners a chance to remove their stock. These were poor people with very small businesses. What kind of beautification drive was this? The story reached the censors. We gave it the slug 'Beautification of Delhi', though the footage was of demolition. The story was cleared for release because the censors thought it was a 'positive story'!

Surinder went to the prime minister's house every day, since we were getting stories there too. We had 'accepted' that the Emergency had been imposed, and we would abide by the rules. We knew there was a new way this government was functioning. We had to work within those rules or shut shop, which would have meant virtually no video for the world from India.

I was keeping the window open for the world to see all that was going on in India under Emergency, whether in the name of 'beautification of cities' or 'family planning'. Some other journalists—I will call them 'blacklegs'—began to complain to the authorities against us. They wanted to know how we were able to cover our news stories. These were journalists complaining against fellow journalists. The kind of journalists who had little intelligence to use the system and thus stayed away from covering any event.

Worst atrocities

Other excesses occurred near Turkman Gate, another area occupied by very poor people. It is in Old Delhi, once known as the walled city Shahjahanabad. Turkman Gate is one of the gates along the wall that circumscribed the old city. In the city centre there were the rich and middle-class people. But along the wall lived people from the weaker sections of society, including tonga-wallahs and street vendors. They were the ones most affected by the 'beautification plan'.

People began to object, demanding that the poor be left alone. At one point the authorities assured everyone that these communities would not be removed. But soon enough, bulldozers began demolishing houses. A large number of people died or suffered serious injuries. I have no idea how many died, but from what we saw and from the figures we acquired later we put the death toll, along the Turkman Gate area, at a few hundred. The sheer cruelty of the demolition force was astounding. Nobody dared question the authorities, so profound was the fear of brutality inflicted in prisons.

The next stage of the process began in Karol Bagh, an upmarket, middle-class area in Delhi. The wreckers started bringing down the flower market, apparently because this was a Punjabi area and Punjabis were by and large supporters of the opposition Jana Sangh and RSS. Since they had spoken out against the Emergency, the authorities decided to 'punish' them. A lot of the area was destroyed, and some people died. When the bulldozers moved in, what transpired went beyond what most people would call 'beautification'.

Was this the aftermath of the Emergency or its very purpose? Were the facts not coming to the notice of the prime minister? How could she not have known? It all happened just a few kilometres from her residence. And yet she went about her daily work without any evidence of being affected by the events. In truth, the government was being run by her son Sanjay and the close group around him which included people like Siddhartha Shankar Ray and other Congressmen who were basically sycophants and who'd made themselves indispensable to him.

As a result, Sanjay Gandhi became the virtual prime minister of India. It was clear to most of us journalists that, fond as she was of Sanjay, Mrs Gandhi allowed him to remain active in politics. Soon, officials and ministers began taking orders from him. He suddenly turned into an extraconstitutional centre of power.

Ultimately, the decision to stop him had to come from the prime minister and the government. But she did not stop him. Why was the modern-day 'Durga' so helpless? No prime minister is ever helpless; they choose to abdicate decision-making. And that is what Indira Gandhi did. She would not be the last Indian PM to do so.

The Allahabad judgment had led to many demonstrations by Indira loyalists, who tried to build a political case for her by suggesting that forces inimical to India were trying to destabilize the government. The so-called demonstrations supporting her were organized at the roundabout outside the prime minister's residence at 7 Safdarjung Road. These protesters were apparently herded by people like Bansi Lal, from Haryana, and Arjun Das, a small-time mechanic from somewhere in Delhi. These strange characters appeared from nowhere. They did Indira Gandhi's bidding and thereby rose in importance in the 'Delhi environment'.

Then there were people like H.K.L. Bhagat, V.C. Shukla and Om Mehta, who positioned themselves around Sanjay Gandhi, thinking he could be influenced for personal gains. They tried to suggest that Sanjay was emerging as a new leader and natural heir. It must be said that Mrs Gandhi really had little regard for them, but she could not dismiss them, because they derived their power from their proximity to her son.

Extraconstitutional PM

Sanjay's whims and fancies were a law unto themselves. The late Vinod Mehta, editor of publications like *The Pioneer* and *Outlook*, was perhaps Sanjay's first biographer. His book, *The Sanjay Story*, was published in 1978, two years before Sanjay's violent death in a plane crash. Incidentally, Sanjay was clad in a white kurta-pyjama and wearing Kolhapuri slippers while piloting the aircraft. This should tell us how casual he was about his own life.

In his book, Mehta asked the same question many of us continue to ask almost forty years on: 'Why did a nation of over 600 million people bow to the whims and fancies of a prime minister's pampered son?'

The many episodes of excesses committed during the 'beautification of Delhi' were reflected in other government initiatives. The forced sterilization programme to check population growth, and the harassment of journalists through misuse of government machinery come to mind.

My dear friend I.K. Gujral, formerly the information minister, was moved to the Planning Commission, and Vidya Charan Shukla took charge as information minister. Why was Gujral removed? Because he wouldn't have been able to initiate the kind of rough tactics expected to be used against journalists. He was too friendly with them.

The Sanjay coterie seemed hellbent upon teaching the 'presswallahs' a lesson. I was at that time president of the recently developed journalists' colony of Gulmohar Park, home to many working journalists and editors. For three days on the trot at least, one journalist's house was found to be ransacked, with no clue as to who did it, except that it was clearly a job carried out by intelligence experts. Our protest to the police led nowhere.

Late one evening, I got a telephone call from a friend of mine who said, 'Prem, we are visiting you tomorrow.' He was a senior income tax officer in Delhi.

I said, 'My dear fellow, it will be good to see you after so long. Where have you been all this while? You are most welcome. Bring your wife along.'

He said, 'Try to understand me.'

I told him in Punjabi that he was welcome to my home.

He once again said, 'Prem, please try to understand. We are coming to you.'

I understood what he meant but tried to keep the tone light, in case my phone was tapped.

He went on: 'Just one thing I want to tell you. You should leave for your office as you usually do in the morning. Do not stay at home. We will take care.'

As the president of the colony welfare association, I called an urgent meeting of the executive committee. I told them about the phone call. I said whatever happened, I did not want any journalist arrested. I added that if anybody had any money lying around at home, they should clear it and spread the word around the colony.

At that time we were all simple journalists going about our work, trying to make ends meet. The authorities, led by Sanjay, wanted to prove that journalists were corrupt, and if they were to find cash or other valuable items in the homes of journalists, it would prove their point.

Having advised the executive committee of the welfare association, I now had to look after my own home.

The most 'valuable' things in my house were about a dozen bottles of imported whisky. I knew this attractive collection would be deemed illegal, as keeping more than six bottles—or more than nine, I think—was against the law back then. I had to call a friend to take the few extra bottles away. And I never got them back. When I asked for them after the Emergency was lifted, he told me that he drank them all!

The other thing that happened, very sadly for me, was that at the time of the surrender of the Pakistani forces in Dhaka, I had travelled as part of General Aurora's party, which had accepted the surrender. Afterwards, I was presented with a Pakistani POW's pistol and a pair of binoculars as mementos. Unfortunately, I had misplaced the papers issued to me when I accepted these trophies. So I gave these, too, to the gentleman who took my whisky in safe custody. Tragically, I never got these back from him as well.

It so happened that the following day Gulmohar Park was subjected to intense scrutiny by income tax enforcement and other income tax officials. I came home just before lunch and found three officers going about their work in my house. I told them that if they wanted to check on the house I had built, I would give them a copy of the completion certificate. They said they had checked everything. So I insisted they stay for lunch. The senior officer (it's a pity that I have forgotten his name) and his two lady assistants sat down. As we talked, the officer revealed he had been among the party that had raided the home of Maharani Gayatri Devi of Jaipur.

I was quite surprised that senior cops had been deputed to raid journalists. He also said that never during their raids had they ever been abused as much as in the Gulmohar Park raids. In one case, he said, he had gone to search a house and the owner told him, 'Mrs Gandhi expects me to have a sofa suite. She expects me to have a fridge. Go tell her to get them installed immediately!'

We were all working journalists. Most had built their houses with loans. We were not wealthy people accustomed to such raids or inquiries about our meagre possessions. We had worked hard and developed the colony into an aesthetically pleasing place where we could live with pride. We had ensured that all the rules and regulations of town planning were observed.

That spell of raids on Journalists Colony Gulmohar Park ended there. But the Emergency's darkness continued.

Before we set up ANI, we had a production unit called TVNF, where we produced a fortnightly show for Doordarshan, covering development news that showed what kind of rebuilding was going on. This development news show was conceived long before the Emergency, but now we began to cover stories for it from all over India about developmental works. Despite the possibility of government interference, we stuck to our guns and covered all aspects of economic development, and covered stories only if there was visual evidence of real development work.

Family planning

Another major thrust of the Emergency was family planning. India's population at the time of Independence was only 330 million. As I have already mentioned, during my first TV interview with Jawaharlal Nehru, one question I asked him was about the population explosion. But he was in no hurry to introduce a family planning programme in the country. He felt that with full industrialization India could support a population twice as large. Yet by 1975, the population had already reached 600 million.

The Sanjay group seemed convinced, and Mrs Gandhi appeared to be on board, that its very large population had caused the economic problems India was facing. So they introduced enforced population control. They set targets, aiming to complete the programme within a year. To achieve this, every school teacher in Delhi had to produce proof of having persuaded a given number of persons to undergo the necessary operation. Failure to do so meant his or her salary would be withheld.

A very dear friend of mine was married to a teacher. Although in his late fifties, this gentleman had the operation solely to help his wife meet her target. That was the kind of thing that was going on. We received coverage from Uttar Pradesh and Madhya Pradesh, where men and women were being herded like cattle on to tractors and taken to vasectomy and tubectomy camps.

Height of insensitivity

One day, screening some footage in the TVNF viewing theatre, I saw something horrifying. It bothers me even now that such a thing could happen in India. This was an item about a family planning camp in a small town in Uttar Pradesh, where several women were kept. They were lying half-naked on beds with their legs spread apart. Doctors and nurses were walking up and down laughing and even touching the private parts of the women. I refused to see any further and said: 'We will not view it. Throw it away.'

The memory of that clip still haunts me. It was shameless exploitation of poverty-stricken women from rural areas and city slums. The doctors, both male and female, showed how insensitive they could be. The bigger shame is that, after the Emergency ended, no action was taken against the authorities who inflicted such grievous wounds on the poor people's bodies and psyches.

Many women caught serious infections. Several died. In any civilized society those doctors and their staff would have been tried for crimes against humanity. Instead, these criminals are probably living respectable lives among us even now.

Despite such cruelties, the family planning programme was pushed through all over India. It caused great anger. But why were people accepting it? I imagine it was the fear of the police. There were reports of police excesses in many areas. When people resisted forcible sterilization, it sparked violent police reaction.

On 18 October 1976, the police in Muzaffarnagar killed scores of people who had protested against this barbarity. The police never revealed the figures, and the Emergency seemed to have validated their actions. Moreover in 1976, the Supreme Court, by a majority decision of a five-judge bench in the ADM Jabalpur vs Shrikant Shukla case, had suspended Fundamental Rights (and this includes the right to life).

The much-touted campaign against corruption, another favourite objective of the Emergency, had failed. Corruption at all levels became the norm, since there was no way for anyone to report it. The media had been muzzled. But nonetheless, the government continued to claim the great success of the new order.

There was darkness all around. Wherever I travelled across India, I heard stories of excesses and inhumanity inflicted by the dictatorship. Shooting newsreels was becoming increasingly difficult. Nobody was willing to speak on camera or allow shoots. Yet the tyrants, despite their best efforts, had failed to suppress the mounting protests.

I will never forget my dear old friend, the late Mohammad Iqbal Malik, deputy director general of Doordarshan. He had chosen to stay on in India at the time of Partition, even though he was from Lahore. He did not accept Jinnah's two-nation theory. He always believed in India's democracy and in leaders like Jawaharlal Nehru. Now, his ideal of Indian democracy had fallen apart. We commiserated with each other and prayed the horrors inflicted on our nation would end.

In Punjab, the agitation against the Emergency, led by the Akali Dal and the Jana Sangh, was gaining strength every day. Jails were full, yet the demonstrations and arrests continued. The rulers in Delhi were becoming increasingly frustrated at their failure to contain Punjab. Narendra Modi, a young Jana Sangh worker, having escaped arrest in Gujarat, was among those leading the agitation in Punjab together with the Akalis.

In November, Parliament—with most opposition members in jail—gave itself an extension of life by a year. This was a rubber-stamp Parliament. Earlier, it passed the Constitution (Forty-second Amendment) Act, 1976, and amended the Preamble of the Constitution, making the nation a 'socialist, secular' republic. The two words were perhaps meant to hide the reality. Socialist perhaps meant dictatorship, as in the Soviet Union. There were other widespread changes made to the Constitution. The act is known as 'mini Constitution'.

Jawaharlal Nehru at the Durgapur Steel Plant, West Bengal, in 1959. He called this project one of the new temples of India.

Lal Bahadur Shastri at Parliament House, soon after his election as leader of the Congress Parliamentary Party and thus the prime minister of India, succeeding Nehru.

The author on top of the Haji Pir Pass during the 1965 war against Pakistan as the mountain guns go into action.

Stuck in heavy snow on the way to Daulat Beg Oldi in Ladakh, 1963.

The author with Indira Gandhi, soon after her election campaign in 1971.

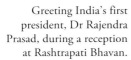 

Greeting India's first president, Dr Rajendra Prasad, during a reception at Rashtrapati Bhavan.

Lt General J.F.R. Jacob (*right*) with Lt General A.A.K. Niazi in Dhaka, where he negotiated the unconditional surrender of the Pakistan Army in 1971.

With Prime Minister Rajiv Gandhi in his office. Also present: Julian Kerr (*left*), managing director, Visnews; and G. Parthasarthy (*second from right*), information adviser to the PM.

Interviewing Prime Minister I.K. Gujral on board an aircraft.

With Atal Bihari
Vajpayee at the ANI
studios in New Delhi.

With President Mohammad
Najibullah of Afghanistan
in his Kabul office.

With cameraman Arun Kapoor
(*centre*) and sound man Harbhajan
Singh (*left*) in the deserted town
of Balkh, Afghanistan, during the
Afghan war.

Three days to leave

In the middle of all this, I took a telephone call from Harry D'Penha, the chief censor and a very dear friend of mine. He said, 'Prem, long time since we met. Can you drop in at my office for lunch?' I agreed.

I went there the next day. When we sat down for lunch at the Janpath Hotel restaurant, I simply asked him why, after all this time, he had suddenly called me and asked me to lunch.

He replied: 'Prem, you understood it well. I want you to disappear.'

I was astounded. 'You want me to disappear? But what is my crime? Have I broken any censor laws?'

'Prem, you have been too smart for my officers,' he said. 'We have nothing against you. All your reports have been duly cleared by us, and we have no adverse comment from any Indian embassy abroad against you concerning whatever material you have released.'

Then came the bombshell. He said I had only two options: either to go abroad, or to stay put and get arrested!

They had already arrested a few journalists, including Kuldip Nayar, under which law we did not know. They could arrest anybody, since the Supreme Court had already suspended Fundamental Rights.

I asked Harry how soon I needed to leave, and he told me quite clearly that if I did not go away immediately, I would be in prison.

Harry had given me a maximum of three days to leave Delhi. Before long, a mysterious tea stall appeared across the road from my house. Things were turning eerie.

I moved quickly, and within twenty-four hours I was on a flight to London, leaving everything else in the hands of Surinder and Jagdish, my trusted colleagues, and telling them not to worry about me but to keep the unit going.

Our telephone lines to Reuters had been cut off. The teleprinter and telex line had been cut. India's largest news agency, the Press

Trust of India (PTI), had been subverted and merged with three other agencies—UNI, Samachar Bharti and Hindustan Samachar. The new agency created by this merger fell directly under the control of the Government of India. The other news media were suppressed as well by the censors. As for the official media, they were told not to forget that they were owned by the government. They were told to carry out the government's orders. What could we do in such circumstances?

I arrived in London, where I got every form of support and understanding from the editors at Visnews. They said I need not worry. I could decide on whatever work I wished to do. They offered to put me in charge of office operations in New York, since they understood I would not wish to work as a news cameraman in London. I wasn't sure if I wanted to accept what was offered. Did I want to get posted to New York? I gave myself a month to decide. Meantime, I watched the situation in India getting worse.

I must acknowledge the great support and friendship that I received from my editors at Visnews in London, and from my friends at the BBC, ITN and NBC among others. Through my contact with them, almost every newsroom in the UK and the USA came to understand the plight of journalists in India.

The Western media had a high regard for India because of the image Jawaharlal Nehru had built. India had earned immense respect, even during Lal Bahadur Shastri's time, as well as during the early years of Indira Gandhi. It was not that she was not respected. She was held in high esteem (especially when I recounted her vision for the Congress and how she fought the old guard that had opposed her). But somewhere, she got blinded by her son's emergence. Sanjay seemed to have such power over her and ruled India by proxy.

Time passed and reports from India were not good. If anything, they were getting much worse. Foreign journalists had been ordered to move out. The BBC office was closed. The communication lines to Reuters, as I mentioned earlier, had been totally cut.

Six weeks later, Visnews again asked me what my plans were. I told them I felt I should go back. My work was in India, however difficult the circumstances. Soon afterwards, to the surprise of my editors in London, I announced my intention of returning to India. I firmly believed that I could not afford to close the only window I had managed to keep open for the world to see what was going on in my country.

I slowly made my way back. I stopped off in Geneva and stayed with a very dear friend of mine, Peter Jackson, and his wife, Adrianne. The duo had been Reuters correspondents in India.

When I finally reached home, it was sad to see what was going on. Hoping that the journalists, who had worked against me and 'leaked' to the government information about my reports, would have by now forgotten me, I returned to work in Delhi in November 1975.

Fresh elections

Let me not forget an earlier instance during the Emergency. The state of Bihar was severely flooded, and Mrs Gandhi was planning to go there. I rang her media adviser, Sharada Prasad, and said I wanted to go with the PM. And I did so. Meeting her again seemed different. I used to address her as Indiraji. That day, I addressed her as Prime Minister. She noticed it and looked sharply at me. I said it was a slip of the tongue.

In Varanasi, there was a crowd of Congress workers standing quietly with folded hands. She did not look at even one of them but just walked straight by. I sensed a strange atmosphere and found the prime minister rather unhappy, far from her usual self. It couldn't have escaped her notice that those folding their hands in line were doing so with resentment and fear in their eyes, not affection or respect.

Under Sanjay's hawkish gaze the Congress had managed to crush the spirit of the nation. It seemed the Emergency was here to stay. The communist nations and the Non-Aligned bloc were silent. There were demonstrations in Western capitals, where

Indian immigrants exerted a considerable influence, but no world outrage over the suspension of Fundamental Rights in India. India's Emergency fell off the news cycle.

After travelling abroad and mixing with other world leaders, Indira Gandhi and her senior colleagues found themselves isolated among Western nations. She did travel to Sri Lanka in August 1976 to attend a summit of Non-Aligned nations but made sure to avoid the international press.

In January 1977, I was in Calcutta, covering a sports event, when, late one evening, I took a phone call and heard that Mrs Gandhi had called for fresh elections. My immediate reaction was—she has had it! Though world interest in the Emergency had slipped, and though my editors in London were not assigning political stories to me because they were censored at source, I had managed to travel around the country, doing feature stories and meeting with people in cities and towns. I could sense that disillusionment with Indira had taken root.

The nemesis

Having extended Parliament's life by a year, but feeling isolated internationally, Indira took the nation by surprise in deciding to hold elections in March 1977.

The decision was apparently taken after the Intelligence Bureau assured her that the Congress would return with a thumping majority. I am told this is the kind of feedback given to many Indian ministers by IB, because if they were to say anything to the contrary, elections would be delayed! The world knows what happened in the elections. Both Indira and Sanjay Gandhi met their nemeses and were trounced at the polls. Sadly, the party never apologised for the atrocities of the Emergency.

The Emergency was over. The people of India had overthrown it in the elections of 1977. As elections began on the first polling day of 16 March 1977, I managed to create a bit of history that day. With the help of N.L. Chowla, additional director general and head of news at Doordarshan, I sent the first news feed via satellite out of India.

I had known for some time that the Overseas Communications Service (OCS) of India was carrying out tests in cooperation with Intelsat to send and receive TV films via satellite. When I checked this formally, I was told that it was true but that the playout facility would need to be arranged via Doordarshan, as OCS did not have it. I discussed this with Mr Chowla, who said it wouldn't be a problem, as this was an important election and the government was keen that it get maximum international coverage. I then discussed this with Andrew Ailes, chief news editor at Visnews. He got as excited as I was and proceeded to book satellite time with Intelsat, even though everyone else in the newsroom was sceptical. Even people at the BBC and European Broadcasting Union were not sure if it would work.

As polling started on 16 March, we quickly carried first footage from Delhi and nearby areas for processing at Asian Films, which was the only company that had the facility in Delhi other than Doordarshan. After editing it, I took the news story to Doordarshan and at the appointed time of 6.30 p.m., Mr Chowla himself was present at the playout suite—this was as important a day for Doordarshan.

The feed started just one second late, with Doordarshan's logo and some background music. And lo and behold, black-and-white pictures of this historic poll were received in the newsroom of Visnews and simultaneously delivered to BBC and the European Broadcasting Union in Geneva. We had scored a world exclusive. All the global channels carried Visnews's pictures, even as other media organizations were preparing to send their material via airlines. Andrew tells me that the one-second delay had brought smiles to the faces of the sceptics, but they were all taken aback when the Doordarshan logo appeared on the screen in London.

The elections of 1977 turned out to be historic, and over the next one week, the polling, the vote counting and then Mrs Gandhi's defeat and her acknowledgement of defeat—it was all seen by the world through the eyes of Visnews and ANI. Our pictures were sent out via satellite, thanks to the lab facilities of ANI.

Mrs Gandhi was no longer the prime minister, and her son Sanjay and others with him were unceremoniously shown the door. This span of Mrs Gandhi's prime ministership was to be forever tainted by the stain of Emergency. All the good work she did was overshadowed by the dictatorial steps she'd taken at her son's behest.

Indira Gandhi faced huge problems from day one, when she took charge of the party and of the country after Shastriji's death. The Bihar drought, food shortages, the upheavals in East Pakistan, and over a million refugees coming into India . . . She faced this last problem with such fortitude and success that perhaps nowhere in the world could so many refugees have been sent back to their homes so successfully. India has a history of mass migration. After Partition, millions came to India and millions left for Pakistan. Those who came here never went back. But the Bangladesh case was different. A million or more refugees, both Hindus and Muslims, returned to their old homes in Bangladesh.

Mrs Gandhi was the prime minister when on 18 May 1974 India conducted its first nuclear bomb test successfully. India was now a nuclear power. This was prompted by that fact that, after the 1962 war, China exploded a nuclear bomb in what was seen as a warning to India. It was Mrs Gandhi who let the Chinese know that we too had nuclear capacity.

The whole crisis of food shortage, the problems in Punjab—she faced them all. Another of her achievements was the expansion of television in India. India was the first country in the world to use modern satellite technology to expand its television network and link the stations to New Delhi. It was my good fortune to cover all these events for foreign media.

Mrs Gandhi was a recognized world leader. She received immense respect from the Commonwealth heads of government when she hosted the Commonwealth meeting in Delhi in November 1983, with Queen Elizabeth opening the meeting as head of the Commonwealth.

Similarly, she earned a huge and positive reputation from her interest in the Non-Aligned Movement and from the great success of the Non-Aligned summit in Delhi, with practically all world figures attending, including Fidel Castro. She was a global leader in her own right.

Mrs Gandhi also ensured that the army continued to grow stronger. She believed that the budgets for the defence forces should not be cut, and she was vindicated in this during the Bangladesh operation. The army finished the Bangladesh war in barely eight days.

On 6 December 1971, Indian forces moved into East Pakistan. By 14 December, General Manekshaw had issued a warning to the commander of the Pakistani forces to surrender. This, despite very heavy opposition from America. In dashing Pakistan's hopes of becoming militarily equal to or more powerful than India, Indira Gandhi delivered a body blow to that country. By facilitating the break-up of Pakistan into two parts, she did yeoman service to India for all time to come.

The US secretary of state, Henry Kissinger, did not approve of whatever Mrs Gandhi did in this case. But when America sent its powerful Seventh Fleet to threaten India with nuclear attack, Indians did not go under.

It has to be remembered that Pakistan attacked us first, on 3 December 1971. General Yahya Khan, president of Pakistan, had hoped that by his pre-emptive strike he would destroy India's air capability—not knowing that the Indians were waiting for him. Mrs Gandhi had devoted further resources to India's external intelligence, and that paid handsome dividends.

Many years later in Washington, I met a former senior American diplomat, Sidney Sober, who had been in Pakistan during the war. I asked him how America allowed Indian forces to defeat Pakistan so easily, why it had not intervened to bail out its ally Pakistan and why Washington threatened to send its Seventh Fleet to India's waters.

His reply was very revealing. This is what he told me: 'Yes, we were supporting Pakistan. My officers went to the forward areas to monitor the preparations being made by the Pakistan Army.

I was advised that they would be capable of capturing Amritsar and maybe even going a little further. That would force India to withdraw from East Pakistan in return for Pakistan's withdrawal from Amritsar. Little did we realize that in the battle in West Pakistan India would have the upper hand and would also gain some parts of Kashmir.'

It is a pity that a tiny technical fault in the 1971 election should have led to her election victory being set aside and the horror of Emergency and dictatorship being imposed on India, with Sanjay Gandhi, an extraconstitutional centre of power, taking virtual control of the government. There had been no corruption in Indira Gandhi getting elected in 1971.

8

Janata Party Takes Over

Indira Gandhi's first term as prime minister ended in 1977. After two years of Emergency rule, she and her new Congress party were swept from power in a landslide electoral defeat.

There were many opposition parties. They contested the election against Mrs Gandhi's Congress under a joint arrangement and defeated her. The main campaign against Mrs Gandhi was led by the great freedom fighter Jayaprakash Narayan, who had refused any office in the government after Independence but continued to serve the country as a social worker.

He suffered from severe diabetes and renal disorder and had to have dialysis every second day. Still, he travelled relentlessly all over India as head of the opposition alliance and ensured their victory.

Compromise candidate

On 25 June 1975, a huge public meeting was held at Delhi's famous Ramlila Ground. I have never seen such a massive crowd assemble. Whichever direction I turned my camera in, I saw thousands of people shoulder to shoulder listening to speeches by hitherto unknown leaders, who were rather rustic in speech and demeanour. At this event, it was announced that various opposition groups had merged into what was to be called the Janata Party. During the meeting, a dear friend of mine who had suffered during the Emergency, Chandra Shekhar from Ballia in Uttar Pradesh, was elected president of the party.

The Janata Party went to elections as a divided house. There were too many candidates for the prime ministership in its ranks. There was considerable infighting between rival factions but, at the end of the day, Morarji Desai emerged as the compromise candidate and was thus accepted—although grudgingly—by all others as the prime minister of India. In my view, this was not right. Swearing by democracy, the Janata Party did not let its parliamentary party elect the leader and, by extension, the prime minister. Thus, Babu Jagjivan Ram was kept at bay and Morarji Desai announced as the consensus prime minister.

The problem with Morarji Desai was that he was never a team player. He was, in many ways, a very egotistic person who cared little what others thought of him. I had covered him extensively with the help of his son and secretary, Kanti Desai. Morarji hated the media in general and my cameraman in particular. But I had to put up with that.

Certain decisions he took under his tenure played havoc with India's external intelligence. Morarji Desai always thought it was a waste to spend money on the Research and Analysis Wing (R&AW), India's external intelligence agency. In a basic change of policy, he strove hard to bring about a closer relationship between the United States and India.

For one thing, he was quite happy for India to collaborate with America's Central Intelligence Agency (CIA). The net result was that India's own Intelligence Bureau and R&AW, which had been built with great respect and care and which used to report directly to the prime minister, were weakened and many of their assets destroyed.

It later transpired that the prime minister even allowed the CIA to install listening equipment in the Himalayas, aimed at China. This was some part of America's attempt to keep a check on China's nuclear programme. But despite the possible danger it posed, the equipment seems to have gone missing—it simply disappeared. What happened to it remains a mystery.

Over all, Desai's policies were not entirely acceptable to those at the helm of the Janata Party. Nor was the government making progress on the economic front. Desai's response to the day-to-day problems faced by the business community was to rely on the age-old policy of the Congress, which was Fabian socialism. Socialist as he was, Desai decided to throw the Coca-Cola Company out of India, after which another brand, known as Campa Cola, appeared in its place.

Media strategy

My first interaction with the Morarji Desai government concerned the issue of independence of the media. The Janata Party had, during its election campaign, announced that the official broadcast media, All India Radio and Doordarshan, would be made independent, much like the British Broadcasting Corporation (BBC).

The information minister, L.K. Advani, held a press conference, at which I asked when they were going to announce the independence of All India Radio and other official media, such as the Indian newsreels. Advani said they would appoint a committee to look into it. I argued that the government, being the owners of the official media, did not need any such committee since it had been made clear during the elections that the pattern to be followed would be that of the BBC.

In any case, my impression was that the Janata Party government wanted to keep control of the media and that an independent media corporation was not of immediate interest to them. I have observed this right from the time of Independence that every political party speaks about less government control over state media, but when they come to power, they are exactly like their predecessors—they just don't let go.

I was by now president of the TV Programme Producers Guild of India, formed to look after the interests of independent producers who made shows for Doordarshan. We compiled a complete document about granting editorial independence to media through a BBC-style corporation and presented it to the government's committee. We also pointed out that the satellite revolution was upon us. Satellites did not see political boundaries. Foreign television channels would be watched in India, so it was important that Indian channels themselves be made independent.

It was as early as 1976 that I, among other journalists, had demanded that private TV channels be allowed to operate in India. But it was not till the Congress government under P.V. Narasimha Rao came to power that the liberalization of media would actually happen.

Meetings with the Janata Party government committee went on for days. We answered all kinds of questions and kept pressing our case. But even though the report of the committee, titled 'Prasar Bharti', did talk of creating an independent media institution, it did not accept the notion of private channels, except only to the extent that universities were allowed to have television channels if they wanted. That was all they had to offer.

Flag of rebellion

Morarji Desai was an individualistic politician. He did start straight away on finding out what had been done during the Emergency. This was sensible, since the party wanted to take steps to ensure that in the future it would be impossible for any leader to impose a similar state of emergency. And the Janata Party managed to do that without much difference of opinion.

Desai then faced a challenge from within, when the deputy prime minister, Charan Singh, raised the flag of rebellion. By now, Sanjiva Reddy had been elected the president of India and thus became a crucial player, especially as he had his own axe to grind and scores to settle. The egos of Janata Party leaders came into play, and it was sad to see even the president's office becoming a part of the game.

When Morarji Desai's government started encountering problems, the president of the Janata Party, Chandra Shekhar, took a delegation, including Babu Jagjivan Ram, to President Reddy, asking him to invite Jagjivan Ram to be the prime minister succeeding Morarji Desai.

Babu Jagjivan Ram was a very generous man, and his generosity did not confine itself to his family. I had been to his constituency, in Sasaram, Bihar, and seen excellent work done by him there. It was part of the tradition of the Jagjivan Ram household that when anybody from his constituency visited Delhi, that person was well looked after.

We covered the story of Babu Jagjivan Ram's visit to the president and saw Chandra Shekhar and the rest of the delegation come out of the meeting looking quite happy. The president had given them the impression that he could invite Babu Jagjivan Ram to be the next prime minister of India, as the delegation had shown him the list of the members of Parliament supporting them.

But by the time they drove from the president's house to Parliament it was announced that the president had already invited Charan Singh to be prime minister and asked him to prove his majority on the floor of the house in two weeks. This was unheard of. Never before had a prime minister been nominated by the president and asked to prove his majority in the house before being confirmed in office.

In 1969, the group known as the Syndicate in the Congress had put forward Sanjiva Reddy's name for president. Indira Gandhi went against the tide and suggested Jagjivan Ram's name. Mrs Gandhi was outvoted. Under no circumstances was Sanjiva Reddy now going to appoint Jagjivan Ram as prime minister.

Charan Singh took charge, hoping to win the support of Chandra Shekhar and Jagjivan Ram and other party members. But they refused. They felt that there had been a conspiracy and that Charan Singh's prime ministership should not be allowed.

Charan Singh never faced Parliament. He never sought any vote. Instead, he took a resolution from his cabinet to the president, recommending the dissolution of Parliament and the holding of fresh elections. This, in my view, was a subversion of both the Constitution and the instruction of the president that Charan Singh prove his majority in Parliament. It seemed to me then, and I believe it even now, that President Sanjiva Reddy never wanted and thus did not let Babu Jagjivan Ram to prove his majority in Parliament. Instead, he quickly accepted Singh's recommendation to dissolve the Parliament, a decision that was not right, for Charan Singh had not been okayed by Parliament as the prime minister. Charan Singh thus became a lame-duck prime minister of India till the elections of 1980, which brought Indira Gandhi back to power.

It was now up to comparatively junior leaders, like Atal Bihari Vajpayee and L.K. Advani, to decide whether they would remain in the Janata Party or take the Bharatiya Jana Sangh out of the Janata Party. This issue became a breaking point for the Janata government. What followed led ultimately to the demise of the Janata Party. The Bharatiya Jana Sangh rechristened itself the Bharatiya Janata Party.

I would rank Atal Bihari Vajpayee as one of the best foreign ministers of India. He carried out his task extremely well both at the United Nations and in maintaining relations with neighbouring countries. George Fernandes, a firebrand socialist, ran the industry ministry very effectively. It must be remembered that Fernandes was not released from jail even after the Emergency was lifted. He contested elections from jail and won with a resounding majority. Madhu Limaye, another socialist, and Madhu Dandavate who was railways minister, did their jobs extremely well.

It was a pity that the individual egos of the leaders were such that the Janata Party broke up. Throughout the Janata government regime, Mrs Gandhi was given a house to live in but was subject to a very strict watch. They even tried to dig up the grounds of her farmhouse, looking for hidden wealth, but nothing was found. They tried to arrest her and again they failed. The drama of her threatened arrest became headline news because, by that time, popular support for the Janata government was in decline. The Janata government had also dug up the 'time capsule' at Red Fort—the Kalpaatra, buried there by Indira Gandhi on 15 August 1973 for future generations—to see if it carried praises of Mrs Gandhi and the Congress. Nothing along these lines was found.

On one occasion, I was interviewing Mrs Gandhi in the garden of her house. When we set up the camera, we heard a strange, intrusive noise coming through the headphones. At first, I could not understand where it came from but suspected it was from listening devices installed all around the house. So we went inside and did the interview there, free from any audio interference.

This was the time when Mrs Gandhi was surrounded by Sanjay Gandhi and a great many fixer politicians who came to be known later on as the Punjabi mafia. Men like R.K. Dhawan, Zail Singh and Buta Singh were prominent among them. They kept her informed as to what the government was doing—and what the government was threatening to do to her. By now Mrs Gandhi had developed a reputation for being paranoid about rumours that she would be subjected to jail atrocities similar to those inflicted by her regime during the Emergency. But nothing of the sort happened. There was no political vindictiveness apparent.

When elections came, she was fully prepared. She had painted herself as a martyr in the eyes of the people. She projected herself as a woman of substance, a real leader, as opposed to the pygmy politicians of the Janata Party who couldn't see beyond their noses.

I travelled a great deal during the election campaign, and I must say that it was clear to me that Indira Gandhi won that election, defeating the Janata Party, single-handedly. She made an untiring effort and was on the move day and night. India is a vast country, but she tried to cover every corner.

The Janata Party's campaign, led primarily by its president, Chandra Shekhar, could not match Indira Gandhi's drive and popularity. Besides, the Janata Party was a house divided.

Thus ended the brief period of the Janata Party in power. Its only real achievement was ensuring that future generations would be saved from situations like the one that began in June 1975, when Emergency was imposed on India.

Morarji Desai and the Janata government, despite all their efforts, were unable to unearth any evidence of serious wrongdoing by Mrs Gandhi, other than the imposition of Emergency. It would take decades for the other political parties to gather strength to fight the might of the rejuvenated Congress party.

Indira Gandhi was now poised for her second term as prime minister.

9

Indira Gandhi Returns

Indira Gandhi launched her 1979 election campaign with enormous energy. Never before had I seen her or anybody else go into a campaign determined to fight it out single-handedly.

Debarred—by the Allahabad High Court judgment—from office for six years, she had undone the court order through the rubber-stamp Parliament she controlled during the Emergency. In its two-year rule, the Janata Party government had failed to disqualify her. Full credit for a successful campaign must go to her. She travelled tirelessly all over the country to remind people of the follies of the Janata government.

The result was that she was back in the saddle for her third term as prime minister of India by January 1980.

She herself had contested from two constituencies, which seems to indicate that she was not sure if her own constituency in Raebareli would still back her. But clearly, the Indian electorate had forgiven her, since she won in both the constituencies she contested— Raebareli in Uttar Pradesh and Medak in Andhra Pradesh. She actually surrendered her seat in Raebareli in favour of her son Sanjay. It was a clear message to her detractors that she would not punish her son for the Emergency. It also, in a way, set a precedent for her family, which is given to not admitting to past political mistakes made by their kin. Rajiv Gandhi never spoke about Sanjay; Sonia and her children have not apologized for either the Emergency or the anti-Sikh riots.

Mrs Gandhi in her third term as prime minister began to take stock of all that had happened in the two years of the Janata experiment.

The big, noisy protests that had started after the High Court judgment in June 1975 had by now come full circle. If India had suffered the agony of the Emergency, the country had also borne the brunt of unstable governments run by Morarji Desai and Charan Singh. Mrs Gandhi was determined to undo all that had been done by the Janata government.

Raj Narain plays black sheep

Not many people know that the man who had defeated Mrs Gandhi in 1977, the maverick Raj Narain, was caught having a secret meeting with Sanjay Gandhi while Charan Singh's Janata Party government was still in power. Sanjay and Raj Narain were clearly contemplating the termination of the Janata experiment. To my mind, the ego of Janata leaders provided a very sad end to the long and distinguished career of Jayaprakash Narayan.

The Punjabi group, or what was known as the 'Punjabi mafia', that stood by Mrs Gandhi while she was out of office, was now back in full strength, both around her and around Sanjay Gandhi. Interestingly, I found one of my childhood friends, Captain Narender Sikand, also joining the Punjabi group, although, uninterested as he was in politics, his affiliation did not last long and he went back to his private life.

Delhi's Rasputin and Sanjay's fatal air crash

Yet another person who appeared on the scene was Dhirendra Brahmachari. He was known as the Rasputin of New Delhi. He made himself very close to Sanjay Gandhi. This long-haired and bearded 'guru', clad in a white dhoti, used to flaunt his own airplane.

He used to fly it himself to his Aparna Ashram in Mantalai, Jammu. He persuaded Sanjay to get his own plane. But Sanjay went a step further and acquired a plane from the Delhi Flying Club that was fit for intricate aerial aerobatics.

Tragically for Mrs Gandhi, the friendship between Sanjay Gandhi and Dhirendra Brahmachari led to her son becoming fascinated by aerobatics. On 23 June 1980, he was flying one such aerobatic aircraft when he lost control and crashed near Safdarjung Airport in New Delhi. Sanjay died instantly from multiple injuries. It was within a few months of his mother taking office.

This was a huge tragedy for Mrs Gandhi. She was shaken—in fact, devastated. I covered Sanjay's funeral; his samadhi was built next to Shanti Van.

Trouble in Punjab

Mrs Gandhi was unhappy with the fact that during the Emergency, Punjab was the centre of maximum political resistance to it, through both the Akalis and the RSS.

Giani Zail Singh, Buta Singh and others sought to control the gurdwaras, which have always been a very strong support base of the Akali party. They are known for raising huge amounts of money. Though this money is usually spent on charitable causes, in hospitals, schools, colleges and universities, political players are always attracted to it. In the early '80s, trouble began again when these unscrupulous profiteers got busy trying to gain power in Punjab.

In Punjab, strangely, the killing of Hindus by Sikh separatists began around this time. There was hardly a day when the newspapers did not report the mysterious murder of a Hindu. Fortunately, there were no Hindu-Sikh clashes. Hindus and Sikhs have lived together in Punjab ever since the birth of Sikhism during Guru Nanak Dev's time. Nonetheless, in some areas Hindus began leaving Punjab and moving to Delhi.

Hindus and Sikhs in Punjab have always intermarried, and so they are related to each other. According to an edict by the tenth

Singh guru, Guru Gobind Singh, the eldest son of Hindu families could become a Khalsa. That used to be the tradition at least in west Pakistan, where I came from. In most cases the elder son in Hindu families was often dedicated to the Khalsa Panth.

It would not be out of place to say that all the ten Sikh gurus preached what was a reform of Hinduism and we can see that in Guru Gobind Singh, who created the Khalsa Panth by fighting against the atrocities of Aurangzeb and by protecting Hindus.

When he created the Khalsa Panth, Guru Gobind Singh chose the 'Panj Pyare', who came from the lowest of Hindu caste, known as untouchables, to lead the Khalsa. The Khalsa was meant to fight the atrocities of the Mughal Army under Aurangzeb, individually and collectively, as guerrillas.

Zail Singh backs Bhindranwale

In Punjab, rival factions were on the move. For one, Giani Zail Singh backed the head of another Sikh organization, the Damdami Taksal, a fellow named Jarnail Singh Bhindranwale, to assume supremacy over the Akali Dal and to move into the Golden Temple.

Akalis at that time were led by the very decent and gentle Sant Harchand Singh Longowal. I met him on several occasions in the Golden Temple when covering the story. Each time, Santji would ask why the government did not conduct an investigation to find out who was killing Hindus. After all, he said, this was a crime. Why were the police not able to trace the criminals? So-called police raids were being conducted here and there but to little effect. There was a suspicion that Bhindranwale himself was responsible for many of these acts.

I had some insight into this because the joint secretary of internal security in the Ministry of Home Affairs, Gurdev Singh Grewal, had been a dear friend of mine since childhood. He was an upright IAS officer of the Bihar cadre. He once told me how the nation's home minister had sabotaged certain security measures. When they planned the arrest of Bhindranwale, which was to be carried out in

Pune, only three people in the Ministry of Home Affairs knew about it. The three were: the home minister, Giani Zail Singh; the home secretary, B.G. Deshmukh; and Gurdev Singh himself. The fourth person kept in the loop was Maharashtra's director general of police.

On the day Bhindranwale was to be arrested, the home secretary and Gurdev took a frantic call from Maharashtra, to say that Bhindranwale, in his speech at the gurdwara, was openly declaring that 'while they are calling me for talks they are planning my arrest'. Clearly, Bhindranwale knew he was about to be detained. The plan to arrest him was therefore aborted. Bhindranwale went straight back to Amritsar and took refuge in, and subsequently control of, the Golden Temple.

My friend Gurdev appealed to the home secretary to relieve him of his difficult position. He said only the two of them knew about the arrest. So who informed Bhindranwale? 'Therefore,' he said, 'it's better that I go.' The home secretary, much against his wish, allowed Gurdev to move on.

The economic situation of the country at that time was not in good shape. Food shortages were still continuing, although they had been sorted out to some extent by the earlier green revolution, accomplished through the efforts of Mrs Gandhi. The economy was in the doldrums because of the Fabian socialistic policies that had been pursued. There were long lines in front of ration shops. The hoarding of food grains was high. In Delhi, efforts were made to dig out hoarded food grains from the wholesalers in the Khari Baoli of Chandni Chowk. However, nothing came of it.

Mrs Gandhi visited the United States during the presidency of Ronald Reagan, hoping that she would at least be able to bring him sympathetically to her side. But the United States continued to complain that India was leaning towards the Soviet Union. The reason for this was obvious. The only nation that would sell weapons to India in exchange for rupees was the Soviet Union. India could not afford to buy weapons from the United States in dollars. And India was certainly not going to compromise its independent foreign policy by aligning with a bloc that had Pakistan in it.

Indira Gandhi was, I don't know why, a very lonely person. She had always been a loner but Sanjay's death left her even more isolated. It was at that stage that she managed to convince her other son, Rajiv Gandhi, to stand for the Congress. Rajiv was hardly interested in politics. Being a qualified airline pilot, he was more of a technocrat. Yet he contested from Sanjay Gandhi's constituency in Raebareli and won. He began taking an interest in, and tried to help the prime minister in dealing with, the Punjab issue. However, the Punjabi mafia around her was too well-entrenched to tolerate his interference.

Rajiv Gandhi was very friendly with the media. He specially took interest in coverages that my colleague Surinder and I would do when travelling with him. He would always ask Surinder why he was using noisy cameras, even when he used the best of that time—an Arriflex. Rajiv, who knew that Surinder had tremendous experience with still and video cameras, was interested in new technology, whether it was light equipment or even something as small as the tripods we used for our cameras. He would not hesitate to look at the frame from the viewfinders of our cameras, even sharing some tips with Surinder.

The situation in Punjab grew worse. Though Mrs Gandhi had done so much work in other fields, such as fighting the Bihar drought, creating Bangladesh, nuclear test, endorsing the use of satellites to expand television, all these things were overlooked. Punjab kept hogging the nation's attention for all the wrong reasons. The Punjabi mafia that surrounded Mrs Gandhi was seen as fomenting all the trouble in the state and was thought to be behind Bhindranwale, who had moved into the Golden Temple.

Operation Blue Star

By the beginning of 1984, Bhindranwale had almost fully occupied the Golden Temple. To add fuel to the fire, he was joined by General Shabeg Singh, who had been, in my view, wrongfully dismissed by the then army chief, General T.N. Raina. Shabeg Singh was one of the most decorated army officers in India. He had fought with distinction in Burma during World War II and was responsible for training the Mukti Bahini in Bangladesh. A devout Sikh, General Shabeg Singh had cut his hair because he infiltrated into East Pakistan several times to oversee counterinsurgency operations there and would have stood out had he sported a turban, becoming an easy target for the Pakistani forces. It is said that General Raina bore a grudge against General Shabeg Singh and had a score to settle with him. Shabeg Singh was dismissed a day before he was to retire.

Bitter as he was about his dismissal, Shabeg Singh found a cause to rebel against the system. He moved into the Golden Temple to join Bhindranwale. Shahbeg Singh was able to attract many other retired Sikh soldiers and noncommissioned officers from Punjab who had served under him. He created a model rebel defence system in the Golden Temple. Indeed, he turned the shrine into a fortress.

It was in June 1984 that Surinder and I, among many others—the whole world's press was there—arrived in Amritsar expecting something to happen. We were at the Golden Temple when Sant Harchand Singh appealed to the government to come clean on who had installed Bhindranwale in the Golden Temple and who had brought armed men into that holy place.

I don't think anybody could be as forthcoming as Sant Harchand Singh Longowal was. By then Zail Singh, Buta Singh and all those who had contributed in bringing the situation to such a pass felt that the only way to deal with the crisis was to march in and forcibly evict them all. But this was not going to be the best solution. An assault on the Golden Temple would create more problems than it solved.

My mind was clear and so was that of all the other journalists who were covering the crisis. We knew that some catastrophic events were going to take place soon. On the other hand, we also met Bhindranwale on a few occasions and found him to be extremely adamant and negative. He seemed to believe he had already gained independence for Khalistan and seemed convinced that he himself was a force for independence.

The Shiromani Gurdwara Parbandhak Committee (SGPC)—guardians of Sikh places of worship—still controlled the Akal Takht

and the rest of the temple complex, but Bhindranwale was keen
to take total control of the place. He, along with Shabeg Singh,
had become firmly established there. It was now their fiefdom.
Bhindranwale expected something big to happen and was ready to
fight. He was a mad man.

On the night of 3 June we were told that Mrs Gandhi was
about to address the nation on radio and television. She came on
air to announce that Amritsar was under curfew and that the army
was moving in. We were surprised to hear this because there was
certainly no curfew in Amritsar at that point, nor was the army to be
seen anywhere. Nobody was certain as to what kind of information
had been passed on to the prime minister that she spoke of an army
movement and curfew. Was she misinformed, or did she really think
that she could announce something drastic and hope to instil fear
in the militants at the Golden Temple and get them to surrender?
None of us knew for sure. Officially, however, a curfew was on
and the army had moved into the areas in the corridor around the
Golden Temple.

So we rushed to the Golden Temple to meet the Akali leader.
There, Sant Harchand Singh Longowal said that, sadly, only that
afternoon he had been hoping to sit down and talk. But now, the
prime minister had announced this further escalation. Would
anybody tell him what was going on? What could we journalists
tell him? In truth, not much. On the next day, the police would not
allow anybody near the temple area.

From 3–4 June, announcements were made on the loudspeakers
by the army, threatening the militants holed up inside the Golden
Temple and demanding that they surrender. There was unease in
the media group, as many of us felt that it was just a matter of hours
before the army would take stronger action. Those of us who had
met Bhindranwale inside the Golden Temple knew that he would
not surrender. However, none of us could imagine what actually
happened when the storming of the Golden Temple took place on
4 June, which was also Guru Purab, when the Sikhs serve water and
sherbet to one and all.

Commandos stormed the temple site but found themselves facing a well-organized and well-entrenched defence. No media person was allowed anywhere near the temple. Most of us had been externed from Amritsar. Surinder was virtually locked up in his hotel, as were the few others who had managed to stay on. I was coordinating from Delhi. Though the city was under very strict curfew, Surinder did manage to visit the residential areas on the periphery of the Golden Temple, where quite a few houses were on fire. The army and paramilitary forces were patrolling the city— Surinder filmed all that.

Clearly, the army and the police had not received sufficient intelligence. In any case, they should have known that General Shabeg Singh was a vastly experienced soldier whose military skill ensured the temple was well-fortified.

Tanks moved in. There were several hundreds, if not thousands, of pilgrims inside the temple who had not been able to leave. Many of them were caught in the crossfire and were killed.

There was no way that the armoured units or the infantry could move into the Akal Takht without damaging it. In the end, the 300-year-old Akal Takht was attacked and was damaged. Both General Shabeg Singh and Bhindranwale died there.

During the assault on the Akal Takht, its centuries-old library was set on fire and a great number of valuable manuscripts and books were lost. As the flames leapt from the library building, people in Amritsar thought that the nearby temple itself was in flames. The news spread like wildfire all over the world. 'The sacred Golden Temple had been set on fire,' said the headlines, whereas it was only the library that was burning. Nobody from the media could get near the temple to establish the truth.

There was now anger all over Punjab, and indeed across India, among all Punjabis—Hindus and Sikhs—over the terrible things that had happened. There was anger among the Sikh troops nationwide. Operation Blue Star had left everyone profoundly shocked.

In Delhi, the Punjabi mafia around Mrs Gandhi blamed me for sending out visuals showing the Golden Temple on fire. But no such footage was available or sent out. I tried to explain that none of our cameramen were allowed inside the temple complex. I was in Delhi and, by now, so was Surinder.

Though nobody was allowed to go near the temple, I challenged my accusers to let me go to Amritsar to get pictures showing the Golden Temple undamaged and send them across the world. However, the 'wise' officers refused to pay heed to that. They arranged for their own coverage and rushed their video clips to Delhi.

I do not wish to criticize them, but I would only say that these fools were in such a great hurry to run that two-and-a-half-minute unedited film shot by a Doordarshan crew on television, they were in such a hurry to show to the Punjabis and Sikhs all over India that the Golden Temple was undamaged, that they failed to preview the film. Had they done so, they would have seen that it also showed piles of dead bodies of the many pilgrims who were killed in the crossfire.

Once the tape was given to me, we edited it properly and were able to show the world that the Golden Temple was, in fact, undamaged. The officers and men who had levelled those charges against me and against my team did not have the courtesy or the moral strength to apologize.

Meanwhile, Giani Zail Singh visited the Golden Temple as if to show to the Sikhs that he was not responsible for these sad events. So the anger and disillusionment in Punjab remained completely focused on Mrs Gandhi. Everyone held her responsible.

With people's emotions running high, Mrs Gandhi was advised to replace her Sikh security guards. Some people said that R.K. Dhawan, her secretary, was not in favour of them being removed. Others said that Mrs Gandhi did not wish to be seen as communal and refused to remove them. In any case, the guards remained.

Mrs Gandhi assassinated

On the morning of 31 October 1984, I was getting ready to go to my office at Janpath when I got a call from my friend Inder Sharma. He asked me if I had heard about the assassination of Mrs Gandhi.

Inder was calling me because one of his employees, daughter of a senior police officer, was being dropped by a police car when she had heard the report on the police radio.

Indira Gandhi had been shot dead by her own Sikh bodyguards.

We hurried to the Ram Manohar Lohia Hospital, where we were initially told Mrs Gandhi was being taken. But the bodies of the assassins were brought there. The staff at the hospital did not know that the bodies they had received were those of Mrs Gandhi's killers.

It was odd that a lot of time was lost in taking Mrs Gandhi to the All India Institute of Medical Sciences (AIIMS). The whole system seemed to have collapsed at that point. Moving her to that hospital only added to the confusion. The doctors at AIIMS could not save her.

Thus ended the four years of rule by Indira Gandhi.

10

Rajiv Gandhi Takes the Plunge

Rajiv Gandhi joined the Congress party following his brother Sanjay's unfortunate death in a plane crash. He had been elected from Sanjay's constituency, Amethi, and on 31 October 1984, he was travelling in Kolaghat, in the outskirts of Calcutta, when he was informed that his mother had been assassinated. He was flown in a chopper to Calcutta and immediately took a flight, with senior Congressman Pranab Mukherjee, to Delhi.

Since the precedent of having a stand-in prime minister had not been followed, there was no prime minister of India for several hours till Rajiv Gandhi arrived in Delhi. He then went to AIIMS, where his mother had been brought after being shot. Later that evening, he went to the president's house, where he was administered the oath of office as prime minister by Zail Singh, who was the president of India from 1982 to 1987. Rajiv Gandhi thus became the sixth prime minister of India since Independence. Soon after taking office, he asked for the dissolution of Parliament and called for fresh elections.

Another catastrophe hit Delhi soon after Mrs Gandhi's assassination and it was to have its own impact on Rajiv Gandhi's premiership. This was the unprecedented killing of Sikhs in Delhi.

I was at AIIMS with my colleague Surinder on the day of Mrs Gandhi's death, with all the Congress leaders standing and waiting for Rajiv Gandhi to arrive. When Rajiv Gandhi did arrive, shocked as he was, he went straight to see his mother. He emerged from the room with swollen eyes; he must have wept inside. He then left for his home, and later that day he was sworn in at the president's house.

As Surinder and I were returning from AIIMS we saw the beginning of the riots opposite Kidwai Nagar. The rioters were stopping taxis and autos and beating up Sikh drivers. Some buses were also burnt there.

As we passed the Taj Mahal Hotel at Man Singh Road, we stopped several Sikhs and warned them against going out. We told them to remain inside the hotel. I also cautioned my friend Lashkar Singh, who was the owner of the All India Tourist Taxi Service at the Imperial Hotel.

What followed over the next few days was terrible, particularly in places like Karol Bagh, Trilokpuri, the Filmistan area, etc. Even the funeral of Mrs Gandhi became a low-key affair as the procession had to be rushed through.

Those riots, or that thinly veiled genocide, was perhaps the most unfortunate episode not only in Rajiv Gandhi's prime ministership but in the history of India. It was to have far-reaching consequences for India's social fabric for decades to come.

Bhopal gas tragedy

It was while Rajiv Gandhi was on his election campaign that, on the night of 2–3 December 1984, the country was hit by what was arguably the world's biggest industrial disaster—the leakage of lethal gas from a pesticide plant in the city of Bhopal. The factory was owned by the American company Union Carbide Corporation.

It was reported that faults had already been detected in the gas tanks at the factory, but preventative steps had not been taken on time. The result was the leakage of poisonous gas which led to the deaths of thousands of people and animals across Bhopal.

When the story broke, I spent the whole of 3 December trying to charter a plane to fly to Bhopal, since there were no commercial flights from Delhi that late at night. Such things were never easy in our country in those days.

By the time I managed to charter a flight in the evening, I was told the plane could not land in Bhopal, because that airport did not have night-landing facilities. I rushed back to the office and found an alternative. There was a train leaving for Bhopal within the next hour, scheduled to arrive in Bhopal at around six o'clock in the morning.

I sent Surinder and his team to the railway station, asking them to stop only to buy blankets to protect themselves from the severe cold in the train. And Surinder, my true lieutenant, did not once think about the hazards of doing this story. We cameramen have our minds focused only on the story when we go to cover such events.

Having shot the footage of the disaster, Surinder rushed to Bhopal Airport, where a plane was due to land from Delhi at around ten o'clock. It was carrying Indian and foreign journalists. My own second team was also travelling in that plane. Surinder flew back to Delhi on the same plane. While shooting the footage in Bhopal, he had covered his face with a wet cloth, which was his only protection. Fortunately, he suffered no health issues after the coverage. I met Surinder at the airport in Delhi and we rushed straight to the Overseas Communication Service, from where we transmitted the pictures, via satellite, all over the world.

Thus, we succeeded in sending out the news of the Bhopal gas tragedy almost twelve hours ahead of the competition, who had chosen to wait for the flight to Bhopal. As we were sending out our videos worldwide, they were still in Bhopal. We must remember that in those days one didn't have broadband connectivity, so transmission could only be done from Delhi or Bombay. Our camera units kept travelling to Bhopal and back for almost a fortnight. The scenes of disaster they had captured ran on all networks. Meantime, my other team members, who had taken the flight to Bhopal, were busy covering the different aspects of the story, which was dominating the world's news networks.

BBC's Mark Tully, who went to Bhopal with the rest of the press, had given a stand-up report to Surinder's visual—which was part of an arrangement between BBC and Visnews. The visuals and his report were transmitted to BBC via Visnews. Mark won a journalism prize for that story, when in fact it was primarily based on the visuals that Surinder had shot. But alas, cameramen get no awards or citations.

Rajiv Gandhi arrived in Bhopal on 4 December, soon after the scale of the tragedy had become clear. He took stock of the situation and personally reassured people that all assistance would be provided to those who had suffered.

Then, the Bhopal story fell off the headlines. The victims of the tragedy were denied full justice in the settlement made by this huge American corporation. Whether it was the fault of the Indian authorities who didn't disburse the settlement money properly or it was the matter of the government not taking punitive action against the perpetrators, the fact remains that this story didn't get covered properly.

A ray of hope

Rajiv Gandhi continued with his election campaign. He was soon to become the first prime minister since Independence to win an election with over 50 per cent majority. Jawaharlal Nehru, in his time, had not gone beyond 46 per cent, nor had Mrs Gandhi. The Congress invariably used to win elections with around 42–45 per cent votes.

Rajiv Gandhi became the first prime minister to get such a high percentage of the vote because of the public sympathy following the assassination of his mother. He was seen as a ray of hope, the man who would take India into the new millennium. He won 404 out of the 542 seats in Lok Sabha.

It's true that Rajiv Gandhi's term had begun with a spate of problems: Mrs Gandhi's assassination; the anti-Sikh riots in Delhi and north India; and the Bhopal tragedy. But he got down to work straight away. The first thing on his agenda was to see what could be done about the crisis in Punjab. To begin with, he met Sant Harchand Singh Longowal, leader of the Akali Dal, and signed what came to be known as the Rajiv-Longowal Accord. Under this accord, the government accepted the demands of the SGPC, and they, in their turn, agreed to end the agitation in Punjab. Soon after, the Punjab assembly elections were announced, giving Punjab a proper state government of its own.

Longowal was a considerate and highly respected figure among Hindus and Sikhs. In Delhi he visited several areas where Sikh families had suffered during the riots, and I still remember vividly the emotions of the Sikh women when Longowal visited them at their homes. The wailing of the widows of the Sikh riots still haunts me at times.

Sadly, less than a month after signing the accord, Longowal was assassinated by Sikh militants who opposed it.

Fresh momentum

Among the things that Rajiv Gandhi embarked on to drive employment in India was the establishment of technology missions. These were specific projects aimed at training the youth of India in different aspects of emerging technologies.

He pushed ahead with the widespread introduction of information technology, and it can be said that if India dominates the world in IT today, much of the credit must go to Rajiv Gandhi. He not only initiated these developments but sustained them with great determination.

In those days, owning a telephone was the preserve of the rich or of those who had influence. Rajiv Gandhi was intent on changing this. So he called on his friend Sam Pitroda from the United States. Pitroda was an expert on telecommunications and was given charge of the mission to make telephones available for everyone in India.

Pitroda established what was known as C-DOT exchanges to upgrade and simplify the telephone system. If all of us in India today have easy access to telephones, it is mainly due to the efforts put in by Rajiv Gandhi and his team.

Around this time Rajiv Gandhi simultaneously paid attention to the north-east, where insurgency and the issue of illegal Bangladeshi immigrants in Assam were causing serious problems. Here, he moved as fast as he had done in Punjab by drawing up and signing the Assam Accord. This accord was really a memorandum of understanding between the Government of India and the leaders of the Assam Movement, a popular front against illegal immigration. The agitation in Assam had been launched in 1979 and was causing immense instability and violence in the state. Nearly 900 people had died because of it. While covering the signing of the Assam Accord, I believed that tensions and the violence in this region would soon end. Through this legislation, anyone who came to Assam after 1961 was denied citizenship rights. This removed a source of popular discontent in the north-east and ensured that development projects could go ahead in Assam and other areas.

Rajiv survives attack

Rajiv Gandhi was anxious to examine India's relations with its neighbours and particularly the problem of the Sri Lankan Tamils. The issue had been troubling the country for quite some time and was a very sensitive matter for Tamil Nadu, because of their sympathies for the Sri Lankan Tamils.

In Sri Lanka, the Tamil population had been demanding that the Jaffna province to the north of the island (where the Tamils were in majority) be separated from Sri Lanka. This was, of course, not conceded by the Sri Lankan government. Ever since the departure of the British, the Sinhala government in Colombo had been discriminating against the Tamils in matters of education, employment and so on. This had given rise to violent groups like the Liberation Tigers of Tamil Eelam (LTTE), led by Velupillai Prabhakaran.

At one stage, to subdue the Tamils, the central government in Colombo, under President J.R. Jayewardene, cut off all essential supplies to Jaffna. Rajiv Gandhi immediately ordered the Indian Air Force to drop relief supplies to Jaffna. This was seen by the Sri Lankan government and the majority Sinhala population of Sri Lanka as a hostile act that interfered with their sovereignty. However, Rajiv Gandhi offered to fly to Colombo and talk the problem through.

Rajiv Gandhi did travel to Colombo, taking me and several other journalists along with him. We arrived to find the city under curfew. The prime minister and the other Indians were not made to feel very welcome but, nonetheless, the talks began the next day and the two countries agreed on several bilateral issues.

We were all staying at the Taj Hotel and were supposed to fly out soon after the signing of the agreement. But something at the hotel disturbed me. I thought that instead of being on location where the prime minster was, I was stuck at the hotel. Most of the newspapermen had decided to stay back as well, waiting to be briefed later on. I asked the Indian embassy to take me to the president's office, where the talks were being held, so that I could see the prime minister leave.

A very efficient Indian diplomat, Laxmi Puri, managed to get a car through the curfew and took me to the president's house. As I arrived there, Rajiv Gandhi was just preparing to leave after signing the agreement. He was to be given a guard of honour before his departure. I now started walking by the prime minister's side, covering his ceremonial inspection of the guard. As I did so, I noticed, out of the corner of my eye, one of the soldiers (this was a Navy guard of honour) raising his rifle to strike the prime minister with it. But, young as he was, Rajiv Gandhi ducked sideways, just in time. The butt of the rifle hit him hard on his shoulder. This was an attempt on his life by a Sinhala soldier. I had captured it all on camera.

I asked Rajiv Gandhi, right there in the presence of President Jayewardene, why had this happened. Rajiv pointed towards Jayewardene and replied: 'Ask him.'

Jayewardene simply said that he would take appropriate action. I then hurried back to the place from where the press helicopter was taking off for Colombo Airport, where the prime minister was also due. In Colombo, when the press party got on the plane for Delhi, all the journalists surrounded me to ask what had happened. They were not present at the guard of honour as it was basically a photo opportunity, not considered essential for print journalists. I was giving them the details when suddenly the information adviser to the prime minister, H.Y. Sharada Prasad, appeared on the scene. He demanded to know what I was telling the press. I said I was only telling them what I had seen.

He said that I was misinforming the press and that 'there was no incident'. While this argument continued, my dear friend Binod Mishra, editor of the Hindi daily *Hindustan*, angrily stood up and went to the prime minister's compartment. Moments later, he brought the prime minister himself into the press cabin.

Rajiv Gandhi asked me to come to his compartment and to bring my camera along. He was a great technocrat himself. He knew how these cameras worked and that I could play back the tape. So he asked me to do so.

I said, 'Sir, this was clearly an attempt on your life. You ducked.'

I put my hand on his shoulder and I saw this huge swollen bump where the rifle butt had hit him. I asked him if it was painful. He told me that it was very painful. I said it could have hit him on the head, and he said, yes, it could have.

By this time, it was clear that both the Sri Lankan and Indian governments wanted to play down the incident or avoid mentioning it altogether. I pointed out that the international press had been out there—Reuters, AP, everybody. As if to reinforce my point, the captain of the plane confirmed that the news breaking throughout the world was that an attempt had been made on the prime minister's life.

I told Rajiv Gandhi that it could not be hidden. His secretary for internal security, T.N. Seshan, who later became the chief election commissioner, tried to confiscate my tape, saying he was going to make a copy. I protested and the prime minister backed me. He asked Seshan to wait for a copy from me later on. The rights of the footage rested with me; the government could only request me for a copy.

Talks with the LTTE

Back in Delhi, Surinder was waiting for me at the airport. My videotape went straight to the Overseas Communication Service, and the news about an attempt on Rajiv Gandhi's life was beamed through satellite to the whole world.

Just as we were leaving Colombo, we had heard that Indian troops were landing in Jaffna. This came as a surprise. We wanted to know what they planned to do. But there was no information coming our way as yet. It seemed that the agreement between Rajiv Gandhi and Jayewardene was that India would ensure the disarmament of violent groups like the LTTE while the Jayewardene government in return would see to it that the Tamils got their rights.

But this was not going to be easy, because the LTTE was not a party to this agreement. They refused to lay down their weapons, and it proved impossible for the Indian military to disarm them. Later, the LTTE leader Prabhakaran and his colleagues were invited to Delhi for talks, which went on for a long time but failed. The LTTE was still not willing to abstain from violence.

One day, I headed to meet with the Afghan foreign minister, who was staying at the Ashok Hotel in Delhi. I arrived on the floor where the minister was staying. Leaving the elevator, I saw quite a few policemen. They allowed me to go towards the minister's suite. As I was walking towards it, I passed a room with the door wide open. Sitting inside were Prabhakaran and his men.

They were being 'held' in the five-star hotel, even though their talks with the Indian government had failed. They were eventually allowed to leave, but it was clear that serious bitterness had developed between Rajiv Gandhi's government and the LTTE.

Attempting to take control of Jaffna, India's peacekeeping force went into action but it only resulted in very heavy Indian casualties. Over a thousand were killed fighting the Tamil Tigers. The Indian defence forces had been sent abroad on such a mission for the first time—and it ended badly.

Bofors slur

The other problem that hit Rajiv Gandhi's prime ministership had to do with India's defence capability. Since Independence, India had been totally dependent upon the import of weapons for its armed forces. When the British departed, they left behind a large number of ordnance factories that were built during World War II. But India had neglected these factories in the mistaken belief that there would be no need for huge armies in the second half of the twentieth century, with nations refusing to use war as a means of settling political disputes.

So India depended on imported weapons. For one thing, the Indian Army was extremely short of long-range artillery. After protracted negotiations, the government decided to import the guns from the Swedish manufacturer Bofors. Their guns had been found fit for the purpose and were later to play a major role in helping India win back Kargil, when it was occupied by Musharraf's Pakistan Army.

However, soon after the order for Bofors guns was placed, Rajiv Gandhi's finance minister, V.P. Singh, who had been working in the finance ministry before moving to defence, declared that there was something wrong with the Bofors contract.

V.P. Singh had raised doubts about the Bofors deal, suggesting that over 600 million US dollars may have been paid out as commission to the Gandhi family and other Congress leaders. This was Rajiv Gandhi's own minister, a person who was assumed to be clean and who had been made whatever he was by the late Mrs Gandhi. She had made him the chief minister of Uttar Pradesh. Rajiv Gandhi trusted him and had invited him to join him in Delhi. Now, Rajiv Gandhi had no alternative but to remove V.P. Singh.

Meanwhile, there were extremely bitter exchanges over the issue of the Bofors guns both inside and outside Parliament.

The media cast V.P. Singh as the next ray of hope for India—a middle-class messiah who would bring the corrupt dynast to his senses. Rajiv Gandhi's own corruption-free image suffered a terrible setback because of an Italian named Quattrocchi, who was involved somewhere in this deal. His relationship with the Gandhi family was used by the press and everybody else to attack the prime minister. Many of us were unable to fathom how Rajiv Gandhi frittered away his goodwill. The affable, media-friendly PM started becoming bitter.

V.P. Singh, as I had observed over time, had his own ambitions. He was actually a small-time raja of Manda—a place in Uttar Pradesh I had never even heard of—and was basically a feudal lord. But he carefully cultivated his image as a socialist, and the media bought it. Interviewing him was quite a task. He took long pauses, and every response of his had something to do with either Bofors or caste.

V.P. Singh had launched a campaign against Rajiv Gandhi, and in this he was joined by some of the latter's friends, including Arun Nehru, who had helped him come to power. Having formed the Janata Dal group, V.P. Singh got the support of left-wing parties and communists who were unhappy with Rajiv Gandhi's economic reforms.

These reforms were introduced in a very limited manner, but the left-wing parties wanted India to continue under the communist-style 'licence permit raj', which imposed severe regulations, hindering all industries and encouraging corruption.

Rajiv Gandhi was always, in my view, anxious to push India ahead. He had watched the progress China was making after Mao's death and was actually aware that India had failed to keep pace. India had slipped from the dominant position it was at, with a robust economy, at the time of Independence. In the '80s, India was busy making so many new things, but the issue of poverty was still staring us in the face. Rajiv Gandhi was doing his best to address this. But then came the accusations from people who, latching on to the link between Quattrocchi and Rajiv's Italianborn wife, Sonia, began to hurt him.

An investigative journalist named Chitra Subramaniam wrote that there had indeed been leakage of funds from the Bofors gun deal. But no one could say if these had reached Rajiv Gandhi, although by implication the prime minister's reputation was being questioned. It was sad to see this man, who had won such a huge electoral majority, have his name dragged through the mud. As the 1989 elections came around, the so-called Bofors scandal became the prime issue in the campaign strategies of V.P. Singh and other opponents of the Congress party.

It can be said for sure that Rajiv Gandhi had made an earnest and concentrated effort to speed up the economy. He made doing business in India less complicated. He ensured that businesses adopted new technologies and, towards that end, even amended the income tax laws to encourage businesses to modernize and so create employment.

This was a period when the demand for television news was starting to grow in India, and in recognition of that I, along with a group of professionals—P.D.P. Rao from Chennai, Durgadas Chatterji from Kolkata, A.V.G. Thampi from Mumbai and others—launched the Tele Trust of India or TTI, which would provide three to four major news stories a week from across India. Thus the TTI service was launched. It was then felt that the name TTI did not have a global appeal. So the service was rebranded as ANI, Asian News International, which was globally publicized by my son, Sanjiv Prakash, and daughter-in-law, Smita Prakash.

A 'highly responsible' opposition

Rajiv Gandhi's term was soured by several blunders. India's peacekeeping efforts in Sri Lanka had been repulsed with great losses, failing to disarm groups like the LTTE. There were demands that the troops be called back from Sri Lanka. V.P. Singh made it a leading electoral issue. We covered the bitter election campaign led by V.P. Singh in 1989, which mostly centred on the theme of corruption. The opposition parties often used replicas of Bofors guns in their rallies. The impact of their campaign was felt the most in the Hindi heartland.

The Bofors scandal and the stationing of Indian troops in Jaffna together did serious damage to Rajiv Gandhi and his election campaign. The Congress, which had previously won the biggest-ever parliamentary majority, was now reduced to 197 seats. Not that V.P. Singh could claim victory. His Janata Dal won only 143 seats. Rajiv Gandhi could have rightly formed the government again, being the largest single party. But he was denied support by the leftists, and others who commanded a sizeable presence in Parliament.

With only 143 seats, V.P. Singh managed to get the support of the left and communist parties, DMK, TDP and all others who wanted to keep the Congress and Rajiv Gandhi out of power. Thus, V.P. Singh was able to stake his claim to be the prime minister, while Rajiv Gandhi became the first recognized leader of the opposition in the Indian Parliament. It was for the first time that an opposition party had more than sixty seats, the minimum required to have the office of the leader of the opposition.

In his short first term, Rajiv Gandhi had done a lot to push India towards a newer economy. He laid the foundations of the IT industry, which, in due course, came to dominate the world and gave India its prime place in that field. He also ensured that the administration adopted modern methods and that all government staff were trained in computer technology.

As leader of the opposition, too, Rajiv Gandhi assured the nation that his would be a highly responsible opposition, ready to work for the best of public interest, allowing the government to work the way it wished to, but still fighting to represent the minority voice.

However, the Congress party was not comfortable sitting in opposition, believing itself to be the natural party of governance in India. Rajiv Gandhi was convinced by his cronies—and there was a galaxy of them—that his calling was to be a prime minister and not an opposition leader. His quest to depose his successor began soon after his first term ended.

11

V.P. Singh Checks In

V.P. Singh's rise and then his success in projecting himself as the middle-class messiah were also due to the media strategy of some of Rajiv Gandhi's former friends turned foes. One was Rajiv's own cousin, Arun Nehru. The two had a falling out in the second half of Rajiv's term as PM. V.P. Singh had made Arun Nehru the junior minister for internal security in the home ministry under Mufti Mohammad Sayeed, a Kashmiri politician not considered senior enough for the post he held.

It is also a fact that V.P. Singh's election as prime minister was mired in controversy from the very first day. There seemed to be no agreement in the Janata Dal as to whom to appoint prime minister. Chandra Shekhar was a serious contender. Then Devi Lal emerged as a consensus candidate, and it was decided that when the parliamentary party met, he would be elected as prime minister.

I was present in Parliament when this strange, cloak-and-dagger game was played out. V.P. Singh rose and proposed that Devi Lal should be the prime minister. This was to be seconded by Chandra Shekhar. But before Chandra Shekhar could get up, Devi Lal rose to thank V.P. Singh for proposing his name, and then he, in his turn, proposed V.P. Singh's name for the prime ministership. It seemed too staged to be true. Chandra Shekhar had been checkmated by V.P. Singh and Devi Lal. But he had no proof of any wrongdoing

147

and decided to swallow the bitter pill. Chandra Shekhar, together with several of his supporters, quietly walked out. V.P. Singh was thus elected the prime minister.

The first crisis the V.P. Singh government faced was the kidnapping of Mufti Sayeed's daughter, Rubaiya, by Kashmiri terrorists. In return for setting her free, the kidnappers demanded the release from prison of several hardcore terrorists. This was opposed by officials in the home ministry and by most political commentators. There was anger throughout the nation and among the opposition parties. Yet V.P. Singh gave in and the terrorists were released. Rubaiya Sayeed was set free, but the country continues to pay heavily for this decision of V.P. Singh to this day.

Could the government have taken the tough decision of not negotiating with terrorists? The fact is that all governments, even globally, are prone to resorting to such conciliatory measures, though officially they might have a policy of not negotiating with hostage-takers.

Severe criticism of V.P. Singh over the Sayeed affair came particularly from the Bharatiya Janata Party, which had previously given him support. In order to placate the BJP, V.P. Singh nominated Jagmohan to be the governor of Jammu and Kashmir. Jagmohan was also a friend of mine and a very upright officer. It has always puzzled me as to how, during the Emergency, he joined Sanjay Gandhi in implementing his horrendous pogrom under the guise of 'beautification of Delhi'.

Jagmohan had the reputation of being a top administrator and began his tenure in Kashmir to stem the rot created by the release of those hardcore terrorists. But the situation in Kashmir began to deteriorate further, and V.P. Singh's government struggled to control it. The terrorists released by V.P. Singh opened new divisions in a state which has had a long history of peaceful secularism. There were attacks on Kashmiri Pandits, Hindu scholars. There were slogans and threats, telling Kashmiri Pandits to leave or be ready for slaughter.

At this time, Soviet troops had withdrawn from Afghanistan, releasing many terrorists and Islamic fanatics, who moved from there to Kashmir to fight as mercenaries. The entry of terrorists from Afghanistan began to cause further troubles. Fundamentalists who arrived there began to attack both Hindus and Kashmiris. This was a direct assault on traditional, all-inclusive Kashmiri society. We covered the events in Kashmir, but there was little or no international interest for these stories.

Adding to the troubles in Kashmir was the rise of the Muslim United Front leader, Muhammad Yusuf Shah, who took the name Syed Salahuddin and became a powerful rebel commander. He is now based in Muzaffarabad, capital of Pakistan-occupied Kashmir, and continues to wage terror against India.

While all this was going on, V.P. Singh was more or less a silent observer. He was powerless to stop the exodus of Pandits from Kashmir. He was hardly able to control what was going on in Kashmir, despite having a Kashmiri Muslim at the helm in the home ministry. V.P. Singh was an indecisive and weak prime minister, and the cabinet took advantage of it. Mufti Sayeed and his deputy, Rajesh Pilot, were at loggerheads, and the PM did nothing to resolve their differences. Within a couple of months, the V.P. Singh government became extremely unpopular, thanks to the failures in Kashmir and the deteriorating economic situation.

V.P. Singh had made a wise choice in appointing Inder Kumar Gujral as his foreign minister. Gujral had a number of friends in the media scene in Delhi and was seen as a gentleman politician. I travelled with him to Canada and America, when he visited the United Nations in New York in 1990. Gujral had suggested that I meet Robin Raphel, the US assistant secretary of state for South Asia, in Washington, D.C. I met her and conveyed the message from the Indian foreign minister, that the country wanted closer relations with the United States. She responded positively and asked me to convey her good wishes to India's foreign minister in return.

I must add here that I took the occasion to discuss with her the reasons why the United States had failed to recognize the Najibullah government in Afghanistan for three long years after the departure of the Soviet troops, while continuing to back fundamentalist forces in

Peshawar, Pakistan. When I mentioned to her that Afghan women had been the worst sufferers under the Taliban, with their society having been forced back into the Stone Age, her cruel response was, 'They have always been like that.'

I strongly disputed this and told her that she had not seen Afghanistan in its happy days. I left her office with the impression that she was perhaps the most stonehearted of all women and certainly not fit for the office she was holding.

And I wasn't too far off the mark. Raphel's hatred for India was barely concealed. Why India did nothing to stop her frequent trips to Srinagar will always be a mystery. We were too much of a soft state, in awe of the power of the United States of America. Raphel was instrumental in getting the USA and other Western nations to tacitly support the separatists in Kashmir. Intelligence officials and even Kashmiris say that she was the one who spread the idea that Jammu and Kashmir was self-sustainable and that it was morally and ethically right for Kashmiris to want to secede from India. She had caused enough damage in Afghanistan, and she now thrust her attention to India like a wrecking ball.

Mandal djinn unbottled

In order to deal with his growing unpopularity and other problems, V.P. Singh dug out the Mandal Commission report, which had been lying in cold storage for decades, and decided to implement its recommendations.

The Mandal Commission, set up in 1979 by the Morarji Desai government, was charged with identifying backward castes other than those that were already known and documenting the social and economic issues faced by them. This report provided up to 27 per cent reservation in government jobs for other lower castes, in addition to the reservation quota set out under the Indian Constitution.

The moment V.P. Singh announced the implementation of the report's recommendations, serious rioting erupted in Delhi, mainly by students, who believed the new conditions would raise difficulties for them in finding jobs. Rajiv Goswami, a student protester, attempted to self-immolate on 19 September 1990. He suffered severe burns. His attempt fuelled the agitation, which spread all over India, bringing V.P. Singh's government's popularity to an all-time low.

I suggested to Gujral Sahab that the PM should go on All India Radio and assure the students that full justice would be done to everybody and that the implementation of the Mandal Commission recommendations would not result in injustice for any social group. I was with Gujral Sahab when he made that call to V.P. Singh, who agreed with his foreign minister. But when V.P. Singh addressed the nation, he did nothing more than try to justify his own actions, let alone mollifying the students and those who were upset by the report. The agitation spread further after his address.

Earlier, in order to divert attention from his domestic problems, V.P. Singh undertook a tour of the Soviet Union and other Central Asian republics. I travelled with him. It was a lacklustre tour, which was really dominated by the foreign minister, Gujral, who was well-versed in diplomacy, having been India's ambassador to Moscow when Indira Gandhi was PM. Gujral Sahab knew many in the upper echelons of power in the former Soviet countries.

For the accompanying journalists and other officials, there is often a lighter side to the foreign visits of political bigwigs. During V.P. Singh's visit to the Soviet Union and Central Asia in July 1990, we went to Samarkand and Bukhara. These places are known for, among other things, very large watermelons, some weighing between eight and twelve kilograms. I was reminded of the early days when these watermelons came all the way from Afghanistan and Central Asia to be sold in Delhi. But because of trade restrictions with Pakistan we had not seen them for ages.

It so happened that, when our Soviet hosts took us on a tour, I found myself in a vegetable-and-fruit market. I bought three watermelons, which weighed around 27–28 kilograms, and I had to carry them on my back. I arrived at the Samarkand airport just as our flight was announced. The entire media party was waiting for us, watching me stagger in with my load. Everybody laughed at what I had managed to carry. I told them they had apparently forgotten that there were quite a few Punjabis in our group who knew of these watermelons. They said they regretted not having gone to the market. That was the only lighter part of that trip, enjoyable because the rest of V.P. Singh's tour through this region had no political interest or value.

We came back to Delhi to find that L.K. Advani, leader of the BJP, was addressing a huge rally. Here, he announced his famous Ram Rath Yatra, in support of the call for the construction of a temple in honour of the Hindu God Ram at the site of an ancient Ram temple which, it was said, was razed by Babur and replaced with a mosque.

V.P. Singh was again a silent observer as the Rath Yatra moved on. His lethargy in taking decisive steps was the reason he always seemed incompetent as a prime minister. Advani had even waited in Delhi for some days to provoke the central government into arresting him. But the government failed to take up the challenge, thinking arresting him would make him a martyr.

ANI was covering the Rath Yatra as it set off from the Somnath temple in Gujarat on 25 September 1990. As it moved on, it enthused Hindu crowds and in some ways became a symbol of Hindu resurgence. As we planned the coverage of the Rath Yatra, we realized that this journey of Advani was going to change the nature of Indian politics. We mapped the yatra and had teams following the rath all through the route.

V.P. Singh's friend and colleague Lalu Prasad Yadav, who was then the chief minister of Bihar, allowed the yatra to continue into Bihar, only to arrest Advani there on 23 October. It was a watershed moment in the history of this county. Yadav came to be viewed as the upholder of secular politics in north India even as Ayodhya was in turmoil. Communal riots broke out in Uttar Pradesh. Twenty-eight kar sevaks were killed in police action when they tried to storm the Babri Masjid.

V.P. Singh and the Janata Dal lost the support of the BJP. It was known as the Mandal–Kamandal government, because V.P. Singh had come to power with BJP's support—caste politics supported by right-wing Hindutva. But ultimately, the combination of the two was not tenable and as a result the government fell. Even Devi Lal was unhappy with the way V.P. Singh was running the government, which meant the end of V.P. Singh as prime minister.

His government crumbled after just 343 days to be precise, in November 1990, following an agitation by students.

Lasting scars

It is strange that the V.P. Singh government, which projected itself as one that offered a clean new start, pushed the country back by many years. V.P. Singh did not build his team before becoming PM. He co-opted disgruntled elements from Rajiv Gandhi's team, the socialists who had no ideological unity with him and the right-wing BJP, which was totally at odds with him. This hotchpotch experiment failed. And quick to capitalize on V.P. Singh's collapse was the Congress, offering to prop up his rival, Chandra Shekhar.

When Chandra Shekhar walked out with sixty-four of his MPs, the government was reduced to a minority, and V.P. Singh was left with no option but to resign. This must be one of those rare cases in parliamentary democracy where a party was not technically thrown out by the opposition; it threw itself out.

V.P. Singh's government had caused huge damage to India at a crucial moment. The momentum for progress that Rajiv Gandhi had given to the nation had been broken. V.P. Singh had turned the clock back.

Like the government, Indian society itself almost imploded on the Mandal issue. Kashmir's inclusive Kashmiriyat, signifying peaceful coexistence of all religions in the Kashmir Valley, had been disturbed with the exit of Kashmiri Pandits. How would ensuing governments deal with these problems?

The fact is that many of these issues continue to haunt India even today.

Chandra Shekhar seizes the moment

V.P. Singh's fall led to the ascent of Chandra Shekhar as prime minister. Chandra Shekhar was a fiery young leader from Ballia in Uttar Pradesh, who had appeared on the national scene earlier as a socialist activist under Dr Ram Manohar Lohia. He was wedded to socialism and, to some extent, to extreme idealism.

He joined the Congress party in 1964 and became very popular with its young leaders, who were part of a group known as the Young Turks. I met him first during a routine news coverage, and that developed into a lifelong friendship. I was always impressed with his sincerity and decisive nature.

During the Emergency, he came into direct conflict with Indira Gandhi. He was arrested and spent time in the Patiala jail. He had the distinction of being the only Congressman to be arrested by Mrs Gandhi's regime during the Emergency. After being released, Chandra Shekhar was elected as president of the Janata Party, which was formed in 1977.

He was a great friend. I will never forget one incident in 1978, during Morarji Desai's government. A group of disgruntled TV producers, failing to compete with TVNF (the predecessor of ANI), complained about me. They used Murli Manohar Joshi, a senior Jana Sangh leader, to raise an issue on the floor of the Lok Sabha, asking how a person like me, an alleged blue-eyed boy of Mrs Gandhi, could be allowed to continue producing syndicated documentaries on development news under a Janata Party government. Joshi's sister-in-law was married to one R.C. Pandey, part of the disgruntled group opposed to me.

When I heard this, I met the then information minister, L.K. Advani, to lodge my protest against this intervention by a leader of his party. I pointed out that I would not be able to defend myself in Parliament. This kind of thing was never done in the House.

Advani said that he would be unable to help, even though he agreed that this kind of action was uncalled-for and that Joshi should have spoken to him first. But even though not a minister, Joshi was too senior for Advani to disagree with him.

I then called my friend Chandra Shekhar. After all, he was the president of the Janata Party. He was furious on hearing this and said: 'Premji, just leave it to me.' On the next day, when Joshi tried to raise the issue in the Lok Sabha, he found to his surprise several MPs from within his own Janata Party standing up to challenge his action against me—someone who was not in the House to defend himself.

Chandra Shekhar had effectively shown that there was no scope for personal agendas in this government, nor was there going to be vindictiveness against journalists who had been perceived to be close to the previous regime. When I rang to thank him, he responded graciously. 'How can I, as president of Janata Party, allow such motivated attacks by any member of the party?' That was his idealism.

In 1983, Chandra Shekhar decided to undertake a countrywide *padyatra,* walking tour. He decided to walk all across India, starting from the southern tip of the country in Kanyakumari. He wanted to get to know each and every area at ground level by walking from village to town to cities across the nation. I walked with him on several stretches while covering the progress of his padyatra.

He also wanted ordinary Indians to know him. I had the privilege, admirer as I was of my friend, of walking with him and seeing how he interacted with the people he met. It was a great experience for me. I could see why he was such a popular leader. The stories I did of his tours got great global play on television as well as in print.

Row over donations

There was a controversy within the Janata Party over funds collected during the padyatra. The fact was, as I myself witnessed, that wherever Chandra Shekhar went, people would offer all kinds of small donations, even though he did not call for them. Along the way, people would donate Rs 5, Rs 10 or, occasionally, Rs 100–200. Wherever he stopped, money was collected.

Indeed, it was great fun to watch a large group count the money in the evenings. To avoid controversy, Chandra Shekhar had decided that, since this money had been donated by the people for the padyatra, he would create fifteen Bharat Yatra Kendras, to promote social welfare in different parts of the country and to train social workers. He also created a centre at Bhondsi, Haryana, to study what could be done to improve the lives of the rural population.

Chandra Shekhar had, from day one, disapproved of V.P. Singh as prime minister. He had quietly walked out when Devi Lal had proposed V.P. Singh's name. Chandra Shekhar never liked the way V.P. Singh worked against his own prime minister, Rajiv Gandhi, and felt that many of the charges V.P. Singh levelled against the latter were not substantiated.

When V.P. Singh's government collapsed, Chandra Shekhar seized the moment and was assured of support from Rajiv Gandhi in his drive to become the next prime minister.

Chandra Shekhar accepted Rajiv's support and became the seventh prime minister of India, but with only a meagre sixty-four MPs to back him. I could never tell him this, but knowing that he was a Congressman at heart, I thought he should have joined the Congress party way back and asked Rajiv to take charge. It remains a mystery to me why he didn't do that.

In any case, having taken the decision, Chandra Shekhar formed his government with his sixty-four MPs and ran it well. This surprised many in the media. Obituaries of his government had been written in advance. People thought that this experiment would be as short-lived as Charan Singh's or Morarji Desai's.

Soon after his government assumed power, Chandra Shekhar got down to work. He took a bold decision, which was to allow US Air Force planes to refuel in Calcutta while on long flights to and from the Far East. This was a distinct change of policy.

He was never shy of taking tough decisions. The Indian economy at that point was in serious trouble. Decades of communist-style management had left India with huge debts. The country was unable to meet repayment deadlines on certain loans. It was not earning enough foreign exchange, and international organizations were refusing to lend India any more money. All this left India's economy in a mess, if not in a state of bankruptcy.

Indian industries were even importing raw material, something for which we always used to fault the British. We always claimed that Britain took raw material from India and sent back finished products. Now, our industries were importing raw material.

Faced with the option of defaulting on debt repayments, the finance ministry approached the prime minister and offered a solution. The PM was told that we could make the payments by mortgaging a part of India's gold reserves. Chandra Shekhar's immediate reaction was, Indians love their gold at individual, family and national levels. As the nation's leader, he felt that if he were to mortgage India's gold there could be serious repercussions. But the prime minister was not given proper advice.

He was not told that he could give the kind of impetus to the economy that Rajiv Gandhi was trying to effect, during his first term, in consultation with the World Bank. And that, perhaps, could have helped in getting further loans. If he had been told all this by the concerned bureaucrats, including the then economic adviser, Dr Manmohan Singh, perhaps Chandra Shekhar would have accepted the World Bank's conditions for the loan and Indian gold would not have been mortgaged.

So Chandra Shekhar was left with limited options. India could either default on the repayments or pay by mortgaging some of its gold. Manmohan Singh, who later rose to be the finance minister and then prime minister, advised Chandra Shekhar that the mortgage deal could be kept secret while the government made every effort to recover the gold as soon as possible.

Though Chandra Shekhar knew that such a move could not be kept secret, he went ahead with the gold mortgage plan. India was not going to ruin its reputation by defaulting on payment. He allowed the gold to be moved. And lo and behold, even as the gold was taken out of the vaults of the Reserve Bank of India in Bombay, the guards at the bank began asking where the gold was going. The gold had not even reached the airport when the city of Bombay was awash with rumours that gold was being moved out of the RBI. Sure enough, the entire country knew before the gold left Indian borders.

Chandra Shekhar suffered a serious setback to his career because of this very unnecessary decision. Looking back, he would always express regret over the decision, which cost him so much in terms of his reputation. Having suffered this shock and lost the public's faith, Chandra Shekhar was never the same person. He spent a lot of time brooding. I have often wondered why he did not go back to the Congress. Instead, he simply withered away in the evening of his life.

Then, in the midst of all this, Rajiv Gandhi withdrew his support for Chandra Shekhar. Rajiv alleged that Om Prakash Chautala's government in Haryana was spying on him. (A Haryana state policeman was found loitering outside Rajiv Gandhi's house.) Whether or not that was true, Chandra Shekhar was concerned. With Rajiv's support gone, the scene was set for another election.

LTTE assassinates Rajiv Gandhi

In the 1991 election campaign, Rajiv Gandhi did extremely well. Just like his mother in 1980, he made an all-out effort to get his point of view across. He was widely expected to win the election. People were tired of another experiment with a non-Congress coalition, which created instability and brought international disrepute.

I met Rajiv Gandhi the day before he was to leave for south India. He had specially asked for me because ANI's crews had been travelling with him during the campaign and he had been very happy with them. I went to his house that evening. He was hosting a tea party for all the media people who had been travelling with him. He thanked me and wanted to know how soon I would make ANI into a really big television news agency. I said, 'Sir, it will all happen in time. It's all moving quite well.'

Next morning, he was to cast his vote at Udyog Bhavan before proceeding to the next stage of his campaign. A woman was there to perform aarti, and as she started the puja thali fell down—a bad omen. While meeting the journalists assembled there, Rajiv Gandhi asked me who from ANI would be joining him in south India. I told him that since he would be arriving in Tamil Nadu very late in the day, we would be joining him in Kerala, which was going to be very colourful. He was quite pleased.

Sadly, that was not to be. For Rajiv Gandhi was assassinated the next night, by a female agent of the LTTE. (The Sri Lankan terror group had not forgiven Rajiv Gandhi for sending the Indian peacekeeping forces to Jaffna to disarm them.) She detonated a bomb that killed Rajiv Gandhi and fourteen other people.

With Rajiv Gandhi gone, the election campaign went astray. Many people claim that the second half of the campaign, after Rajiv Gandhi's demise, brought more seats for Congress. But that did not seem to be the case, as the Congress's overall tally was 244. It was a minority government by the largest single party, with outside support.

Out of that election, overshadowed as it was by tragedy, there emerged another prime minister, Narasimha Rao, a man who was to have a huge impact on Indian economy and politics.

12

The Mantle Falls on Narasimha Rao

P.V. Narasimha Rao took over after the 1989 election results were announced. He became prime minister without a majority in Parliament but with a lot of drama. Not even he could have imagined that one day he would be PM.

Rao was only the second Congress leader outside the Nehru–Gandhi family orbit to become prime minister, after Lal Bahadur Shastri. (Dr Manmohan Singh would be the third a few years later.) It was the talk of the town that Rao was not Sonia Gandhi's first choice. Her advisers had pitched for Shankar Dayal Sharma, considered a Gandhi family loyalist unlike Rao, who was his own man. The coterie around Sonia wasn't sure of Rao, who had a reputation of being unbending and a private person. Moreover, Rao had virtually retired from politics. But fate had more in store for this polyglot Telugu Brahmin.

When Sharma was offered the PM's position, he refused, saying his health did not permit the responsibility. Another prime minister candidate was Sharad Pawar, who lost out in the last lap at the hands of the Congress's backroom boys. Pawar was the popular choice among the media, but the kitchen cabinet picked Rao, thinking he would be more pliable.

Soon after Rao was sworn in as prime minister, in a very sombre oath-taking ceremony, I requested an interview with him, and I was very lucky to be the first one to be granted an interview. I asked him what his vision was, given that he was assuming office in very difficult times and with an empty treasury.

Rao was candid and quick to respond. He said he expected a tough situation, thanks to the previous two years of loose control and mismanagement of the economy. It was already widely recognized that the Indian economy had suffered the most during the V.P. Singh–Chandra Shekhar period. Forty-seven tonnes of India's gold had been pledged in the Bank of England. Rao's first job was to bring the economy back on track. That is what Rajiv Gandhi would have done had he lived to be the PM, Rao said to me at the interview.

Having appointed Manmohan Singh as finance minister, Rao asked him to deal with the economic situation as a matter of priority. Many speculated that Singh had actually been placed in the ministry at the behest of the World Bank.

Rao was faced with the same predicament as Chandra Shekhar: either to repay the international debt or default. The shrewd politician that Rao was, he was certainly not going to mortgage any more gold. But he also knew that Rajiv Gandhi, who had already introduced some remarkable reforms in his first term, could not fully eliminate licence raj with all its attendant restrictions.

Rao ushers in liberalization

Greater liberalization was on the cards. Rao knew that under the current economic order of Fabian socialism, the country could not go any further. He therefore agreed to the terms set out by the World Bank in return for further loans. This meant major economic reforms.

The World Bank needed to be sure that India would generate enough revenue to meet its financial obligations. Once this assurance was given, the World Bank agreed to the loan. The Rao government's response was immediate. India was going to welcome foreign direct investment (FDI), which it had previously shunned (and in doing so, it had taken away majority shareholding rights in foreign companies).

Tariffs on all imports were immediately reduced. Duty rates were scaled down to 25 per cent. Even gold imports were to be allowed, because gold smuggling had become a major source of the outflow of India's foreign exchange resources. The government also announced that it would embark on the privatization of the public sector.

The response to these reforms was rather favourable. People were taken by surprise, but they welcomed the move. To begin with, India began receiving hot money, that is, investment in the stock market, where Indian industries, by and large, have always been rich due to their captive markets.

Foreign companies knew that if liberalization was really to happen, it would help generate business and profitability in India. As a result, a lot of investment came into the country, even though many international investors approached India with some reluctance. Some Indian industrialists, who complained that they were not getting a level playing field, accepted liberalization grudgingly. I remember how a group of industrialists, who were used to a protective economy but were now exposed to competition with foreign companies, formed something known as the Bombay Club, out of a sense of sheer insecurity.

I must say that, on the whole, Indians welcomed these steps. They could now go ahead and do business freely. Licensing, in most industries and businesses, was removed. Now it was possible to launch a business enterprise without first having to go through the corrupt practice of seeking a licence, which itself would come with all kinds of restrictions. This was Rao's first success. He had achieved the almost impossible task of reforming the Indian economy.

To the foreign media, this was an interesting news story. However, as a visual story it was hard to shoot. Business houses and businessmen are by nature reluctant to speak to the media in India, unless it is a PR-padded story. And that we didn't do.

Better ties with the US

Rao made conscious efforts to improve India's relations with the United States and western Europe, while curtailing the country's dependence on the Soviet Union. It was not that easy, considering India's precarious foreign exchange position and the fact that trade with the Soviet Union had always been rupee-based.

Rao undertook a number of foreign tours to spread the message that India was open to business. I remember a time when you could not buy an air ticket to travel abroad; you had to fill something called a 'P Form', which was submitted to the Reserve Bank of India, and then the RBI approved or rejected a person's foreign travel plans but without release of any foreign exchange.

I remember a great comedy movie from the late '60s, *Around the World*, about an Indian who travels the world with only eight dollars, because that was all the foreign exchange someone going abroad (other than a business traveller) would get. Once, on an international flight, I saw a man untie his shoes and take out foreign currency from his socks. After decades of such restrictions, the opening up of the economy was almost unbelievable.

Rao had given clear instructions to Indian diplomatic missions abroad: to remind the world that Indian foreign policy would now be driven by economics and not simply by non-alignment.

Our view of industrialists

I was speaking with our ambassador in the United States, a very fine gentleman named Abid Hussain. The subject of Indian economy arose and he was lamenting the fact that all his efforts to convince Americans that the Indian economy was open for business were falling on deaf ears. The Americans simply did not believe it. They felt that the shackles of communist control were still in place and that India was not a safe investment area.

I told Abid Sahab that it was the job of Indian businessmen to convince the American business community. The Americans were hardened investors; they would listen to their Indian counterparts than to an ambassador, because they wanted to invest their money carefully. I pointed out how strange it was that while India's biggest industrial houses had close relations with US industry, we should both be left wondering how to get American investors interested in India.

I gave him one example. The hugely important Tata Group had always had an America-first, Britain-second policy. At that time it was headed by the most respectable of the Tatas, J.R.D. Tata. I asked Abid Sahab, 'What kind of respect or recognition has the government in India shown to the Tatas? Don't we treat businessmen as corrupt people who should be kept at a distance? And have not the Tatas been dealt with rather roughly?'

I suggested that perhaps the time had come to involve Tata Group, to get them to open up and see what might be done on the question of American reluctance to invest in India. I said it was very strange that we Indians don't give recognition to those doing great work. J.R.D., as the head of the Tata Group, was one of the cleanest industrialists in the world. But, I asked Abid Sahab, have we recognized him?

I left the question in the air. But I was gratified in less than a year when, in 1992, J.R.D. Tata was honoured with the Bharat Ratna, India's highest accolade. This was a rare occasion when a living person was honoured with this decoration. That alone sent a message, not only to businessmen abroad but to Indian entrepreneurs as well, that the Government of India recognized wealth creators as people who did service to the country.

In the early '90s, satellite television came to India with the launch of Zee TV. Soon after, dedicated 24/7 news channels started appearing. And with that came the demand for video news content. The opening up of the media market—by accident and not by design—had led to this demand for video news. And it was fulfilled by ANI.

I had the good fortune to have met J.R.D. when I had just turned twenty-one. We'd met in Switzerland but were never really in touch with each other. I never interviewed him or covered any of the events of the Tata Group. Years later, I was sitting in the lobby of St James' Court hotel in London when I saw him walking in. He noticed me and came up to me. I was so touched that he had remembered me. He asked what I was doing there. He then said he was about to take a walk in St James's Park and wondered if I would care to join him. Of course, I did. It was a great and very memorable day for me.

Around this time, Narasimha Rao began a series of overseas tours, mixing foreign policy with economic matters. Though Rao was not much of a statesman-like figure—as, say, Rajiv Gandhi was—he had an air of an academic about him which many world leaders appreciated. I travelled with him to South Korea and China. Since the liberalization of the economy, South Korea had become a major investor in India. South Koreans had taken an interest in a multitude of Indian businesses—motor cars, television sets, refrigerators, washing machines, you name it.

After South Korea, the prime minister travelled to China. India's relations with China had been very difficult ever since the Chinese moved into Tibet in 1950, which raised many other problems. Nonetheless, once in Beijing, Rao pitched for Chinese investment in India. I was with him and saw how he was introducing an economic flavour into his discussions, to improve bilateral relations with this complex neighbour. This, I have noticed, is something that the Chinese love.

Nowhere else in the world has communism been so happily married to American capitalism as in China. Look at all the cities that have emerged there. Guangzhou is one of them. Another, Yiwu, was built only to produce lights. A lot of investment has come from America. On every visit that I have made to China, I have felt a sense of awe as to how China has zoomed ahead despite its ideological baggage.

Of course, the Chinese worked the Cold War to maximum advantage. They used the Soviet Union as long as they could get the best out of them. Then they realized that real prosperity lay with America. The practical Chinese have always had a largely American view of economic affairs.

The emergence of China as a major power could only have come through its embrace of the American economic model. When Henry Kissinger arrived in China to wean them away from the Soviet Union, they welcomed the idea. How cleverly they have managed to avoid compromising their communism, their one-party rule, their

own way of government, while bringing American investment, and
every American brand name, to their country.

China's prosperity is no doubt due to their own hard work, but it
is based mainly on American investment and American technology,
which, tragically, India failed to accept, for all the opportunities it had.

Punjab to Kashmir

At home, Rao faced numerous difficulties but also enjoyed
considerable successes.

Punjab was still suffering in the aftermath of Operation Blue
Star, with Pakistani involvement in Khalistani terrorism adding fuel
to fire. But it is to the credit of Rao that the terror of Khalistani
elements in Punjab was brought to an end. He gave chief minister
Beant Singh a free hand to deal with it in any way he saw fit.

The chief minister, with his military background, ordered his
police chief, K.P.S. Gill, to finish it. Gill led the campaign from the
front, and there are allegations that in the process many innocent
people were killed. But Punjab was free from terrorism.

News coverage of such events proved one of our toughest
challenges. ANI and Reuters TV—which I headed—were the
main source of information for the global media and millions who
watched television. Yet the stories from Punjab were some of the
most difficult stories that we had to cover.

Another difficult story broke in Hazratbal, Kashmir. In 1993, the
revered Hazratbal Shrine was captured by terrorists who occupied
the building. In dealing with this sensitive problem, Rao was anxious
to avoid a repeat of Operation Blue Star and the Golden Temple
disaster. In this volatile situation, any damage to the shrine would
have created serious problems for him. However, he managed to get
the shrine cleared without any damage to the structure.

It was during Rao's term that Benazir Bhutto, as prime minister
of Pakistan, upped the ante on Kashmir. She said, 'We support
Kashmiris today and will continue to support them till we die, and
even if we die we will support them. We will fight for the right of

Kashmiris for self-determination.' Her 'Azadi Azadi Azadi' slogan resonated in Kashmir.

Rao did not match her speech with his own rousing speech. Instead, he took a step which in my view was one of the most significant steps taken by Rao in his political career. On 22 February 1994, the Indian Parliament unanimously passed a resolution on Kashmir. It read:

(a) The State of Jammu & Kashmir has been, is and shall be an integral part of India and any attempts to separate it from the rest of the country will be resisted by all necessary means; (b) India has the will and capacity to firmly counter all designs against its unity, sovereignty and territorial integrity . . . (c) Pakistan must vacate the areas of the Indian State of Jammu and Kashmir, which they have occupied through aggression . . . (d) All attempts to interfere in the internal affairs of India will be met resolutely.

The '90s saw the beginning of one of the most vicious campaigns by Pakistan to wrest Kashmir from India, through proxy war. And the US completely backed Pakistan, pushing to declare Jammu and Kashmir as a dispute.

In April 1993, an Indian Airlines flight from Delhi to Srinagar was hijacked. It was made to land in Amritsar. Refusing to negotiate with the hijacker, Rao asked the security services to deal with it. The hijacker was killed in Amritsar and the passengers were freed. This was in contrast to what V.P. Singh had done in the case of Rubaiya Sayeed's kidnapping, or what even a great prime minister like Atal Bihari Vajpayee was later made to do when, in 1999, another Indian Airlines flight, IC 814, was hijacked and taken to Kandahar. We continue to suffer from the fallout of those decisions to this day.

Babri demolition

Rao faced a great many other crises. There was the Babri Masjid issue—a terrible situation. This sixteenth-century mosque had been occupied by a large group of Hindu activists who threatened to destroy it. Rao was assured by the state government of Uttar Pradesh that nothing would happen. Yet on 6 December 1992, the mosque was demolished, provoking riots in the city of Ayodhya. Some 2,000 people died in that episode.

I was in Delhi at the time to coordinate coverage, but up in Ayodhya my cameramen were attacked and their cameras smashed to pieces. A policeman helped the crew escape the mob. They were able to save some of their videotapes and brought them back to Delhi, from where we transmitted the footage.

Rao was incommunicado for several hours. The incident had serious repercussions for him. There were elements within the Congress and outside who blamed him, accusing him of being a silent spectator. It took a commission of inquiry, set up under Justice M.S. Liberhan, to exonerate him of all blame. And the commission took seventeen long years to finish its inquiry. The report said that several BJP leaders, including L.K. Advani, were involved in the demolition of the mosque.

It was suggested that Rao had connived in the destruction of Babri Masjid. But the fact is that the administration of law and order in India is a state subject. Central government can only intervene if the state seeks such an intervention. Government forces cannot be moved in, unless asked. In this case, the Uttar Pradesh government had assured everyone that the situation was under control and nothing would happen.

Meanwhile, miscreants who wanted to prevent the news of the demolition from being broadcast began attacking newsmen and damaging their equipment. Our cameras had been destroyed and needed replacing. But the customs duties on imported cameras were exorbitant, at about 360 per cent. So importing new cameras was going to be a very expensive affair.

We approached both Rao and his finance minister, Manmohan Singh, pointing out that our security was the responsibility of the central and state governments. So how were we to get our equipment back? Finally, an agreement was reached. The government would waive the customs duty as long as we could prove that all customs dues had been cleared on the destroyed equipment. That's how we got our cameras replaced.

The Babri incident resulted in riots all over India, and this had a bearing on Rao's reputation. The worst riots took place in Bombay, claiming hundreds of lives.

In 1993, a series of bomb blasts in Bombay killed several hundred people. Thirteen explosions hit different parts of the city, beginning with the Bombay Stock Exchange. Both these events—the riots and the bombings—brought the city to a complete standstill and were covered extensively by ANI.

After the bombings, Rao flew to Bombay to review the damage personally and to find out who was responsible. The moment he discovered Pakistani involvement, he asked Indian intelligence agencies to invite their counterparts from the United States, Britain and other nations and investigate the extent to which Pakistan had been involved in the attacks.

That was a great diplomatic step—to convince the world that Pakistan was involved in global terrorism. Rao was not going to send troops into Pakistan. He simply asked other nations to send their own intelligence agencies to Bombay and verify what the Indian government was saying.

The happening years

Rao's term was an eventful one. A lot of action on the economic, social and political fronts marked the span of his coalition government, which worked fairly well for five years. All kinds of unexpected events kept the prime minister and his government busy. And he responded boldly by running a Congress government that stepped away from the Nehru–Gandhi dynasty mindset.

His biggest contribution was to steer the Indian economy away from the Fabian socialism that had been in place since Nehru's days. Rao had put the nation on the path to globalization. There were elements within his own party who were hostile to him and did not approve of the right turn that the economic policy of the country had taken.

One of his government's severest tests came with the Latur earthquake. It was one of the deadliest earthquakes the state of Maharashtra has ever seen. It struck at about 3.56 a.m. on 30 September 1993. Some fifty-two villages were destroyed, approximately 10,000 people were killed and over 30,000 were injured. Rao's government earned great praise for its handling of this crisis and for the way it used modern technology not only to bring immediate relief but to rehabilitate the survivors.

Then came a dark day in parliamentary politics. A no-confidence motion was moved against his government, backed by elements on the left who were unhappy with the economic reforms that he was implementing. There were also those who were unhappy with the way Rao had handled the Babri Masjid demolition issue.

When the government had to finally face a vote it got mired in an unseemly controversy. With the help of the Jharkhand Mukti Morcha leader Shibu Soren, Rao managed to defeat the no-confidence motion and his government survived. But his enemies continued to harass him. They tried to prove that Soren and his people had been paid money for their support.

Then, there were people within Rao's party who disapproved of the way he was trying to take the Congress back to its days when it was more active and held regular elections. This was seen by many as a threat to Sonia Gandhi, who now had virtual control of the party. Men like Sitaram Kesri and several others were merely dancing to her tune. Kesri was done in later by Sonia Gandhi, when she decided to take charge of the party herself.

Rao was very keen, it seemed to me, to restore the Congress party's former greatness. He didn't want a political outfit that depended upon a few individuals, including himself, for relevance, even if that meant losing the support of his own base within the party.

The aftermath of the no-confidence vote, which he won by a hair's breadth, left a sizable opposition ranged against him.

Thus, in 1996, when the country was preparing for yet another election, there were conflicting interests galore. Various elements, the hostile left, and status quo-ist people against economic reforms, those critical of what happened at Babri Masjid and the ones who now pushed ahead for a Ram temple in Ayodhya, all lined up against Rao.

Having spent five years in office, he simply faded away. Perhaps it was because, during the election campaign, he had failed to emphasize how successfully and completely he had turned around India's economy. Surely, among the factors that led to the defeat of this very successful government was Rao's failure to remind the nation of the huge successes he had achieved in every sector of governance. The communication policy of his government was very poor. But whatever the reason, Rao's Congress lost the elections, and once again the nation was faced with the trauma of multiparty infighting.

It's a pity that Rao did not use his finance minister in the election campaign to highlight how successful his economic policies had been. By the time he began making use of him it was too late. So the general impression was that Rao was at best a reluctant party to all those economic reforms which, as I saw it, he certainly was not. He was determined not to mortgage any more gold to meet India's commitments abroad and was not going to let India default on its debt repayments. When he adopted the new liberal policy, he adopted it consciously.

There were regulatory mechanisms still in place to control any rogue elements in the economy. India's was not a laissez-faire economy. It was a system where free enterprise was starting to be recognized, where wealth generators or economic generators were honoured, just as J.R.D. Tata had been. It was very unfortunate that Rao lost the election and that the country was once again in the hands of ragtag coalitions.

Another of his achievements, which remained hidden for a time but was well-known to those close to him, was that Rao had worked hard to turn India into a nuclear power. He backed the development of nuclear weapons, even though he was unable to carry out nuclear tests for fear of sanctions which could derail the economy.

No less a person than A.P.J. Abdul Kalam, the noted scientist who later became president of India, acknowledged that under Rao scientists had been asked to carry out tests on nuclear devices, including the hydrogen bomb. But although these devices were developed and prepared, the tests could not be undertaken, mainly due to American pressure on India to refrain from conducting nuclear tests.

India's nuclear experts were certainly very keen to see India take its place among the nuclear powers. Thanks to Rao's efforts, the Department of Atomic Energy was ready to demonstrate its nuclear capacity. But it was only when Atal Bihari Vajpayee came to power that he, as the new prime minister, could order the nuclear tests to proceed without delay.

13

War in Afghanistan

Afghanistan is an ancient land civilizationally interlinked with India. If we were to draw an outline of the subcontinent in its original, ancient form, the land of the Indian civilization would begin from the mountains of Himalayas and extend all the way to Central Asia.

I visited Afghanistan for the first time in 1976 and found it fairly prosperous. Kabul was a very clean city. The Afghan currency, known as the afghani, traded better than the Indian rupee. Afghan women moved about freely, and many of them wore Western dresses. They freely worked side by side with men. I noticed the same in other Afghan cities, such as Herat, Mazar-e-Sharif and even in Jalalabad.

I greatly admired the entrepreneurial spirit of the Afghan people and the peaceful coexistence of different faiths and communities I witnessed there. There was a prosperous minority of Afghan Hindus and Sikhs living in perfect harmony. Few people remember that the Afghans were innovative businessmen and traders and that they were dealing in money markets and currencies long before the West adopted currency hedging and trading. Kabul was known as the Paris of Central Asia.

Though Afghanistan was a peaceful country, it slowly became embroiled in the policies and machinations of the Cold War, as was the rest of the world in the twentieth century. In 1972, Mohammad Daoud, the Afghan prime minister and cousin of King Zahir Shah, staged a bloodless coup and declared the end of monarchy in his country. Thus, Afghanistan became a republic. King Zahir Shah went into exile with his family, in Italy.

Daoud, who became the president of Afghanistan in 1973, had serious differences with his country's immediate neighbour, Pakistan, including disputes over their common border. During the Cold War, Pakistan was a close ally of the United States; it fell under the influence of the United States following alliances with the Southeast Asia Treaty Organization and the Central Treaty Organization. Peshawar was used as a secret US Air Force base, from where America would send U-2 spy planes over the Soviet Union and Central Asia.

Although never formally a Soviet ally in the Cold War, Daoud took Afghanistan closer to the Soviet Union. The Soviets certainly treated Afghanistan as their area of influence. But Daoud had his own plans and ambitions. Afghanistan joined the Non-Aligned Movement (NAM), which the Russians found hard to accept. The Russians had been suspicious of NAM ever since the Yugoslav leader Marshal Tito had left the Soviet bloc.

The three founding leaders of NAM were Jawaharlal Nehru, Gamal Abdel Nasser and Marshal Tito. Although power was in the hands of Daoud, the communists of Afghanistan had strong factions and their leaders were politically aware.

Daoud's various agreements with the Soviet Union made his army totally dependent upon the Russians, who supplied weapons to Afghanistan's armed forces and trained them. Thousands of Afghan students went to the Soviet Union to study—and came back as confirmed communists.

Wanting to chart a different course, Daoud tried to mend fences with Pakistan on the border issue. He was increasingly influenced by the United States, via the Shah of Iran. The US wanted this country of great strategic importance on its side. Daoud himself was widely regarded as behaving like an aristocrat, like the monarch of Afghanistan.

To further steer his country towards an independent foreign policy and non-alignment, Daoud hosted a meeting of foreign ministers from the non-aligned nations in Kabul in April 1978. The Soviet Union was then under the leadership of Leonid Brezhnev, who expressed his unhappiness at this proposed meeting and his displeasure at Daoud hobnobbing with the Shah of Iran, whom the Russians always treated as an American stooge. Daoud was thus on a collision course with the Soviet Union.

The radicals in the Afghan parliament, particularly the communists, did not approve of the non-aligned summit in Kabul. The support of the radicals was crucial for Daoud, but the Soviets and the Afghan communists had given plenty of hints to Daoud to refrain from hosting the meeting.

With the Soviet Union and the communists in Afghanistan convinced that Daoud was moving closer to the United States, events moved fast. Afghan Army tanks moved into the presidential palace on 27 April 1978 and quickly brought Daoud's rule to an end.

Kabul calling

With the date of the Kabul summit fast approaching, Surinder and I applied for an Afghan visa to cover the event. My neighbour in Delhi at that time was an Afghan diplomat, Enayat Madani, a counsellor at the embassy. Our visa applications, he told me, were being processed. But the embassy shut down, following the news of the coup in Kabul. As soon as it reopened, we picked up our passports and, to our own surprise, found that we had been granted Afghan visas. We left for Kabul the very next day, 30 April.

Luckily for us, there was a flight to Kabul. I messaged my friend S.K. Singh, the Indian ambassador to Afghanistan, informing him of our arrival. He sent a senior officer of the embassy, Daulat Singh, to meet us with a car and drive us into town. The aftermath of the coup could be seen all around. We stopped at the presidential palace and saw damaged tanks standing on the road outside, with crowds of Afghans looking into them and shaking hands with the soldiers.

Cameras in hand, we went inside the palace, where signs of fighting were all too visible. There were no bodies, but Daoud's whole family, including women and children, had been killed. There were torn clothes and other telltale items strewn outside the living quarters of the president and his family—a detritus which spoke of the violence that had engulfed the palace. It was all a terrible sight. Daoud himself was said to have put up a fight. His bodyguards had stayed loyal and were killed.

As we filmed these scenes, crowds of people were swarming into the palace grounds—a place they had never seen before. I drove to the residence of Ambassador Singh, who briefed me on all that had happened. Clearly, it had been a well-planned and efficiently executed coup. And enough warnings had been given to Daoud not to host the non-aligned meeting.

Since Daoud took over from King Zahir Shah in 1973, he had taken Afghanistan close to the Soviet Union. For all practical purposes, the country was considered a military outpost, if not a formal ally, by the Soviet Union. Afghanistan was heavily dependent on Soviet assistance in many fields, including defence and education.

Surinder and I checked into Kabul Hotel in the heart of the city. It had been built by the Russians, as were several government buildings in Kabul. We went around the city and found everything to be normal. The people of Kabul had taken the coup in their stride. If there was any regret or anger, it was over the killing of the women and children in Daoud's family.

Almost nobody in the bazaar had any reservations about the coup, because Daoud's ways had changed things and many Afghans had disapproved of his earlier coup against King Zahir Shah. We filmed everything and rushed our coverage back to Delhi, from where it was shipped to London for syndication. In that way, the world got an eyewitness account of the overthrow of Daoud and the coup in Kabul.

The leaders of the coup moved quickly. The communist party installed Nur Mohammad Taraki as the new president. He had once lived and worked in Bombay. Afghanistan's communist party, known as the PDPA (People's Democratic Party of Afghanistan), had its own major factions within—the Khalqis and the Parchamis.

Babrak Karmal, from the Parchami faction, was made the deputy prime minister, while Taraki himself came from the Khalqi faction. Hafizullah Amin, another Khalqi, emerged as number two in the government.

Surinder and I were given the privilege of covering the first meeting of Taraki's cabinet. We could see all the men behind the coup, including General Abdul Qadir, who had led the military in what came to be known as the Saur Revolution or April Revolution.

We then went into the city to cover the packed Friday prayers at Kabul's famous Pearl Mosque. Kabul was a happy city despite the coup, the violence and the political uncertainty. We saw people enjoying their meals and fruits by the side of the Kabul River. Many women in Western dresses were on the streets. The shops and stores were busy. Life seemed normal and not at all disturbed by the change of government.

We also undertook short journeys outside Kabul to see the situation in the country. At these places, too, we found absolutely no opposition to the coup. But I did get the sense that the Afghans would have welcomed back King Zahir Shah rather than have the communists succeed Daoud.

After a week's stay, we returned home. On the way back, Surinder and I made a stopover in Istalif, a lovely mountain resort village outside Kabul. People of Kabul would go there for weekends, and it used to be a regular tourist destination.

Once back in Delhi, I kept an eye on developments in Kabul. I was helped in this by my neighbour, Enayat Madani. Enayat and other Afghan diplomats were honest enough to tell me that the communist takeover of the government in Kabul was not a good sign.

Things were not looking good in Kabul in general. After the Saur Revolution, Afghanistan's history would be marked by several violent and dramatic events. Tourism had taken a hit. Several far-reaching communist reforms had been met with resistance from the public. The national flag was changed from the usual Islamic green to a Soviet-style red. Rumours were rife that Brezhnev was going to turn Afghanistan into another Soviet republic.

The new regime also began to eliminate its political rivals. The repercussions of these events could be felt at the Afghan embassy in New Delhi. There were rumours that the opponents of the regime were being picked up and eliminated. But despite these desperate tactics, the unity of the government did not last long.

Taraki and Amin together moved against the Parchamis and sent Babrak Karmal as ambassador to Czechoslovakia. General Qadir was arrested and imprisoned. Soon, Amin fell out with Taraki and executed him. There were rumours that Amin had been in touch with the Americans. It was, I thought to myself, time to head back to Kabul.

We were again lucky to get a visa in 1979, thanks to Enayat. We landed in Kabul and found Hafizullah Amin in complete control. He accused the United States of being involved in a coup against Taraki. The American ambassador to Afghanistan was killed in a Kabul hotel where he was said to be meeting some political activists. That was perhaps the strongest warning by the Soviet Union and the communists that they did not approve of US meddling in Afghan affairs.

This time, more security and police personnel were visible in the capital. The tension in the air was palpable. Business had suffered. Unlike on our earlier visits, Surinder and I were not allowed to move about freely. The Afghans had provided a 'guide' to help us. In fact, he was a senior intelligence man.

Our movements were closely monitored. I will not forget an incident when I visited a street famous for its shops selling antiques. I went inside one of the shops and the owner recognized our so-called guide. He rebuked him and scolded him for the way the new government had made it difficult for tourists to visit Afghanistan.

As I was looking at the wonderful collection of antiques in his store, the owner walked up to me and asked me if I was a Hindu. I said, yes. And he said, 'Wait, I have something special to offer you.' He unlocked his huge steel cupboard and brought out an ivory statue of Lord Krishna. He said he believed it to be a few hundred years old but had no certificate to prove that. He said he did not want the communists from Soviet Russia to take it away. He offered it to me, asking me to take good care of it (which I have done). I told him that, the statue being so valuable, I would not be able to afford it. He replied, 'You can give me whatever you think you can afford. I know it is a valuable piece, but I do not want it taken by the Russians. They have no money and come here to barter with liquor and caviar for my precious goods.' I was touched that he understood the cultural significance of finding a Hindu home for a Krishna statue. I could not spare much for the idol as I had to save to pay for my essentials.

Another memorable incident occurred when our guide insisted on taking us to Jalalabad. He wanted us to see how the Afghan Army there was carrying out operations to deal with saboteurs from Pakistan. At the end of this staged show, we heard that three Afghan soldiers had run away!

I was unhappy to see Afghanistan tense and its political situation deteriorating. We covered several stories and travelled to many places. Our 'guide' was not very committed to his job, and we managed, from time to time, to get eyewitness accounts of how the conditions were worsening in Afghanistan. We were denied permission to meet Hafizullah Amin. So we returned home.

Peace in Kabul did not last long. It was clear to me that Amin's communist regime was not popular. It was moving far too fast in enforcing communist state control. And Afghans, by nature being a very free people, resisted such political repression.

Then came yet another coup. This was around Christmas 1979, and it was carried out by the Parchamis, who overthrew Amin. He and his colleagues were killed. Babrak Karmal flew in from Czechoslovakia to take charge of the country.

Karmal's first move, soon after the takeover, was to invite Soviet troops into Afghanistan to deal with what he alleged was 'foreign intervention'.

Surinder and I once again flew into Kabul, with two other men as part of our team, Dharampal Mehta and Harbhajan Singh. We checked into Kabul Intercontinental, where there was a useful media centre.

Soviet troops had already started landing in large numbers and taking up positions in and around Kabul. The city was being patrolled by Soviet tanks, ready to repel any resistance from the Afghan Army. The West called this a Soviet invasion. We sent eyewitness accounts of Russian troops in Kabul and other stories demonstrating the way they were taking charge of the country.

Karmal called a press conference, which was a disaster. Most questions were about the 'Soviet invasion', while Karmal insisted that these were friendly forces, 'invited' to Afghanistan by the Afghan government.

'American agents'

The next day, we travelled by road to Ghazni, to see how far the Soviets had moved. What a sight it was! Outside Kabul, the Soviet troops were dug in on both sides of the road, ostensibly in defence of the city.

Having shot one sequence, I decided to try for closer views. As our car turned around, I noticed a barricade being erected in the distance. Reacting quickly, I locked and hid my main camera and took out the smaller one. I asked a Reuters reporter, who was accompanying us, to hide his notes too. Sure enough, our vehicle was stopped. Each one of us was placed individually in a truck and taken to the field headquarters of the Soviet forces. Our driver and car were taken away separately.

There were snow-covered fields all around us. We were detained and told to stand in the open. I protested, telling them that we were from India, with valid permissions to work as journalists, and that they had no right to do this to us. But the Russians ignored our protests. They looked at our cameras and, seeing the words 'Made in USA' on them, concluded that we were American agents!

It was extremely uncomfortable, standing on the icy, frozen ground for well over two hours, not knowing what fate had in store for us. We kept stamping our feet to avoid frostbite.

Another hour passed before we saw our vehicle and driver return. He seemed dishevelled. We were not allowed to speak to him. Then, another hour went by until suddenly, a cavalcade of black limousines arrived, and two men in suits stepped out from each car. Each one of us was separately packed into the back seat of a car, with one of the suited men sitting on the left and one on the right. Our driver was told to follow the limousines in his vehicle.

I will never forget being driven through Kabul in limousines as prisoners—to see people outside moving about freely, while there was nothing we could do for ourselves. We were driven to the headquarters of the Afghan secret police, KHAD (as feared as the KGB in Moscow), and taken to the room of the deputy chief of KHAD, Mohammad Najibullah, who would one day become the president of Afghanistan.

He spoke in Urdu and, addressing us as 'Indian brothers', asked why were we filming their guests, the Soviet troops. Being on safe grounds, I mustered courage and protested against the treatment meted out to us at the Soviet Army camp. As for filming, I explained that wherever I pointed my camera in the city, the Soviet troops were plainly visible. Najibullah ordered us to destroy the film and go back. 'I don't want to see you again,' he said. I replied that we had hardly shot any film and left saying that I did not want to come back to 'this place'. We returned to the hotel.

It was the end of a very tense day. Tired and exhausted, we were much relieved to reach the hotel alive. I had managed to talk myself out of a nasty situation and also to retain my film—a great report which showed exactly how the Soviets were entrenching themselves in Afghanistan.

The next day, speaking with my friend and journalist M.L. Kotru, I wondered why we were staying in Kabul. We decided we ought to go to Ghazni, to see the tomb of Mahmud of Ghazni, who had attacked the Somnath temple seventeen times. Besides, it would take us outside Kabul. No one was allowed to travel outside Kabul but, being Indians, we took the necessary risk! Anyway, the Afghans were very friendly towards us.

On the way to Ghazni, we passed deserted villages and saw Soviet troops patrolling the countryside. There was no sign of the Afghan Army. It was snowing heavily as we arrived. The tomb of Mahmud was outside the city—a neglected monument of a once-powerful man.

Some of the people we met in Ghazni got angry with us when they found we were Indian. India's representative at the United Nations had welcomed the arrival of the Soviet troops—at the invitation of the Afghan government. This was not the view of the Afghans we met. They considered the Russians to be invaders.

In Ghazni, I learnt of the great respect the Afghans had for Hindus and Sikhs. Ghazni had a small population of Hindus and Sikhs, mostly businessmen. They lived peacefully and carried on with their trade. That night, we were told that one Lala Hukam Chand was to settle a dispute between two tribal clans.

Having covered Ghazni—a city where hardly any correspondent had ever gone—we returned to Kabul, happy with our coverage.

Calm before the storm

My next trip was to Jalalabad. We found the city peaceful. The great Pashtun leader Khan Abdul Ghaffar Khan lived there in exile. This city is an extension of the Pashtun areas that stretch right into the North-West Frontier Province of Pakistan—areas that were once annexed by Maharaja Ranjit Singh. Khan Abdul Ghaffar Khan, nicknamed 'Frontier Gandhi', had been ill-treated and jailed by the Pakistanis when he started his fight for a greater Pashtun area to be known as Pakhtunkhwa.

Reaching the house of 'Badshah' Khan, as he was also known, was quite an experience. As I, along with journalists D. Mehta and M.L. Kotru, entered the courtyard, the great Gandhian was sprawled on his cot, enjoying the crisp winter sun. From a distance he looked like a great pharaoh.

After the initial pleasantries, we asked him about the Afghan situation. He said Amin's rule had been cruel for many in the country. He spoke of his conviction that the only way to attain prosperity and peace was through the non-violence that Mahatma Gandhi had taught us.

I shall always remember that day and how this great man still lived by Gandhian ideals, which had all been forgotten in India. As I interviewed him, he spoke about the issue of poverty and said that the problems faced by Pashtuns and by Afghanistan could only be cured through non-violence.

While driving to Jalalabad, I had filmed convoys of Soviet troops moving towards the city and maybe towards the Pakistan border. The Soviet troops were now settling down. There had been no resistance to their arrival, even though most locals did not approve of their presence, apprehensive that the Soviet Union might turn Afghanistan into yet another satellite country. At the same time, Western propaganda was at full throttle, calling it an invasion of Afghanistan.

I stayed for a fortnight. During this period, most Western journalists were asked to leave Afghanistan. All was calm. However, this quiet interlude proved to be a lull before the storm.

The Afghan war

Western powers, assisted by Pakistan and Saudi Arabia, started an intervention in Afghanistan with a new line that 'Islam was in danger'. And the communist government in Kabul did little to change that view. They had tried to control the mullahs and imams of mosques. Skirmishes were reported between Soviet troops and locals, and in some cases Soviet troops had attacked whole villages.

Babrak Karmal was trying to bring some kind of rapprochement between different factions of the PDPA and also to win back the support of the Afghan people. He quickly changed the flag of Afghanistan from the communist red to its original green. He started approaching other Afghan intellectuals, inviting them to join his government. But now, with America intervening, via Pakistan and Saudi Arabia, Afghanistan was soon to become a battleground between the Soviet Union and the United States.

'Islam was in danger' was the call first given by Pakistan and the Saudis. They began to encourage and send in what were then known as Mujahideen to fight the Russians. The CIA was providing weapons and openly training these men to join the action. The Western powers turned the conflict into a religious fight for Islam which ultimately gave birth to Islamic extremism.

For the CIA, it was a proxy war against the Russians. Afghanistan, a poor country, was now a victim of the Cold War between two superpowers. Babrak Karmal's efforts to bring peace and stability to the nation were being thwarted by the United States, Pakistan and Saudi Arabia.

Karmal even announced a general amnesty to release all the non-communists arrested by the regimes of Taraki and Amin. He offered government jobs to non-communists and sought their active participation in the government. But he was always 'a subject', planted as he had been by the Soviet Union.

Meanwhile, the US-supported Mujahideen were failing to push ahead in the war against the Soviet troops. The Afghan Army and the Soviet forces continued to control the country. Kabul and major cities were still functioning, though tourism and business fell to an all-time low.

I was now travelling more frequently to Afghanistan. The Afghans would not allow anyone to be based permanently in Kabul, so I returned as often as I could get a visa, which was not too difficult to obtain for me.

With all his efforts at political reconciliation having failed, Karmal resigned in 1981 and was succeeded by Sultan Ali Keshtmand, who tried to continue the national reconciliation policy.

The war against the Soviet presence in Afghanistan was becoming more intense. I travelled to Jalalabad, on what was my last visit by road, because 1982 onwards road travel had become risky, with the Mujahideen forces having taken control of strategic passes.

As the war raged, Afghans started moving out of the countryside and into Pakistan. The numbers of refugee camps there increased every day. And the refugees, the able-bodied ones, became willing recruits in the fight against Soviet invaders.

I was now travelling all over Afghanistan by air. Many visiting foreign correspondents wondered how I managed that. Well, the trick was to take my crew to the nearest airport and just wait for whichever commercial flight was going anywhere. There were no scheduled flights.

When I landed in Herat, I travelled from the airport to the centre of the city in an armoured car, because the road from the airport was under Mujahideen control. The only way to commute was by armoured cars, provided by the Afghan Army. That was a clear indication that parts of Afghanistan were beginning to fall outside the control of the Afghan civilian government.

I also visited Balkh and found the place deserted. This city was a centre of civilization in the Middle Ages. The Afghans had advised me not to go there, but I took the risk anyway.

The war was beginning to take its toll on what were once bustling cities. In Pakistan, the CIA-led alliance went a step further. They began recruiting young boys from among the Afghan refugees and training them as the 'Taliban'. They also recruited from among the Pashtun population of the NWFP.

The Soviets and the Afghan Army began suffering heavy casualties as more well-trained elements from across the Pakistan border joined in the fighting. In many areas, it was suspected that the Pakistan Army itself was involved.

In the northern areas of Afghanistan, resistance to Soviet incursion was led by Ahmad Shah Massoud. He was an ethnic Tajik and did not seek help from Pakistan or its allies, the US and Saudi Arabia. He did not want Pakistan involved in Afghan affairs. In this, he had the complete loyalty of his people.

If there were genuine Afghans who fought the Soviets and other foreign forces, Massoud and his men were among those. He first ensured that his base in Panjshir was fully and securely under his control. Then, he started with guerrilla attacks on the Soviet forces. He took control of the strategic Salang Pass, which meant the control of supply lines to Kabul. The Russians were forced to seek truce with him every now and then. During these ceasefires, Massoud took the opportunity to strengthen his forces. When I first met him, I could see in him a true nationalist Afghan leader. All the areas in the north of the country, with Panjshir as its capital, were well-administered by Massoud's men.

Meanwhile, the war in Afghanistan was dragging on and years passed by. Regular units from the Pakistan Army, dressed as the Taliban, were now said to be involved in the fighting, since victory did not seem within grasp of the ragtag Mujahideen. In 1989, Najibullah took over control of the government in Kabul. The Soviet Union was now tired of Afghanistan and was running into trouble at home. The war had hit the Soviet economy and casualties among Soviet troops had been mounting each year, leading to civilian unrest in Russia.

The task that Najibullah undertook was to bring about national reconciliation among all sections of Afghan society. It was easy to talk about, but impossible to achieve. The Russians also wanted some kind of rapprochement to bring an end to the stalemate. In the north, Massoud had begun to create problems in neighbouring Soviet Tajikistan.

Unfortunately, Najibullah got no response from the Peshawar-based Afghan leaders like Gulubuddin Hekmatyar when he approached them. With America anxious to install Peshawar's Afghan mob in Kabul, it meant an opportunity for Pakistan to dominate the country.

Khan Abdul Ghaffar Khan, Frontier Gandhi, passed away in Peshawar on 20 January 1988. He had asked to be buried in Jalalabad and not in Pakistan. For him, Jalalabad was part of the great Pashtun land that extended from the Pakistani Pashtun areas.

On the day of the great Pashtun leader's burial, Afghanistan saw its first ceasefire—only for one day—so that over 200,000 mourners, who had travelled with the body from Peshawar and other tribal areas, could safely reach Jalalabad and return. They were all wearing red shirts, as had been decreed by Khan Abdul Gaffar Khan during the Indian freedom struggle. His followers were known as Red Shirts.

I arrived in Jalalabad in the middle of the night because the aircraft could land only in darkness. The hills around the airfield were controlled by the Taliban. For incoming aircraft, the runway light was switched on for a few seconds. I must commend those Soviet and Afghan pilots who operated these flights in such dangerous conditions.

On the next day, the great Frontier Gandhi was buried in the presence of the Afghan president, Najibullah, and a government delegation from India. Even as the funeral was underway, we heard the noise of a huge explosion. The Taliban had bombed a part of the mourners' procession and over forty were killed.

Back in Kabul, I called on President Najibullah. He now understood that the Soviet Union, under the leadership of Mikhail Gorbachev, wanted to pull out of Afghanistan, even though the war was far from over. But Najibullah's efforts at reconciliation had not received a positive response from either the United States or its allies.

Eager as he was for the withdrawal of Soviet troops from Afghanistan, Gorbachev was equally keen on building friendship with Washington and ending the Cold War. It's not easy to guess as to which of the two was his priority. But it became clear to me that Gorbachev's principal aim was to get out of Afghanistan and end the Cold War with the West, even if that left the Afghan government in serious trouble.

Thus it was agreed that the Soviet troops would begin their withdrawal on 15 May 1988 and complete it by mid-February 1989.

I covered the Soviet withdrawal from Jalalabad. The contingents moved towards Kabul by road. It was a perfect and orderly withdrawal, as had been guaranteed by the United States and its allies. When the Soviet troops had withdrawn from Jalalabad, the Taliban forces, assisted by Pakistani regulars in Mujahideen uniforms, launched a serious attack. When the battle ended, the Afghan Army had successfully repulsed Pakistan-backed attacks, inflicting heavy casualties.

That came as a shock to America and its allies. They could not take immediate advantage of the Soviet withdrawal. It was clear that the Afghan Army was in control and President Najibullah was now running the government in Kabul entirely on his own, albeit with the support of Ahmad Shah Massoud. Although Soviet aid to his government had ceased, other friendly countries, particularly the neighbouring Soviet Central Asian republics, gave him support, as did India. None of them wanted Afghanistan to fall under Islamic rule.

The United States, in the meantime, refused to recognize Najibullah, and Pakistan took the same stand. India, on the other hand, had given the Afghan government full recognition. The Afghan president even came to India on a state visit in 1988.

In Washington, D.C., I interviewed Robin Raphel, the US under secretary of state for South Asia. In the course of that interview, it became clear to me that the US was far too committed to Pakistan and the Taliban and was thus not going to recognize Kabul under any other dispensation. Raphel, who was also viciously anti-Indian, wanted all Indian aid to Kabul to cease.

By 1992, it became clear that Kabul was undergoing major changes. Massoud, who had single-handedly fought the Soviet forces in north Afghanistan and controlled the Salang Pass, now decided to quickly move into Kabul and take charge of the government to forestall the Pakistani-backed and Peshawar-based leaders, like Hekmatyar, from moving in, even though he was said to have signed an accord with Peshawar-based Afghans to avoid civil war in the country. Known as the Lion of Panjshir, Massoud arrived in Kabul with his great convoy to a huge welcome and took charge of the government there.

Massoud had tried to prevail upon the Peshawar-based Afghan leaders, especially Hekmatyar, to ensure a collective government,

but Hekmatyar, backed as he was by Pakistan, refused. As Massoud settled in Kabul, Nawaz Sharif, the then prime minister of Pakistan, suddenly decided to visit Kabul, to get Massoud to agree to let the Peshawar-based Mujahideen groups join his government. However, since Sharif had arrived without an invitation, Massoud refused to see him. A day later, a disappointed Sharif flew back to Islamabad. As his aircraft took off, a missile was fired at his plane, but the flares from his plane deflected the missile and he safely landed back in Islamabad.

Several Afghan warlords switched allegiances, including Abdul Rashid Dostum of Mazar-e-Sharif, who withdrew his troops from the Pakistan border. That single act made it easy for the Taliban and other forces to cross into Afghanistan. Thus began the movement of Taliban from Peshawar into Afghanistan.

In July 1992, when ANI and Visnews sent a large team of eight people, including a young woman, to Kabul, I decided to lead them. I was not going to expose them to serious danger, knowing the Afghan situation as I did. When we arrived in Kabul, it was a shock for me to see that the city had lost its morale. The Taliban and the Mujahideen were arriving in the outskirts of the city.

The journalists were putting up at the Intercontinental Hotel. There were large television news teams from the BBC and Independent Television News (ITN). ITN had managed to install a satellite uplink dish in the hotel. Visnews ought to have been given the permission for its use, but it was denied, despite the BBC protesting on my behalf.

ITN had no access to ANI or Visnews material. This one refusal to share uplink facilities meant I could only send my coverage from the Afghan TV station, which involved a dangerous dash across the city to reach the Kabul TV station. But ITN did not budge. Their attitude was thoroughly unprofessional to say the least. I had reported from several conflict zones with international media; we'd all cooperated with each other, though we were competitors. This was my first exposure to the changing face of conflict journalism.

The outskirts of Kabul, and even parts of the city, became scenes of aggressive fighting between the opposing forces. Yet every day

I had to drive through the city, in the middle of the battle, in a car hoisting a white flag, to send my material via satellite from the Afghan TV station. On three occasions I was stranded at the television station with no way back.

Luckily, the Indian ambassador lived opposite the TV station. This meant I could spend the night there. The ambassador, Vijay Nambiar, was very kind. On each of those three occasions he himself drove me back the next morning in his diplomatic car.

Kabul had still not quite fallen under alien control and Massoud was very much in charge. But the Mujahideen, Taliban and others now surrounded the city. It became increasingly dangerous for me to travel each evening to the Afghan TV station. But it had to be done!

One day, a young ANI journalist, Soumya, came back with an excellent tape of Taliban forces marching towards Kabul. I was really impressed by her coverage, for which she had to face great danger. Looking at the tape closely, I pointed out that what she had filmed were regular Pakistani soldiers in Taliban fatigues. 'See the way they are marching in military order,' I said. This was a big story, showing Peshawar-based elements getting closer to Kabul. The city was coming under siege.

Then, some so-called senior officers from the Taliban arrived at the Intercontinental Hotel. They went from room to room to see how we journalists were operating. I could clearly see that most of them were regular Pakistani officers. One even became friendly with me, soliciting my help in bargaining for a small Afghan carpet from the hotel shop!

A war-torn mess

I realized that it was now time to leave Kabul. The city was erupting in nightly battles. The sky would light up with the firing happening all around. Massoud was certainly not letting the Taliban forces come into the city. We booked our return flight— but it got cancelled due to the Kabul airport being rendered dysfunctional that day. I kept my fingers crossed, hoping the airport would reopen.

We were able to leave Kabul safely a couple of days later. That great, happy city was now a war-torn mess. The women of Kabul had begun either staying indoors or going out in hijab, fully covered. The modern and vibrant Afghanistan I knew was dying.

Once on the flight home, I thanked my young ANI and Reuters TV teams for the wonderful work they had done. They had been the eyes and ears of the world in Afghanistan. As a bonus, I told them to buy whatever they wanted from the duty-free shop in Delhi and that I would take care of the bills. But all they wanted was to get home, to a warm bath and home-cooked vegetarian food.

In April 1992, India succeeded in getting President Najibullah's family out of Afghanistan, but, for some reason Najibullah could not come with them. He was later killed by the Taliban in the most illegal, heinous and cruel manner after being pulled from the United Nations quarters in Kabul, where he had been given refuge.

As the Taliban took charge of the country, Afghanistan regressed almost into the Stone Age. It became the centre of what has come to be known as Islamic terrorism, with Osama bin Laden fuelling sectarian hatred. And the war continues.

Events have come full circle. The war in Afghanistan today is being fought by American rather than Russian forces. The United States and its allies now fight Al-Qaeda and other elements that they had themselves created to fight against the Soviets. Afghanistan has thus become a victim of the American Cold War against Russia and continues to suffer. America itself suffered the horrendous attacks on the World Trade Center in New York at the hands of the Taliban.

With the Taliban taking full control of Afghanistan, the Hindus and Sikhs who had lived in that country for generations left their lives behind and sought refuge in India and other parts of the world, from Germany to Canada.

India has been one country that has given solid and meaningful support to Afghanistan, and Indian aid continues to help rebuild the infrastructure of that country. As and when the sea port at Chabahar in Iran becomes fully functional under Indian management, Afghanistan will be rid of its dependence on Pakistan and the port of Karachi for its trade. At present, though, the story of Afghanistan is far from over. The war rumbles on. There have been many twists and turns to the tragedy that began on that day of April 1978 and continues to haunt Afghanistan forty years later.

14

Unstable Alliances

The general election of 1996 threw up a hung Parliament, despite the very successful term of the Narasimha Rao government from 1991 to 1996. His administration made a qualitative change to the way India was governed.

It was strange that in this election campaign the Congress did not use Manmohan Singh, who was the finance minister. The party was distancing itself from economic reforms, even though these had been so successful in changing the Indian economy and boosting growth.

When the election results were announced, the BJP emerged as the largest single party, and its leader, Atal Bihari Vajpayee, was invited by the president, Shankar Dayal Sharma, to form the government. Vajpayee was sworn in as the new prime minister on 16 May 1996. Sadly, his administration failed to draw support from any of the non-BJP parties. The government lasted until 27 May, when Vajpayee resigned, just before the confidence vote.

I was in the press lobby, and Atalji made a great speech, before telling the house that he was leaving for the president's house to resign. Thus, he foiled the attempts of those who wanted to bring him down in a vote to prove his majority, which he did not have.

Soon after, all the opposition parties began looking for an alternative. They were not willing to cooperate with the Congress.

The non-Congress, non-BJP parties were looking to run the government, but all of them put together could not muster a majority.

Since the nation could surely not afford to go to the polls again, the parties kept working for a solution. The leaders could not agree on anybody who was already a member of Parliament and came up with the name of H.D. Deve Gowda, who was then the chief minister of Karnataka.

Deve Gowda had been a Congress man once, and his single most important credential was that he had opposed the Emergency and was imprisoned in the process. After the Emergency, he had joined Congress (O), the faction opposed to Mrs Gandhi. He'd then become a member of the Janata Party and the president of its state wing. So he was a natural choice for all the non-Congress opposition parties. Deve Gowda came to Delhi and got himself elected to Parliament, thus maintaining the tradition that the prime minister of India should come from the lower house.

It really wasn't easy for him, being a state leader, but he gradually got established as prime minister. The conglomerate of other leaders thought, perhaps, that they could push him around, but, as I saw it, he was no pushover. He would argue and put forward his view on everything, determined not to run the prime ministership at their beck and call.

I remember how he came into conflict with his home minister, Indrajit Gupta, who was from the Communist Party of India. Gupta had issued a strongly worded statement against the Congress. And that did not go down well with Deve Gowda, since the Congress was supporting the government. If Gupta did not retract the statement, Deve Gowda told him, then he would himself do so as prime minister. He would not let this issue bring down his government.

The priority for Deve Gowda were the problems faced by farmers, and he devoted a lot of time to those. The fact that he focused on farmers' issues, I would say, was a significant and successful political ploy, because it became the prime focal point for all successive governments.

But Deve Gowda's real achievement was that he resolved the Farakka Barrage issue. I can say that because I was involved in covering this story for several years. India had built a barrage over the Ganga in Farakka, West Bengal, to hold the water and release it when necessary. Bangladesh complained that enough water was not being released and that this hurt the country's agriculture.

Bangladesh had inherited the problem from former East Pakistan. Even after the birth of Bangladesh, the government in New Delhi had never sat down with Bangladeshi leaders to find a sympathetic solution to this problem. But Deve Gowda did. (Another water dispute, though, often on Deve Gowda's mind—regarding the supply from the Kaveri, which runs through Karnataka and Tamil Nadu—lingers to this day.)

Deve Gowda undertook several tours abroad and, following in the footsteps of Narasimha Rao, went to Davos for the World Economic Forum in 1997. But he could not make much of an impact there. One of the problems with him was that he would go to sleep at any lengthy meeting. It was strange for me to witness this when covering a story. In Davos, most of the work was done by the large delegation of businessmen and finance ministry officials that Deve Gowda had taken along.

I accompanied the prime minister on his visit to Russia, from 24–26 March 1997. Again, this was a routine tour, really managed by his foreign minister, I.K. Gujral.

Deve Gowda always took as many members of his family as he could on such tours and attracted severe criticism over their expenses. But let's face it, India had come a long way from the time of Jawaharlal Nehru and Lal Bahadur Shastri, who always took scheduled commercial flights of Air India and diverted them to their chosen destinations. It was rare for them to use a special flight.

Deve Gowda's foreign policy was mainly handled by Gujral, whose efforts to improve India's relations with its neighbours came to be known as the Gujral Doctrine. This annoyed Deve Gowda. All through his term, Deve Gowda nursed a grudge that he was not accorded the respect or status that he deserved because he was not as

aggressive as most north Indian politicians. In his view, Gujral was
his foreign minister but the foreign policy was Deva Gowda's. But
this was a personal matter. Ego conflicts between Indian politicians
are common, especially with regard to the ownership of the foreign
policy. The media, too, did not hanker after interviews with Deve
Gowda. He was not cut out for TV.

Meanwhile, there was trouble in the Congress. Narasimha Rao
was still the Congress president and leader of opposition. There were
many in the Congress who wanted to pull Narasimha Rao down,
because he was trying to revive the party's traditional, organization-
level elections and to rebuild it from the ground up.

Sitaram Kesri, a maverick in my view, conspired against Rao.
It was said that Sonia Gandhi was also involved in the plot to do
away with Rao. Kesri was elected as Congress president, and he
made sure that Rao was removed from his posts of party president
and leader of opposition.

When Rao fell ill, Kesri came into conflict with the Deve Gowda
government directly. Perhaps Kesri had dreams of becoming the
prime minister himself. In any case, he tried to move a motion of
no-confidence against the Deve Gowda government. Yet again, the
Congress was playing dirty with a coalition government.

On 11 April 1997, Deve Gowda resigned, after an extremely
long speech in Parliament, refusing to see the office of the prime
minister of India degraded. While quitting, he warned Gujral not to
seek the support of the Congress to form the government. Gujral's
name had not yet been finalized, but Gowda had heard rumours that
there were moves to find an alternative to Gowda rather than go in
for elections.

Gujral makes a short appearance

The United Front coalition was not prepared to allow the Congress
to regain power. So the race began to find a new prime minister.
After several days of discussion, Gujral's name came up. He was
acceptable to the Congress because he had been very close to

Indira Gandhi, and even during the Emergency, when she moved him out of the information ministry, she did not sack him. When Gujral fell out with Sanjay Gandhi, she sent him to Moscow as an ambassador but maintained her friendship with him.

One can't forget the marathon meeting at the Andhra Pradesh Bhavan in Delhi, where deliberations continued for almost an entire day and no consensus emerged. It was the hardcore Marxist Harkishan Singh Surjeet who played kingmaker, along with Jyoti Basu, to install Gujral as prime minister. Like Sharad Pawar, Jyoti Babu was another person in Indian politics who had all the goodwill and qualifications to be prime minister, but fate had other things in store for them.

Gujral became the prime minister of India on 21 April 1997. But again, his term of office was short-lived. He sought election from Jalandhar, in keeping with that MP-to-PM tradition. But his government ran into problems with the Congress.

Within a few months, a report by the one-man commission of Justice J.S. Verma of the Supreme Court, appointed to inquire into the assassination of Rajiv Gandhi, was made public. It said that the political party Dravida Munnetra Kazhagam (DMK), through its support of the LTTE, was partly responsible for the assassination. DMK was part of the United Front, and the Congress wanted it expelled. When the United Front refused to do that, the result was the fall of the Gujral government.

Gujral could have sacrificed the DMK, but he was a man known for his loyalty, which he was not willing to compromise on. The Congress was determined to withdraw its support to him, and thus it pulled down the Gujral government, just as it had earlier pulled down the Deve Gowda government.

Fragile governments force polls

India was thus pushed into fresh elections. A second major attempt at a coalition government had failed because the national party—the Congress in both these cases—wanted to control the government rather than allow the coalition to function with its own agenda.

Gujral's elevation had been a matter of great joy for me in many ways. A refugee from west Punjab who'd come to India during Partition had become the prime minster. Gujral Sahab was also a true friend of the media. He had many friends he had helped over the course of his life.

He was amazed at how, in spite of all the restrictions on the import of equipment and so on, I had managed to use Indian engineers in Bombay to make the processing machines for television film and to install the necessary facilities in Delhi with my own resources, without going to the government or to the banks for finance.

I used to go to his house for early-morning walks. The prime minister's residence, at 7 Race Course Road (now Lok Kalyan Marg) in Delhi, has a fantastic walking track, which was built by Rajiv Gandhi. It was always fun to have that half-hour walk, sometimes a little more, and then take morning tea with him before returning home. We discussed many things, but they will always remain between the two of us.

One day, Gujral Sahab asked me why he shouldn't formally appoint me as his media adviser. I told him that this would not help anyone, that half my journalistic fraternity would oppose me because Indian egos are too big. And anyway, it was never wise to appoint an active media person to be media adviser. I could not give up what I was doing, so I politely turned the offer down.

Gujral would have been a very successful prime minister, but he came up short in the same way as Chandra Shekhar. Chandra Shekhar was a great leader. But can you be the prime minister with only sixty-four seats in Parliament? It was the same story with Gujral. How could he be the prime minister if he relied on the Congress party's support? To be a successful prime minister, you really have to be on your own and win the nation's confidence with your own party gaining majority in the polls.

The passing of a gentle colossus

The death of Inder Kumar Gujral was no small event, especially in the context of the turbulent developments in post-Independence India.

He came from Punjab, which bore the brunt of Partition's violence. Human history has rarely witnessed such a mass exodus of people, such cruel abuse of children and women who were abducted and raped. Punjab and the North-West Frontier Province had 'carried the cross' for India's freedom. In the pantheon of those reaching the most important positions in the nation after opting to make the new India their home, Gujral deserves a very high place.

He was from a political family. His father had thought they could perhaps stay on in what had become Pakistan. But that was not to be. Soon, they migrated and joined the millions whom the Hindi-speaking rulers described as *sharnaarthis* (refugees), the word Punjabis hated most; they urged people to stop using that word, with persistent arguments, which at times turned violent. Rightfully, the Punjabis and Hindu Pathans claimed that India was their land, for which they had to sacrifice everything they owned, leaving it behind in Pakistan. Other than Jawaharlal Nehru, there were few among the heartland Hindi-speaking rulers who understood the pain that they felt. Hard-working and easy settlers wherever they went, the Punjabis and NWFP migrants soon settled down and made homes in this new land.

The Gujral family, too, started life afresh. Inder Kumar even went to England to seek a new beginning. But then, the Indian in him brought him back to the land he loved, and he began to make his way into the intellectual and political circles of the national capital.

For a long time in the Nehru era, India had been dominated by politicians from the Hindi belt. After all, they sent the maximum number of members to Parliament with the ruling party. Uttar Pradesh alone sent eighty MPs.

Until 1950, Uttar Pradesh was called the United Provinces. The Hindi-loving people, who referred to it as UP, said they wanted to retain the abbreviation. And so, they decided to call it Uttar Pradesh, though it is not the northern-most state of India. (Jammu and Kashmir is.) With their caste considerations and vote-bank politics, the rulers from the Hindi belt in the post-Nehru era could not comprehend the Punjabi psyche. The Punjabis, too, had a problem understanding the politics of UP and began calling it 'Ulta Pradesh'.

In New Delhi, Inder Kumar Gujral had steadily made his way into political life. A man who used to have encounters with intellectuals at the famous India Coffee House became a part of what came to be known as the 'kitchen cabinet' around Indira Gandhi. As information minister, he was a great friend of the media and truly laid the foundations of what is today a vibrant, independent TV industry in north India. I was privileged to participate in that drive with his full and unstinting support.

During the Emergency and all that followed it, the myopic political manipulations of Congress leaders in the politics of Punjab led to one crisis after another, culminating in Jarnail Singh Bhindranwale's occupation of the Golden Temple. Then came the bloody and uncalled-for Operation Blue Star—yet another huge tragedy for India, followed by the 1984 riots in Delhi and elsewhere.

The political nitwits from UP and other BIMARU (the economically backward Bihar, Madhya Pradesh, Rajasthan and Uttar Pradesh) states, who controlled Congress, hardly realized the Himalayan blunders they made. In such times, Gujral worked silently yet earnestly among the Punjabis. He applied the much-needed balm on the hurt feelings of the Hindus and Sikhs. He emerged as a unifying factor and a leader whom the Punjabis, be it the Akalis or even the diehard Arya Samajis (Hindus), were ready to trust.

He saw to it that historic bonds uniting the Hindus and Sikhs of Punjab remained intact. He worked quietly but persistently on the Rajiv–Longowal accord, which was meant to bring peace to Punjab following the turbulence of the 1984 anti-Sikh riots.

A true, gentle colossus had emerged among the Punjabis. Destiny had made him the prime minister of India. He could not, however, bring himself to take part in any machinations that lowered the dignity of that high office.

Gujral made attempts at peace with Pakistan leveraging his close relations with Nawaz Sharif, then the leader of Pakistan's Punjab, but it was not to be. Still, he left a legacy that continues to call upon the leaders on both sides of the divide to come to terms with reality and live in peace.

With his death, on 30 November 2012, India lost a great man—someone who made sure that the nation remained united and that Punjab, the sword arm of India, stayed strong and at peace.

15

Vajpayee Ascends

Everyone says Atal Bihari Vajpayee became prime minster too late in life, that he should have had one more term. But actually, he held the office of PM thrice: once for thirteen days, once for thirteen months, and then for a full term.

I had personally known Atalji since his days as a Jana Sangh leader. I always admired his poetry and loved his speeches. He was a master public orator. He was also a very gracious and kind person. I remember one small incident. During the 1996 elections, the BJP could not find a studio to record Atalji's campaign speech. So Atalji himself found the solution. He asked, 'Has anyone checked with my friend Prem Prakash? His company might have a studio.'

We did not have a formal studio, but our news room doubled up as a studio when required. Atalji came to the studio in Vandana Building at Delhi's Tolstoy Marg and then up to the sixth floor where the ANI office was located. Hundreds of people who worked in various offices in the building came to the lobby to get a glimpse of him. Many stood outside our office. Such was his popularity. He took several takes with the teleprompter. He wasn't comfortable at all talking to the camera, but he recorded his broadcast nevertheless. When the election results were announced, Vajpayee emerged as leader of the largest single party. But his government lasted less than two weeks.

His second term in power was prompted by the failure of the two predecessor governments, of Deve Gowda and I.K. Gujral, to last the full term. And so India held another general election in February 1998. On 19 March, Vajpayee was sworn in as prime minister. The government was part of a coalition of fourteen parties, known as the NDA (National Democratic Alliance), which had the support of the All India Anna Dravida Munnetra Kazhagam, the Tamil Nadu party led by J. Jayalalithaa. So an NDA government took charge at the centre, with Vajpayee firmly in place as prime minister.

Diplomatic offensive

Atalji was well aware that P.V. Narasimha Rao had wanted to conduct a nuclear test. Nuclear scientists were only awaiting a signal from the prime minister. So, in May that year, Atalji went ahead with the nuclear programme. Within months of his taking charge, India had conducted several underground tests, including one on a thermal nuclear device. Soon after, ANI and Visnews covered the visit of the prime minister to Pokhran, the site of the nuclear test. The foreign media was extremely keen, for almost a year, on receiving any footage shot at the site—not just of the day of the PM's visit but of anything else from the ground; anything that could prove their preconceived belief that the radiation had caused damage to the locals. Unfortunately for them and fortunately for India, nothing of that sort had happened.

There was extreme enthusiasm among the people of India that the country had shown the courage and backed its nuclear scientists in carrying out the tests. The country now had a proper nuclear deterrent. But worldwide, India faced diplomatic isolation. Advisories were issued by several countries urging their citizens not to visit India.

India went on a diplomatic offensive. The world had to be brought around, and India used all its stored-up goodwill with many countries to that end. France was one of the countries that endorsed India's nuclear status. The United States, on the other hand, imposed sanctions against India. Though a soft-spoken person with a poet's disposition, Atalji was a man of steel when it came to taking tough decisions. The fact is that by May 1998, despite US sanctions, India had established itself as a nuclear power.

In July 1998, I had the occasion to cover the SAARC summit in Colombo, Sri Lanka. There, Atalji made contact with his Pakistani counterpart, Nawaz Sharif, and explored the possibility of improving relations between India and Pakistan. He even travelled to Lahore by bus in February 1999, marking the opening of the Lahore–Delhi bus service. It has long been suspected that the then Pakistan Army chief, General Pervez Musharraf, used Atalji's visit as a cover to continue moving his forces into Kargil. He allegedly kept Nawaz Sharif in the dark about troops having already been deployed. The deniability was a fig leaf given to Sharif, who could welcome Vajpayee to Lahore. That was, perhaps, the reason for Musharraf's absence when Atalji went to Lahore.

In May 1999, it was revealed that Pakistani forces had infiltrated and captured mountain peaks in the Kargil area, thus endangering the crucial road to Ladakh, vital for the Indian Army. Atalji gave the Indian Army clear orders—to engage the enemy.

It was during the Kargil War that the famous Bofors guns went into action. The controversy around the purchase of these guns had caused the defeat of Rajiv Gandhi. The guns, reinforced by laser-guided bombs obtained from Israel, were used to attack the hilltop positions occupied by Pakistan and lived up to their formidable reputation, causing heavy damage to the Pakistani positions.

Pakistan's infiltration and capture of the Kargil hilltop positions was no small achievement. They had used their Northern Light Infantry to lead the invasion and had expected to inflict heavy casualties on the Indian Army. But what actually happened was that the Pakistani forces were vanquished and repulsed.

All over India, people were fully behind Atalji. He inspired the country to fight the enemy. Each Indian soldier who died was given a funeral in his hometown with full military honours; these funerals were attended by thousands. The government also declared a much higher compensation for the families of soldiers who died in action.

In a letter to the American president Bill Clinton, Vajpayee made it clear that if Pakistan did not withdraw from Indian territory, India would throw them out anyway. Meanwhile, concerted attacks by the Indian Army and Air Force inflicted heavy damage on Pakistani-held positions, cutting their supply lines.

Prime Minister Vajpayee visited many positions on the front line amid reports that in areas along the border, villagers were beginning to flee, fearing a full-scale war. By the third week of June, Indian troops captured the strategic 'Tiger Hill' in Kargil. Indian operations had inflicted heavy casualties; Pakistan was said to have lost 4,000–5,000 men, including non-state actors, in this adventure.

Pakistan's prime minister, Nawaz Sharif, flew to Washington to seek American help in relieving the trapped Pakistan Army. He failed. At the same time, India set a deadline of 16 July for Pakistan to vacate the Kargil area.

Finding the United States unwilling to help in any way, Sharif told his generals to leave the occupied areas without delay. This clearly was not to the liking of Pakistan Army's command, but the alternative being a war between the two countries, the Pakistanis began to withdraw. The only assurance India gave was that it would not fire on retreating Pakistani soldiers.

By the end of July, India had achieved a huge victory in a strategically important area which had once seemed lost. Pakistan now had to endure anti-American protests throughout the country, despite the fact that the United States had long been an ally of Pakistan.

Another general election

The Vajpayee government relied heavily on Jayalalithaa's AIADMK, but she withdrew her support in May 1999. With this, the BJP was forced into another general election, with Vajpayee as head of a caretaker government. That government lasted just thirteen months.

Following a hectic campaign, Vajpayee returned to office in October 1999. His alliance came out of that election with a clear majority—over 300 seats. On 10 October 1999, Atalji took charge of the country for the third and last time. It was to prove a very active term in office. Atalji wanted to ensure maximum development of the country. In his address to the nation he stressed two things: economic reform and the issue of terrorism. One of his major projects was the construction of a new set of highways, connecting India from north to south and from east to west—the Golden Quadrilateral.

But just as the government was settling down after the elections, an Indian Airlines flight from Kathmandu to Delhi, IC 814, was hijacked by terrorists. The hijackers didn't allow the pilots to land in Delhi. So the plane flew on to Amritsar, where the pilot managed to land, persuading the hijackers by citing fuel shortage.

Commandos from Delhi were already on their way to Amritsar when the hijackers forced the pilot to take the plane from there to Lahore. At first, the airport authorities in Lahore denied the hijacked plane permission to land and were said to have switched off the runway lights, despite the risk that if the pilots had tried landing in the dark, the plane could have crashed. Eventually, however, the authorities switched on the lights and allowed the plane to land.

At Lahore, after the plane was refuelled, the hijackers forced the pilots to fly to Dubai, where the authorities refused India's offer to send in Indian commandos. In Dubai, twenty-seven hostages, including women and children, were released. The dead body of a young passenger—a newly married man named Rupin Katyal, who was returning with his wife from Kathmandu after their honeymoon and was killed by the hijackers—was also taken off the plane. The aircraft then left Dubai and finally landed in Kandahar, Afghanistan.

There has been a lot of confusion as to what happened in Amritsar. The simple fact is that no rescue operation took place in Amritsar when an opportunity presented itself. Why Punjab Police commandos didn't storm the plane is something that remains to be answered. Commandos from Delhi were still on their way to Amritsar when the hijackers forced the pilots to take off for Lahore.

Pressure mounted on the Vajpayee government, with sudden protests at India Gate, ostensibly by the family members of the hostages, demanding that the government give in to the demands of the terrorists. TV channels, in my opinion, irresponsibly ran the footage of wailing family members. The government was left with no wiggle room, and there was no international pressure on Pakistan or Afghanistan to release the hostages. With the public demanding that the authorities get the passengers safely back to India, the Vajpayee government was forced to agree to the hijackers' terms, one of which was the release of the dreaded terrorist Maulana Masood Azhar, who was, at that point, in an Indian prison. The man continues to harass India to date.

Vajpayee also came in for severe criticism for sending his foreign minister, Jaswant Singh, all the way to Kandahar to hand over the released terrorists to the hijackers. This remains a bit of a dark shadow over that government. But was there any possibility of refusing the hijackers' demands? Initially, the government had rejected the hijackers' terms. But public pressure, particularly after the killing of Rupin Katyal, was such that the government was forced, after a seven-day stand-off, to give in.

International relations

The first high-profile visit to India of a foreign dignitary during the Vajpayee era was that of President Bill Clinton, in March 2000. The United States took notice of a stable government in Delhi, as the Vajpayee administration had initiated a series of reforms that opened up the Indian economy in many ways. Foreign companies were allowed major shareholding in many sectors, while in some they could hold even 100 per cent equity.

Travelling in the media contingent with Atalji, as I did, was an interesting experience every time. He was not given to rushing through his international tours. He wanted, wherever he went, to develop good relations with the leaders as well as to get to know the people.

One visit that I remember with great fondness was to Indonesia and the island of Bali in October 2003. At one point, in Bali, Atalji sat on a hilltop, watching the Indian Ocean merge with the Pacific. He asked me especially to sit by his side and watch the great *sangam* of the two oceans. I understood then that the poet in him was very much alive.

The other thing I remember was Atalji's love of seafood. In January 2001, we were in Hanoi, where we were invited to a fantastic banquet organized by the Vietnamese authorities. Among the dishes on offer was a gigantic lobster, the likes of which I had never seen. Atalji enjoyed it thoroughly. As we walked back after the banquet, he asked me if I had liked the lobster. I said it was the best I ever had. I asked him if he enjoyed it too, and he replied, 'Yes, of course.'

Atalji had his own way of relating with other world leaders. In China, he was completely at ease and never allowed his hosts to feel any pressure in dealing with the very serious issues between the two nations. Despite the ongoing border disputes, the two countries moved towards developing closer economic ties. These continue to grow every year.

Agra summit

On 12 October 1999, General Pervez Musharraf, still smarting from his failed Kargil adventure and holding Nawaz Sharif responsible for it, overthrew Sharif's government in a coup d'état. Musharraf was also making overtures to India to settle the Kashmir problem, seeking official talks with Vajpayee. The historic two-day summit was held in Agra from 14–16 July 2001. I was there to cover it, and ANI had installed its own satellite dish, in cooperation with British Telecom, to transmit the news globally from Agra.

There were several meetings between the two leaders, who discussed various issues like Kashmir and cross-border terrorism. However, they slipped into a deadlock after a point. General Musharraf invited a select group of journalists for a breakfast meeting—I was among them. The general explained his position, and his stand seemed unyielding to my mind. It was one of the several games of brinksmanship that Pakistan has played at such talks.

But Atalji was not the kind of leader who could be pressured in this way. Musharraf threatened to call off the talks and return home, even cancelling his planned visit to the Ajmer Sharif Dargah. Atalji's reply was polite but firm. How could he decide for the president of Pakistan, he asked and said that if Musharraf wanted to leave, it would have to be his own decision. Musharraf departed for Islamabad late that night.

Terror at Parliament

I was in Delhi on that cold December day in 2001 when Parliament House was attacked by a group of terrorists. All credit for resisting and warding off the attack goes to the security personnel there. They managed to seal the building so that none of the attackers could break in. Among those who died was one of ANI's cameramen. He was critically injured while covering the attack and later succumbed to his injuries.

In an immediate response to the assault on Parliament, Vajpayee ordered a complete mobilization of the Indian Army along the borders of Pakistan, as though in preparation for war. In due course, this storm passed, but the army remained in a state of full alert along the borders for several months.

The Godhra blot

A most tragic event, and a very difficult one to come to terms with, occurred in 2002, during Vajpayee's term, when a train carrying Hindu pilgrims returning from Ayodhya was burnt down in Godhra, resulting in not only the deaths of fifty-nine people who were on the train but very serious Hindi–Muslim riots breaking out in Gujarat. More than a thousand died and thousands were injured in these riots.

The prime minister was unhappy with the way the state government had tried to deal with the riots. Atalji expected Gujarat's chief minister, Narendra Modi, to resign for his failure to curb the riots. He referred to this in his own way, by quoting Raj Dharma, the righteous duty of the ruler. However, Modi maintained that he had taken all necessary steps to curb the violence.

Growth story

What impressed me most about Atalji was that in spite of all the terrible situations he faced—like Kargil, the IC 814 hijacking, the attack on Parliament—he pushed ahead with the necessary economic reforms that really helped the growth of business and industry in India.

What really should have been done by Manmohan Singh and Narasimha Rao was done very effectively by Vajpayee. Under him, India's highways system grew along with the rest of the economy. Economic growth and the inflow of large amounts of foreign direct investment helped India build substantial reserves for the first time since Independence.

There were even demands that the rupee be made a convertible currency. That never happened, but travel to foreign countries and the release of foreign exchange for such travels became much easier as the economy grew.

This economic success, close to the end of Vajpayee's term in office, encouraged his deputy, L.K. Advani, and another important minster, Pramod Mahajan, to call for early elections, since the government was winning widespread approval. I am quite sure Atalji was not in favour of advancing the elections, but then, being the team player that he was, he agreed.

For that 2004 election campaign, Advani and his team, which included Mahajan, invented the slogan 'India Shining'. It was not a good idea, and it backfired on the government. True, millions of people had improved their lot during Vajpayee's term. Bicycle-riders now rode scooters, but they still considered themselves deprived and poor in many ways. An Indian middle class was still emerging but had not yet arrived.

When the elections were announced, most political pundits expected the NDA, led by the BJP, to do well. But the 'India Shining' slogan hit the coalition hard. Vajpayee's party was defeated. Congress emerged as the largest single party, with 145 seats as against 138 of the BJP. The NDA was not invited to form the government as the Congress managed to ally itself with other parties to get a majority. Manmohan Singh was invited by Congress party's president, Sonia Gandhi, to become the next prime minister.

Singh was not a member of the Lok Sabha, nor did he try to become one after his nomination. He was the first Indian prime minister to come, as he did, from the upper house of Parliament, the Rajya Sabha, breaking the convention that had been followed since Independence of Lok Sabha members becoming prime ministers.

As for Vajpayee, he moved into the sunset of his career after this defeat.

BJP pays dearly for the swagger

The year 2004 was a disastrous one for the BJP in terms of electoral performance. Going into the elections six months ahead of the due date, overconfident in the good work done by the Vajpayee government, the BJP slipped and tumbled before the post.

Without doubt, the country was well-embarked on the road to economic development by that time. Massive infrastructure projects were underway. Vajpayee's Golden Quadrilateral highways project was well-advanced. As Vajpayee's infrastructure projects moved ahead, they helped the Manmohan Singh government prosper in its first three years.

All in all, the Vajpayee government could claim an excellent record of progress in economic growth. From here on, development of the country became the prime objective of the governments that followed.

16

Manmohan Singh and Narendra Modi

I have had only a ringside view of these two prime ministers, as I'd left active field journalism by the time Dr Manmohan Singh took over as the thirteenth prime minister of India in 2004. I played an advisory role in ANI and looked on with keen interest as the agency I had dreamt of and nurtured with love and affection expanded and became the very best in the country. My son and his family were at the driver's seat, and I couldn't have hoped for a better transition.

As a Punjabi, I felt a sense of pride in 2004 that a Punjabi—that too a migrant from west Punjab, like my family members—had become the prime minister of this great country. The earlier one being I.K. Gujral, and I knew Gujral Sahab well. As for Dr Singh, though I didn't really know him, I was aware that many of his experiences were similar to those of the people from my family—who'd left home and hearth to make their lives in a city that resented them initially as interlopers and then embraced them and allowed them to prosper.

My early interactions with Dr Singh happened when P.V. Narasimha Rao was the prime minister and I would visit my friend Ramamohan Rao in the South Block. Dr Singh was the antithesis of the Punjabi stereotype. He was soft-spoken, mild-mannered and always talked to me in English, even though he knew I was a Punjabi and I did try speaking to him in our native tongue.

I knew of some Punjabi journalists in Delhi who claimed to be close to Dr Singh, but I had also heard that Dr Singh was a very private person who hardly had any friends. His polite and courteous manner was deliberately mistaken as friendship by pushy journalists.

Centre cannot hold

Dr Singh did not contest the Lok Sabha elections after he became prime minister. I have always maintained that he should have done so. He set a bad precedent and destroyed a convention that holds that the prime minister of a parliamentary democracy should come from the lower house, duly elected by his own constituents.

I am told that he never tried his luck with the lower house after getting his fingers burnt in his earlier attempt, when he contested from the South Delhi constituency in the 1999 Lok Sabha polls. However, after reading Sanjaya Baru's book *The Accidental Prime Minister*, it seems to me that Dr Singh's decision not to contest in his second term might not have been totally his own. Dr Singh's campaign in 1999 was totally lacklustre; even the party workers were sullen over the Congress's decision to field a non-politician from the constituency. But Dr Singh should have gained the confidence in later years and insisted on fighting an election to the lower house of Parliament.

Still, Dr Singh is the only Congress prime minister from outside the Nehru–Gandhi family to have completed two full successive terms after Nehru. The economic liberalization of 1991, which he brought into effect as the finance minister under Narasimha Rao, was his lasting contribution to the country. He encouraged the same growth-oriented approach in his first term as prime minister, with the economy touching 8 per cent growth rate and the Indo–US nuclear deal confirmed. Dr Singh was always under enormous political pressure, and it is to his credit that he withstood it with courage. If he was not a politician of calibre, he would not have been able to manage the many bruised egos in his cabinet. Many of his colleagues had more administrative experience than Dr Singh and felt that Mrs Gandhi should have picked one of them rather than him. But whether it was the fear of incurring the wrath of Sonia Gandhi or the mistrust of each other, none of the disgruntled ministers tried to overthrow Dr Singh's government.

Dr Singh had few interactions with the media. He held a couple of press conferences at Vigyan Bhavan in Delhi over his two terms, taking several questions and answering them succinctly. His deadpan manner of delivery inspired many jokes. But his PMO never came down with a heavy hand on columnists and journalists who made fun of him. But then again, it's not as if Dr Singh's PMO was powerful. There was a second power centre: Sonia Gandhi, who wielded as much political power as the PM, if not more.

She kept the flock in check and left the day-to-day running of the government to Dr Singh. But it was she who had the veto power in the party and in the government. This dual power centre shadowed Dr Singh throughout the ten long years of his two terms. Oddly enough, the media seemed to be complicit in this unconstitutional arrangement. There were few articles critical of Sonia's influence on governance; many, in fact, welcomed the working relationship that had apparently evolved between the party president and the prime minister.

Highs and lows

The crowning glory of Dr Singh's first term would have to be the nuclear deal signed between India and the United States of America in 2005, ending India's nuclear apartheid. Dr Singh risked his government when the left parties, which were against the deal, withdrew support. Sonia Gandhi, too, was sceptical. But Dr Singh was ready to sacrifice his prime ministership if it came to that. He is reported to have said that the government had made an international commitment and there was no question of withdrawing from it. The Congress had to cobble together support from the Samajwadi Party and the Bahujan Samaj Party to save its government in the trust vote.

The Civil Nuclear Agreement transformed the nature of India's relationship with the US to one of partnership. There have been bumps on the road, but the progress has been continuous.

Dr Singh's unfulfilled desire to visit Pakistan as prime minister, for improving relations with the neighbouring country, will be a regret for him, I am sure. Every prime minister thinks he or she is the person who will resolve this issue, and every prime minister realizes somewhere towards the end of his or her term that it is a near impossibility.

Dr Singh's adventurous attempt to reset India–Pakistan ties, at the fifteenth summit of the Non-Aligned Movement, held in Sharm El Sheikh, Egypt, in 2009, will go down in history as yet another instance of the Indian leadership naively walking into Pakistan's trap, similar to Vajpayee's Lahore bus yatra in February 1999 or Modi's surprise stopover at Nawaz Sharif's home in Lahore in December 2015. Many leaders mistakenly presume that their personalities override the complexities of geopolitics.

Dr Singh's second term should have been a breeze. Instead, he wasted it by turning a blind eye to the scams of his colleagues. He had won his party a second term, yet Sonia Gandhi took the credit for that. The 'grand old men' of the party would not—and still don't—allow a non-Nehru–Gandhi family person to ever become larger than someone from the dynasty. The grooming of Rahul Gandhi had begun in right earnest, but the young scion was content to bask in Dr Singh's shadow.

The term was overshadowed by the coal scam, the 2G spectrum scam, the Agusta–Westland scam, the Commonwealth Games scam, the cash-for-votes scam, the Adarsh Housing Society scam, the Scorpene deal scam, the Satyam scam and several scams related to the Indian Premier League. (Most of the probes are still underway.) The perception took hold that Dr Singh was not in control of his government. The body blow to the economy and governance was something the UPA (United Progressive Alliance) was unable to recover from.

It remains a bad memory for me that when questions about corruption were raised by his coalition partners, Manmohan Singh simply declared that he had to observe coalition dharma! Did this dharma mean freedom for some coalition partners to indulge in corruption?

The Modi years

There have been questions raised over the quality of Indian data when it comes to gauging the economy. That makes comparative studies between the terms of different prime ministers that much harder. It would also be unfair if I were to compare ten years of Dr Singh to five years of Narendra Modi.

Modi came to power with the promise of ridding the country of corruption. He was a protégé of L.K Advani but had carved a niche for himself as an able administrator as chief minister of Gujarat. He had never been a member of Parliament, so many thought that he would not be familiar with parliamentary politics or foreign policy. But he threw a googly as soon as he arrived in Delhi to take oath of office. He invited leaders of the neighbouring countries for his swearing-in ceremony.

The country's economy was doing well a couple of years into his first term. But in November 2016, the Modi government's demonetization policy hit the economy real hard. While the reasons for it might have been noble, the effects of demonetization were near-catastrophic. The unorganized sector has still not recovered from that shock. Only 0.7 per cent of demonetized currency notes were destroyed in the exercise, whereas the finance ministry had expected to recover a lot more. The government kept shifting the goalposts, at a loss to explain why they had thought it prudent to push India towards a cashless economy when the country was ill-prepared for it. Neither the Reserve Bank of India nor the currency printing press was ready with new currency notes to replace the sheer volume of the older ones. To add to that, the poor implementation of the GST regime was yet another setback for the economy.

But despite having suffered enormous hardships, people forgave Modi in 2019, giving the BJP a resounding vote of confidence and electing the party to power with a thumping majority for its second term. Many have opined that it was the 2019 Balakot airstrike by the Indian Air Force, after the Pulwama terror attack, that changed the BJP's fortunes.

When Pakistan returned the captured wing commander, Abhinandan Varthaman, it was seen as a victory of sorts by Indians, with many thinking that Pakistan had been pressured by the Americans to release the Indian pilot. This made me look back at so many similar stories I have covered, of POWs returning home. The return of captured soldiers can either be seen as a sorrowful event or a victory of geopolitical might. The BJP managed to make it seem like the latter. The media spun the narrative of a victorious soldier coming home after teaching a lesson to the enemy. Opposition leaders who asked for proof of the attacks were labelled as cruel and anti-national for doubting the word of the armed forces.

The sheer energy of the BJP in election campaigns is something I have not seen in any other political party. I have covered elections right from the 1950s, including innumerable rallies of political giants—the likes of Nehru, Indira, JP and Vajpayee—but never have I seen the enterprise and enthusiasm of Modi and the BJP in any other leader and party. The BJP loves elections, loves crowds, has a well-oiled machinery and knows exactly which buttons to press. The messaging changes depending on the audience and yet, keeping in mind that television channels are broadcasting live, the message is always linked to the national perspective too.

Modi launched several projects to improve the lives of Indians in his first term. Among the most noteworthy ones is the Swachh Bharat Mission. In 2014, Modi picked up a broom and symbolically swept a street, tagging people on social media and asking them to do the same. Soon, celebrities and professionals followed suit. Making your surroundings clean and hygienic was to become a national mission, with huge outlays and several thousands of experts working round the clock across the country. As part of this project, several chief ministers launched campaigns to make their states 'open defecation free'. Swachh Bharat Mission is probably one of the most ambitious nation-wide projects launched by a prime minister in recent history with a view to giving dignity to the poor and deprived.

Among the other significant projects initiated by Modi are the Pradhan Mantri Jan-Dhan Yojana, which seeks to bring millions of Indians into the formal economy, and the Ujjwala Yojana, aimed at giving LPG connections to households under the poverty line. As many of us who worked for foreign networks knew, the standard image expected out of Indian cameramen was an Indian rural scene depicting women at the chulha or carrying pitchers of water on their heads. It used to annoy me no end, and I rebelled against this kind of colonial stereotyping. I'm hoping that it will soon be completely extinct.

Ayushman Bharat and Startup India are two more national projects that are admirable in their scope and would hopefully bring affordable healthcare and encourage entrepreneurship in the country.

The second term of Modi began with a bang, marked by the abrogation of Article 370 and conversion of Jammu and Kashmir, and Ladakh into two union territories. Civil liberties were suspended for a good part of a year in the centrally governed union territories after the August 2019 decision. While the situation in Kashmir has largely been peaceful, there has been some blowback from international quarters. Pakistan is naturally outraged, even though it has nothing to do with the matter, which is an exclusively Indian issue. Abrogation of this temporary article had been pending almost since the day it was adopted. Finally, the Modi government did it, bringing J&K on a par with other Indian states.

The scrapping of triple talaq and the Supreme Court's decision on the construction of Ram temple in Ayodhya gave another shot in the arm to the BJP.

As the first year of his second five-year term was drawing to a close, Modi had to grapple with protests against the government's decision to implement the controversial Citizenship Amendment Act, as well as struggle with an economy that refuses to pick up pace.

As far as the citizenship law is concerned, I see nothing wrong with it. But I am at a loss to understand why the government didn't educate or inform the people of its true import.

It is sad to see the manner in which the ruling party and the opposition fail to come together even on issues of national importance. The language used against the PM is sometimes terrible. This trend started during Manmohan Singh's term and has taken on its worst form against Modi today. It certainly doesn't behove a parliamentary democracy.

There is a TINA (there-is-no-alternative) factor associated with Modi, which even most of his detractors accept. They say everywhere they go, people seem disappointed with the BJP government and with the dismal state of the economy but have little or no expectations from the leaders of any of the other political parties.

A double crisis

The year 2020 has been one of unprecedented difficulties for India and the world. The COVID pandemic, which began from Wuhan in China and spread around the globe, has resulted in hundreds of thousands dead and millions infected. It has dealt a body blow to economies around the world.

India under Modi was one of the first to impose a very strict lockdown to deal with the pandemic. India, being a developing nation with a huge population of 1.3 billion, was faced with a challenge like none other. We had neither the expertise nor the resources to cope with a medical emergency like a pandemic of this nature. However, the Cassandras who had predicted that India would have a million-plus death toll in months have had to rework their numbers. The media reports changed to wonder why the death toll was low! The government got its share of bouquets and brickbats over its handling of the crisis.

Like a billion other Indians, I too observed all the rules and regulations imposed by the government during the COVID period. It gave me time to reassess decisions I have made in my life. Introspection is a great thing, but many of us do not have the luxury of time to do it. COVID quarantine forced it upon us. I spent the time reading and watching dozens of films and documentaries on Netflix.

A new crisis was tacked on to our fight against the pandemic when China decided to breach our borders. They entered the northeast part of India in Ladakh and forcefully occupied land that did not belong to them. For the first time in forty years there were casualties on the India–China border. At the time of going to press, Chinese soldiers have still not returned to their original positions. Efforts are on to resolve the issue diplomatically and politically.

Modi's critics in the country launched sharp attacks on the prime minister for his handling of the pandemic and of China. They blamed him for being naive in trusting President Xi Jinping in the past and for misleading the country on the nature of intrusions by Chinese troops. In regard to the pandemic, the accusation was that the lockdown was too sudden and too inhuman. But despite these two monumental events, Modi's popularity remains undented. There is no one to challenge him on the political horizon of the country.

I have seen Gujarat under Modi, when he was chief minister. I have even seen the man in action during Advani's Rath Yatra, and I have been amazed at his energy and drive. I am hopeful that Prime Minister Modi will set the wrongs right and get some able guidance in running in the country.

17

My Life Was a DIY Project

As I look back, I realize that my life certainly was a do-it-yourself project. Of all the things I have done in my professional life, the one thing I am immensely proud of is my role in the creation of ANI, India's first multimedia news agency. The idea of creating something that would be a legacy in Indian media first struck me in 1952, but it was to fructify decades later.

We began small, with one newsroom and one edit studio. But today we partner with almost every news channel in India. I use the word 'partner' deliberately, because while all channels subscribe to the ANI wire, they neither compete with us nor do they dictate the terms. Every channel sees ANI as a credible news source that adds value to their product.

It was in 1988—when Sanjiv, my son, and Smita, my daughter-in-law, put together a news package to send to the US for ethnic news channels to use in their bulletins—that the dream I had of creating a news agency began to take shape. We had already been making news spots for Doordarshan, which were shot, edited and voiced by a staff of six people in the Asian Films newsroom. The packages that we were sending to the US in U-matic tapes were soon in demand in the UK and South Africa.

The Ministry of External Affairs started getting queries from various embassies wanting to know more about this 'news agency' and about how they could subscribe to our 'news service'. But truth be told, there was no news service! Just a weekly tape with edited and voiced news stories to run in news bulletins. In 1992, international sales managers of Reuters TV, David Wratten (Asia and Middle East) and Diana Quay (UK and Ireland), broached the idea of beginning a daily satellite news feed from India for the world. Sanjiv, Smita and my wingman, Surinder, had by then put together a great team of journalists and camerapersons keen on launching a full-fledged TV news agency.

Sanjiv had worked for NBC and USA Today in the US, and he knew how to make slick news bulletins with an international perspective. As the CEO of ANI, Sanjiv has steered the news agency from the conception to the consolidation stage.

Surinder, who had worked with legends like Mark Tully, had the technical expertise like no one else in India. As ANI's chief operations officer, Surinder saw that the production line kept expanding at the agency and the quality kept improving.

Smita had emerged as a formidable television reporter, anchoring for Amit Khanna's Business Plus Channel, for Zee TV's *Ghoomta Aaina* and, in the '90s, for international broadcasters like PBS and NHK. For the past twenty-five years, she has been in charge of the editorial division of the news agency, making sure that channels from across India, and globally via the ANI–Reuters feeds, find whatever they need in the news feeds that we supply.

ANI at the cutting edge

By the mid-'90s, ANI had been registered as a news agency, but we were still a smallish setup. Sanjiv and I had decided very early on that ANI would not be like PTI or UNI, the other two news agencies in India. We would be lean and mean and would hire young, energetic and idealistic people. Private satellite channels had already begun in India; the world was interested in knowing the India story. Sanjiv started creating various TV products, made by this dedicated team, for dozens of TV channels around the world. With its documentaries,

TV news spots and packaged news bulletins, ANI became the one-stop shop for all that a TV news channel would need by the turn of the century.

The cutting edge to ANI was provided by my grandson, Ishaan, the fourth-generation journalist in the Prakash family. After graduating in journalism, Ishaan joined the fledgling web division of ANI. He saw that Indian news channels were moving towards live coverage of events, and we were losing out because we did not have expensive OB vans, as NDTV and CNN–IBN did. Moreover, the channels wanted more content and faster delivery, which we were not able to provide.

ANI had hit a roadblock in terms of the distribution of real-time news content. But Ishaan had begun reading up on how defence forces of various countries relied on 3G mobile communications systems to stream live videos rather than clunky satellite transmissions. 3G technology had also brought more versatility in news production, ending news channels' reliance on archaic satellite dishes lining up with satellites in the sky to provide a steady link.

The answer to our problems came in the way of an Israeli broadcasting start-up called LiveU. With Surinder's vast range of contacts and Ishaan's on-the-spot MacGyvering—which made this technology functional in India's limited mobile connectivity space in 2011—LiveU and ANI entered into a partnership to deploy their units with India-specific modifications.

For a period of four years, between 2011 and 2014, ANI invested heavily in 3G technology and in personnel training, with a view to expanding our live-coverage network across the country. ANI's mantra for live coverage was simple: we would not limit our live reports to just the tony localities of New Delhi, Mumbai, Chennai and Bengaluru; ANI would take live news to tier-2 and -3 cities and set up bureaus in India's north-east, which was often ignored and once dismissed contemptuously by a senior TV journalist with the phrase 'the tyranny of distance' as an explanation of why his network chose to ignore what happens in the region.

Smita, Ishaan and Naveen Kapoor, Surinder's son, who had been with us for almost two decades by then and is an integral part of ANI's editorial section, did not limit themselves to just live videos. We were not going to be a mere 'post office', as a senior political leader once categorized us. In 2011, ANI had a handful of reporters working for its print service; today, the agency employs over 300 people across the country. The goal was clear: be it any media—television, print or social—ANI reporters should be the first with the news.

In 2019, many sponsored magazine hitjobs were conjured up to tarnish ANI's image and to figure out what makes us tick. Unfortunately, the editors of these magazines failed to understand that here is no gimmick. This company is run by journalists, does not have massive cross-holdings unlike other media barons and does one thing well: it gets you the news, credibly and fast.

As 2020 approaches an end, I am proud to say that ANI has kept the ship steady, with no mass retrenchments, and is debt-free. We have grown to two 24/7 live-news feeds, which go to over 200 channels in this country, and a print product that goes to all the major newspapers and websites in India and abroad. The days of running tapes to channels are over.

I wish my father had been alive to see how we have grown from that studio in Janpath to becoming the go-to place for all India- and subcontinent-related news. My younger brother Om Prakash (Kali) was a great photographer who died very young in a car accident. My father could never cope with life after cremating his son. My youngest brother, Satya Prakash (Sati), is a documentary filmmaker of repute. I wish my father had been around to see that we all became filmmakers and journalists like him.

A mixed bag

I bagged many plaudits in my career—including awards for my camerawork in India and an MBE (Most Excellent Order of the British Empire) from the Queen of England, soon after I retired from Reuters—but a shabash from my father would have been more valuable than any of them.

I worked my fingers to the bone for fifty years of my life, to prove myself as a journalist. Nothing came easy to me. I wasn't born with a silver spoon. But what surprises me and, even to this day, makes me look back in wonder is the fact that my legacy is ANI—something that germinated as an idea decades ago. But all the credit for the agency's growth and consolidation should go to my son and his family, and to Surinder and his son.

We are a family that lives and breathes journalism. From the breakfast conversations with my son, grandsons and daughter-in-law to our dinner-table conversations, the talk revolves around current events. We narrate our experiences past and present, since we all have a journalism background. This may seem banal to most, because I am sure something very similar happens in families of, say, lawyers, doctors or actors. I only bring it up here to emphasize the passion for journalism that my son and his family have, which they have inherited from me and my friend Ramamohan Rao, Smita's father. It's this passion that has made ANI a successful venture.

At eighty-nine, I look back at my life as a life well-led. I have achieved a lot and have a few regrets. Is that not what life is all about? A mixed bag? As Frank Sinatra said:

My friend, I'll say it clear
I'll state my case, of which I'm certain
I've lived a life that's full
I travelled each and every highway
And more, much more than this
I did it my way . . .